LONDON & SOUTH EAST ENGLAND

PADDLE BOARDING

100 PLACES
SUP, CANOE & KAYAK

LISA DREWE

WILD THINGS PUBLISHING

West Wittering (92)

LONDON & SOUTH EAST
ENGLAND
PADDLE BOARDING
100 PLACES
SUP, CANOE & KAYAK

Tollesbury Marshes (68)

CONTENTS

PADDLING LOCATIONS

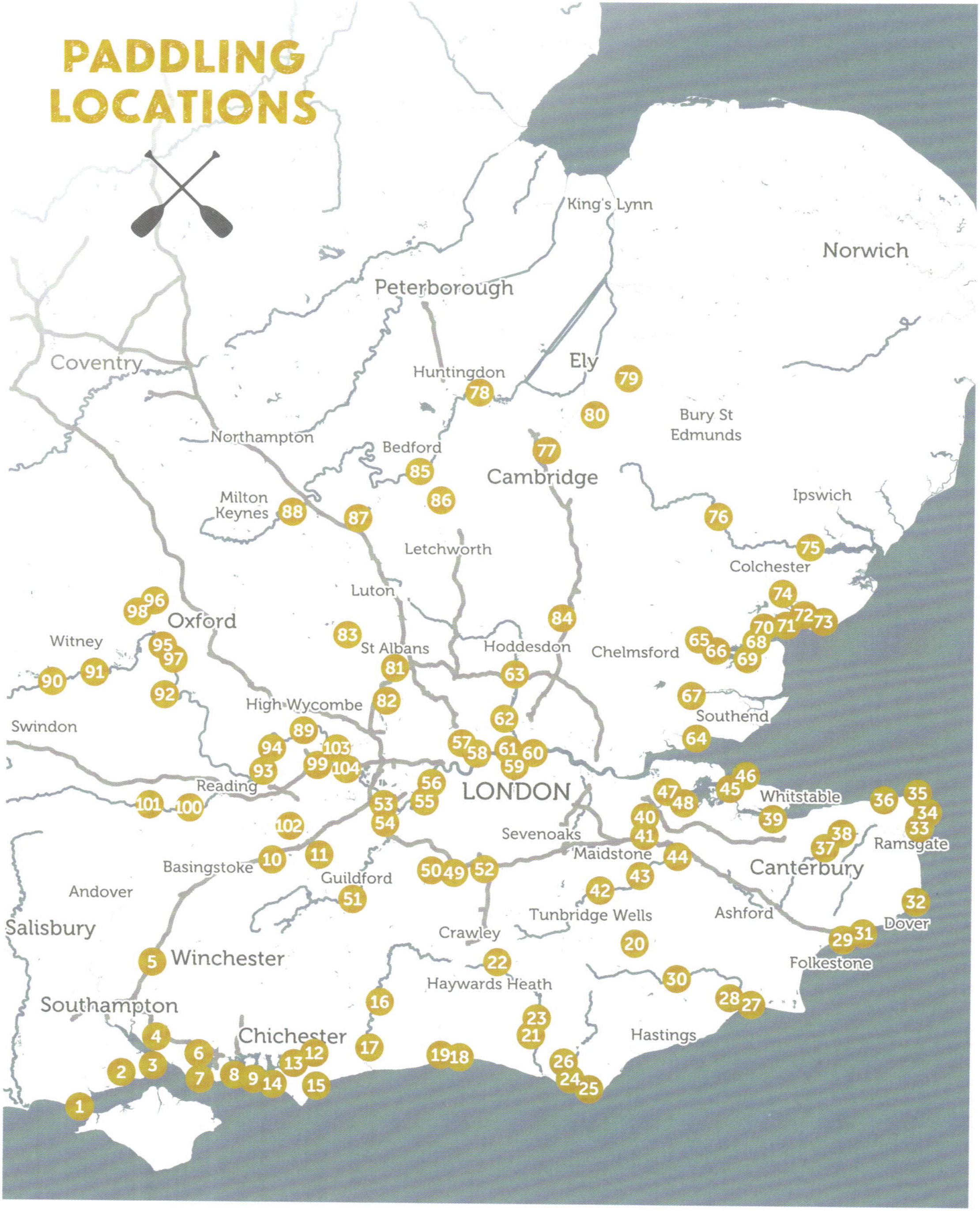

ROUTE	NAME OF ROUTE & DESCRIPTION	PAGE	TYPE OF WATER	GRADE	DISTANCE (km) return

HAMPSHIRE

ROUTE	NAME OF ROUTE & DESCRIPTION	PAGE	TYPE OF WATER	GRADE	DISTANCE (km) return
1	**Keyhaven to Hurst Castle:** Estuary trip across Keyhaven Lake from Keyhaven to Hurst Castle	42	Estuary	4	5.0
2	**Beaulieu River Buckler's Hard to Beaulieu:** A serene river trip, exploring salt marshes, ancient woodlands, and wildlife	44	Tidal river	3	8.3
3	**Calshot Lagoon to Lepe:** Explore Calshot Lagoon or uncover smuggler's tunnels and D-Day history on a Solent adventure	46	Estuary/coast	3 or 5	13.0
4	**River Hamble Swanwick to Botley:** Journey along the tidal Upper River Hamble with plenty of great pitstops along the way	48	Tidal river	3	13.5
5	**River Itchen Explorer:** Enjoy the River Itchen's clear waters near Winchester or enjoy Swaythling's family-friendly pub paddle	50	River	2	1.5 or 3
6	**Portsmouth Harbour Explorer:** The wilder side of Portsmouth Harbour with an imposing castle, a wildlife island, and tidal creeks	52	Inland harbour	4	7 or 8
7	**Alverstoke Lake to Haslar:** A trip through three tidal lakes towards the iconic Spinnaker Tower, and close encounter with a submarine	54	Tidal river	3	5.0
8	**Hayling Island Langstone Harbour:** Discover Langstone Harbour's hidden wilds, wartime history, secret creeks, and serene lagoons	56	Estuary	3	16.0
9	**Hayling Island Chichester Harbour:** Explore the quiet tidal inlets of Chichester Harbour on the southeast coast of Hayling Island	58	Estuary	3	6.0
10	**Basingstoke Canal Barley Mow to Odiham Castle:** Family-friendly rural stretch of Basingstoke Canal to the castle that helped change British history	60	Canal	1	13.8
11	**Basingstoke Canal Mytchett to Ash Lock:** Family paddle on a wildlife-rich canal and lakes, including the charmingly named Great Bottom Flash	62	Canal	1	10.0

WEST SUSSEX

ROUTE	NAME OF ROUTE & DESCRIPTION	PAGE	TYPE OF WATER	GRADE	DISTANCE (km) return
12	**Chichester Ship Canal:** Tranquil trip on a historic waterway with kingfishers, wildflowers, and stunning Chichester Cathedral views	64	Canal	1	4.2
13	**Chichester Harbour Dell Quay to Bosham:** Explore Chichester Harbour's waters with sweeping views, wildlife, and charming hamlets and inns	66	Tidal river	3	14.0
14	**West Wittering to West Itchenor:** Escape the bustling beach crowds to explore the wilder parts of Chichester Harbour	68	Estuary	3	11.7
15	**Pagham Harbour Explorer:** Coastal trip to a wildlife reserve with tranquil creeks, and historic Sidlesham Quay	70	Coast/tidal inland harbour	3	9.0
16	**River Arun Pulborough to Stopham Bridge:** Gentle family paddle along the River Arun through scenic countryside to a welcoming riverside inn	72	Tidal river	2	4.0
17	**River Arun Arundel to Black Rabbit:** Tide-assisted trip with stunning views of Arundel Castle, and the perfect riverside pub stop	74	Tidal river	3	6 (or 21 one way)
18	**Southwick to Brighton:** Adventurous coastal paddle past Brighton's vibrant seaside and iconic landmarks	76	Coast	5	10km (one way)
19	**River Adur Shoreham to Upper Beeding:** Tide-assisted journey from harbour to pub, past bird sanctuaries, rolling chalklands, and industrial heritage	78	Tidal river	3	19.0

EAST SUSSEX

ROUTE	NAME OF ROUTE & DESCRIPTION	PAGE	TYPE OF WATER	GRADE	DISTANCE (km) return
20	**Bewl Water:** Scenic reservoir perfect for outdoor adventures and spotting wildlife amongst a picturesque landscape	80	Lake	1	
21	**River Ouse Lewes to Hamsey Island Loop:** Serene trip through idyllic East Sussex countryside with a touch of history at every turn	82	Tidal river	3	8.0

ROUTE	NAME OF ROUTE & DESCRIPTION	PAGE	TYPE OF WATER	GRADE	DISTANCE (km) return

EAST SUSSEX

ROUTE	NAME OF ROUTE & DESCRIPTION	PAGE	TYPE OF WATER	GRADE	DISTANCE (km) return
22	**Ardingly Reservoir:** Beautiful lake surrounded by ancient woodland, nestled in the stunning High Weald National Landscape	84	Lake	1	
23	**River Ouse Barcombe Mills & Isfield:** Tranquil journey on the serene non-tidal section of the River Ouse	86	River	2	3.6
24	**Cuckmere Meanders:** Family-friendly trip amid the stunning chalk cliff scenery of the Seven Sisters Country Park	88	River/lake	1	3.0
25	**Cuckmere Haven Exceat to Seven Sisters:** Adventurous trip to the mouth of the Cuckmere River under the iconic chalk cliffs of the Seven Sisters	90	Estuary/coast	3 or 5	4.8 (or 6.4 one way)
26	**Cuckmere River Exceat to Alfriston:** Family-friendly river journey through rolling chalk hills past quaint villages and excellent pitstops	92	Tidal river	2	12.0
27	**River Rother Rye & Rye Harbour:** Explore a medieval port and vibrant wildlife reserve where nature meets rich seafaring history	94	Tidal river/estuary	3	7.5
28	**Camber Northpoint Water:** Family fun at this hidden gem outside Rye, offering a peaceful lake with a lively vibe	96	Lake	1	

KENT

ROUTE	NAME OF ROUTE & DESCRIPTION	PAGE	TYPE OF WATER	GRADE	DISTANCE (km) return
29	**Royal Military Canal Hythe to West Hythe:** Gentle trip along a waterway rich in military history and wildlife, with an excellent café to finish	98	Canal	1	8 or 13
30	**River Rother Bodiam Castle to Newenden Bridge:** A serene High Weald trip past stunning Bodiam Castle, charming tearooms, and excellent camping	100	River	2	13.0
31	**Folkestone Harbour Explorer:** Coastal journey of history and art, featuring vibrant sculptures and stunning seafront views	102	Harbour/coast	4 to 5	3.0
32	**St Margaret's Bay & the White Cliffs:** Discover the hidden bay that inspired Ian Flemming—dramatic, secretive, and quintessentially British	104	Coast	5	
33	**River Stour & Pegwell Bay Ramsgate to Sandwich:** Exhilarating coast and river trip with expansive seascapes and a reserve teeming with seals and birds	106	Coast/tidal river	3 to 4	11.5 (one way)
34	**North Foreland Explorer Broadstairs, Kingsgate & Botany Bay:** Discover the seven bays, the jewels of Thanet, between Dumpton Bay and Foreland Point	108	Coast	5	11.5
35	**Margate Walpole Tidal Pool:** Experience one of the largest and oldest tidal pools in the UK	110	Tidal pool	1	
36	**Minnis Bay to Margate:** Hidden bays, historic harbour, and sunset paddles along Thanet's coast	112	Coast	5	8 (one way)
37	**River Stour Chartham to Canterbury:** Experience Canterbury's timeless beauty and highlights from the Great Stour River	114	River	2	2.3 or 5.5 (one way)
38	**River Stour Fordwich to Grove Ferry:** A peaceful and wildlife-rich journey between Fordwich and Grove Ferry	116	Tidal river	2	7.7 (one way)
39	**Oare to Faversham:** Explore Kent's waterways from Oare Marshes to Faversham Quay, with a stop at Shipwright's Arms	118	Tidal river	3	12.5
40	**St Andrews Lakes:** Turquoise waters, sandy shores, and watersports offer a Mediterranean vibe in Kent	120	Lake	1	
41	**Leybourne Lakes:** Relax in Leybourne Country Park's largest lake	122	Lake	1	
42	**River Medway Trail Tonbridge to Yalding:** A calm river journey with great pitstops on the first stage of the Medway Canoe Trail	124	River	2	13.5 (one way)
43	**River Medway Trail Yalding to Maidstone:** Oast houses, orchards, and ancient bridges on the second leg of the Medway Canoe Trail	126	River	2	11 or 15 (one way)

ROUTE	NAME OF ROUTE & DESCRIPTION	PAGE	TYPE OF WATER	GRADE	DISTANCE (km) return

KENT

ROUTE	NAME OF ROUTE & DESCRIPTION	PAGE	TYPE OF WATER	GRADE	DISTANCE (km) return
44	**Mote Park Lake:** A peaceful haven in Maidstone, this river-fed gem is perfect for watersports	128	Lake	1	
45	**Sheppey Island Queenborough to Deadman's Island:** Naval history, wildlife, and a haunting past await paddlers exploring Queenborough's highlights	130	Tidal river	3	
46	**Sheppey Island Barton's Point Coastal Park Lake:** Play in a saltwater lake, a family-friendly alternative to the open sea	132	Lake	1	
47	**Chatham Docks:** A watersports haven in a historic dockyard that shaped Britain's maritime might	134	Lake	1	
48	**Gillingham & Medway Islands:** Explore two River Medway islands, home to the historic forts of Hoo and Darnet	136	Estuary	5	5.5

SURREY

ROUTE	NAME OF ROUTE & DESCRIPTION	PAGE	TYPE OF WATER	GRADE	DISTANCE (km) return
49	**Buckland Park Lagoon:** A pristine lake and watersports lagoon in a nature reserve with a serene beach vibe	138	Lake	1	
50	**River Mole Box Steps to Leatherhead:** An adventurous trip through Mole Gap, where the river carves a lush valley through the North Downs	140	River	2	8.0
51	**River Wey Navigation Godalming to Guildford:** Float downstream on the historic River Wey through lush water meadows, woodlands, and heath	142	River	2	7 (one way)
52	**Mercers Country Park:** A peaceful former quarry near Merstham, famed for its beautiful blue waters	144	Lake	1	
53	**Abbey River & Penton Hook Island:** A Surrey safari, navigating a willow tree jungle and a "Loch Ness monster" before rejoining the Thames	146	River	2	7.0
54	**Wey Navigation Weybridge to Desborough Island:** A river adventure past historic mills, around an island, and a charming Victorian-era café	148	River	2	13.5

GREATER LONDON

ROUTE	NAME OF ROUTE & DESCRIPTION	PAGE	TYPE OF WATER	GRADE	DISTANCE (km) return
55	**River Thames Hampton Court to Kingston:** Discover Thames islands, houseboats, Hampton Court, and riverside scenes steeped in royal history	150	River	2	6 (one way)
56	**River Thames Ham House to Richmond & Teddinton:** Two scenic routes from Ham Street: downstream to Richmond and upstream to Teddington	152	Tidal river	3	4 or 5.6
57	**Grand Union Canal Paddington to Horsenden Hill:** Slip out of London on the Paddington Arm to discover rural Horsenden Hill	154	Canal	1	12 (one way)
58	**Regent's Canal Paddington to Kings Cross :** Experience vibrant boating communities, Camden Lock, and spot an occasional monkey or wolf	156	Canal	1	5 (one way)
59	**Isle of Dogs Millwall Outer Dock:** A 'lake' in the heart of East London's Isle of Dogs	158	Lake	1	
60	**Royal Victoria Dock:** Family-friendly watersports location with beach vibe and plenty of landmarks to spot	160	Lake	1	
61	**Limehouse Cut & Olympic Stadium Loop:** Explore East London's oldest canal with colourful graffiti and a circuit around the Olympic Park	162	River	2	10.5
62	**River Lea Navigation Tottenham Hale to Hackney Wick:** A river trip blending urban grit with natural beauty and the creative vibe of Hackney Wick	164	River	2	6.5 (one way)
63	**Lee Valley White Water Centre:** A thrilling water environment, blending Olympic heritage with calm areas perfect for paddleboarding	166	Lake	1	

ROUTE	NAME OF ROUTE & DESCRIPTION	PAGE	TYPE OF WATER	GRADE	DISTANCE (km) return

ESSEX

ROUTE	NAME OF ROUTE & DESCRIPTION	PAGE	TYPE OF WATER	GRADE	DISTANCE (km) return
64	**Two Tree Island Loop:** Expansive Thames Estuary views and wildlife-rich salt marshes on an island loop	168	Coast	3	6.5
65	**Chelmer & Blackwater Navigation Beeleigh Falls to Papermill Lock:** Tranquil river trip leading to a popular boating spot and tearooms	170	River	2	15.5
66	**Maldon Loop:** Explore tidal creeks and saltmarshes to Beeleigh Falls, returning via the calm Chelmer Navigation	172	River and tidal estuary	2 to 3	9.0
67	**River Crouch Hullbridge to Battlebridge:** Journey along tranquil waters between quaint historic villages	174	Tidal river	3	8.5
68	**Tollesbury Explorer:** Navigate salty boatyards and atmospheric marshes or circumnavigate two islands	176	Estuary	3	5.0
69	**Osea Island Circumnavigation:** Circumnavigate a secluded island in the Blackwater estuary	178	Estuary	3	11.0
70	**West Mersea Explorer:** Discover an island rich in seafood history and a wilderness full of hidden creeks	180	Estuary	3	1.6 or 5.2
71	**Mersea Boating Lake:** Family-friendly sheltered watersports lake backed by the panoramic Blackwater Estuary	182	Lake	1	
72	**Brightlingsea Explorer:** Explore low-lying islands, sandbars, and wide open views	184	Estuary	3	
73	**St Osyth Mill Dam Lake:** Family-friendly watersports lake	186	Lake	1	
74	**River Colne Explorer:** Discover the industrial relics of Hythe Harbour or the hidden beauty of the Roman River	188	Tidal river	3	3.5 or 8.5
75	**River Stour Cattawade to Dedham:** Float through idyllic countryside past Flatford Mill made famous by Constable's paintings	190	River	2	12.0
76	**River Stour Sudbury to Bures:** Peaceful trip through the Stour Valley with a classic pub stop along the way	192	River	2	11 (one way)

CAMBRIDGESHIRE

ROUTE	NAME OF ROUTE & DESCRIPTION	PAGE	TYPE OF WATER	GRADE	DISTANCE (km) return
77	**River Cam Grantchester & The Backs:** Discover the famous colleges of the Backs and the beautiful Grantchester meadows and tearoom	194	River	2	4 or 5.6
78	**River Great Ouse Houghton Mill & Cook's Stream Loop:** Tranquil Ouse Valley trip from a historic flour mill and campsite to discover a quiet backwater	196	River	2	9.5
79	**River Lark Explorer:** Journey on a hidden waterway through fenland landscapes to explore local history and riverside inn	198	River	2	8 or 18
80	**Reach to Wicken Fen:** Navigate two Cambridgeshire Lodes to reach England's most famous Fen	200	River	2	12.0

HERTFORDSHIRE

ROUTE	NAME OF ROUTE & DESCRIPTION	PAGE	TYPE OF WATER	GRADE	DISTANCE (km) return
81	**Grand Union Canal Kings Langley to Batchworth:** A canal journey to historic locks, a hidden waterfall, and parklands that run alongside the River Gade	202	Canal	1	11 (one way)
82	**Grand Union Canal Rickmansworth to Harefield:** Canal trip with wildlife-rich lakes and quirky landmarks with plenty of pitstops along the way	204	Canal	1	7.0
83	**Grand Union Canal Cow Roast to Little Tring:** Enjoy a rural stretch of canal past lush countryside and ancient mills to discover the Wendover Arm	206	Canal	1	9.6 or 14
84	**Stort Navigation:** Journey through ancient parkland and peaceful meadows	208	River	2	7 or 15km (one way)

ROUTE	NAME OF ROUTE & DESCRIPTION	PAGE	TYPE OF WATER	GRADE	DISTANCE (km) return

BEDFORDSHIRE

ROUTE	NAME OF ROUTE & DESCRIPTION	PAGE	TYPE OF WATER	GRADE	DISTANCE (km) return
85	**Great River Ouse Kempston to Great Barford:** A peaceful river journey through Bedford, meadows, villages, locks, and a riverside pub	210	River	2	11 or 16 (one way)
86	**River Ivel Biggleswade to Tempsford:** A hidden river full of wildlife flowing through Biggleswade to the River Great Ouse	212	River	2	13 (one way)
87	**Brogborough Lake:** A friendly watersports hub just a short distance from Milton Keynes and Bedford	214	Lake	1	

BUCKINGHAMSHIRE

ROUTE	NAME OF ROUTE & DESCRIPTION	PAGE	TYPE OF WATER	GRADE	DISTANCE (km) return
88	**Grand Union Canal Wolverton to Thrupp Wharf:** A gentle trip over the Iron Trunk Aqueduct to the Navigation Inn at Thrupp	216	Canal	1	9.6
89	**River Thames Marlow to Maidenhead:** A picturesque Thames journey past Cliveden House, wooded hills, meadows, and riverside inns	218	River	2	11 (one way)

OXFORDSHIRE

ROUTE	NAME OF ROUTE & DESCRIPTION	PAGE	TYPE OF WATER	GRADE	DISTANCE (km) return
90	**River Thames Buscot to Lechlade :** A peaceful Thames stretch winding through meadows, past locks, islands and riverside pubs	220	River	2	7.0
91	**River Thames Tadpole Bridge to Newbridge:** Pub paddle along the remotest stretch of the Thames	222	River	2	10 (one way)
92	**River Thames Culham Loop & Abingdon:** An idyllic trip to a historic town, looping Culham Island and swimming in scenic Sutton Pools	224	River	2	7.8
93	**River Thames Sonning to Wargrave via hidden backwaters:** Explore a peaceful Thames tributary, picturesque islands and historic landmarks on this pub paddle	226	River	2	11.4
94	**River Thames Henley to Wargrave & Hennerton Backwater:** A pub paddle on one of the best Thames backwaters, plus secret islands & stunning riverside homes	228	River	2	6.5
95	**Oxford Canal & River Thames Wolvercote Loop:** A circular route linking Oxford Canal to the Thames with some classic pitstops and landmarks to spot	230	Canal/river	2	11.5
96	**Oxford Canal Enslow to Thrupp:** Peaceful trip along the Oxford Canal and River Cherwell to tearooms and two welcoming pubs	232	Canal	1	8.5
97	**River Cherwell Oxford Colleges:** Explore Oxford's hidden waterways, with views of dreaming spires, meadows, and iconic city landmarks	234	River	2	6.7
98	**Blenheim Palace Great Lake:** Enjoy "one of the finest views in England" from the Great Lake in this World Heritage Site	236	Lake	1	

BERKSHIRE

ROUTE	NAME OF ROUTE & DESCRIPTION	PAGE	TYPE OF WATER	GRADE	DISTANCE (km) return
99	**Bray Lake:** Enjoy the lake's strong community spirit, and diverse range of water activities	238	Lake	1	
100	**Kennet & Avon Canal Midgham to Theale:** A peaceful trip along a canalised part of the River Kennet that retains its chalk stream features	240	Canal	1	9.4 (one way)
101	**Kennet & Avon Canal Newbury to Hungerford:** A gentle trip through the beautiful Berkshire countryside, criss-crossing the River Kennet and railway	242	Canal	1	9 or 14 (one way)
102	**Horseshoe Lake:** A popular family destination on the doorstep of Sandhurst	244	Lake	1	
103	**Jubilee River:** Options for peaceful routes from meadows and wetlands to the iconic skylines of Eton and Windsor	246	River	2	8 or 15
104	**River Thames Windsor to Staines:** Journey through history past Windsor Castle and Runnymede with islands to discover on the way	248	River	2	12.5 (one way)

Iron Trunk, Grand Union Canal (88)

INTRODUCTION

The South East of England isn't just a paddleboarder's paradise – it's a revelation. Here, the waterways have long been the lifeblood of the region; liquid veins of commerce, power, and culture that have shaped this country for centuries. These ancient highways carried kings and queens, merchants, and explorers, threading through some of England's most iconic places. From London's bustling Thames to forgotten rivers that slip quietly past historic gems, paddleboarding offers a secret passage into our great cities: London, Cambridge, Canterbury, and more. Beyond the famed rivers of the Medway, Great Ouse, and Stour, or hidden backwaters like the Ivel and Lark, hundreds of unique adventures lie waiting to be discovered.

It's not all rivers, though. Canals like the Kennet & Avon and Oxford Canal turned sluggish waterways into highways of industry, while navigations like the Lee and Grand Union became vital arteries feeding the capital's supply chain. The Chichester Ship Canal connected the city to the sea, while the Royal Military Canal, originally built for defence, now provides tranquil paddling through history-rich landscapes. Then there are the lagoons and lakes, some of them born from the quarries that once yielded the stone and clay to build the region but now transformed into serene retreats for families. Meanwhile, the vast natural harbours of Langstone, Chichester, and Pagham offer the chance to paddle among thriving ecosystems teeming with thousands of species –

River Cam and The Backs (77)

graceful wading birds, darting fish, seals, and rare plants – creating unforgettable encounters with nature's wonders.

And the beauty of the South East? Whether you're venturing along the coastline beneath the magnificent White Cliffs or weaving through the South Downs, a welcoming inn or café is never far away to round off your journey in style.

PADDLING AND WELLBEING

We intuitively know that we feel better in "blue spaces", and the science behind the mental and physical benefits of being close to water is becoming clear. In my last book I used the term "blue health", coined by Wallace J Nicholls, a Californian surfer and marine biologist, who sums it up perfectly when he suggests that being on, under, or beside water results in a "mildly meditative state characterised by calm, peacefulness, unity, and a sense of general happiness and satisfaction with life in the moment". After another year spent on the water I couldn't agree more. It's little wonder, then, that paddleboarding has become so popular, with more of us discovering this activity every day.

Although every journey can be an adventure, for many people the joy of paddling is simply about being on the water and engaging every one of our senses. Watch ring-like patterns form as heavy raindrops hit the water, or see the light dancing across a river's surface; breathe in the ozone of the ocean or the sweet smell of river water, and enjoy the fresh taste of spring-fed lakes. The sound of a paddle dipping beneath the water's surface, the emptying of tidal creeks heralded by the cries of wading birds looking for their next meal, the gentle song of rivers flowing on their eternal journey to the ocean – all these sensory experiences increase our "blue health", and all are beloved by paddlers.

Alfriston, Cuckmere (26)

MY JOURNEY

I have paddled since I was a child, my school youth club giving me the opportunity to learn how to kayak. I loved the thrill of shooting the Symonds Yat rapids and paddling the length of the Thames, bumping down the many weirs and hanging on for dear life in the locks (not a great idea, even though it was legal then). Later the camaraderie of sea-kayaking trips around the Isles of Scilly, the embarrassing sinus leaks after attempted Eskimo rolls, and the night-time training for the Devizes-Westminster canoe race were certainly character-building for my younger self, and built a firm foundation for later adventures.

It was on a work trip to California that I first noticed the new sport of paddle-surfing. I was amazed that people could not only stand up on long boards in big waves using just a paddle as a rudder, but also move gracefully. Paddleboarding didn't arrive in Britain until a few years later – but when I tried it myself, I was instantly hooked. On recent travel projects I've circumnavigated over 600 islands in the UK, many of them using kayaks and paddleboards as a means of transport, and this book is a way of sharing some of those journeys along with many more. I started this paddleboarding odyssey in the South West, my home and holiday destination for most of my life, continued it in Wales, the country that first inspired me to spend a lifetime exploring the outdoors, and have now thoroughly explored the South East, where I have spent much of my life, including studying in Cambridge, and working Thameside in London.

River Medway Trail (43)

CONNECT WITH NATURE, HERITAGE, AND ADVENTURE

This past year, exploring and documenting the rivers, canals, coasts, and lakes of South East England has been nothing short of extraordinary. Each journey uncovered not only stunning scenery and wild, unspoiled places but also the enduring soul of the region's waterways – silent witnesses to centuries of history, culture, and transformation. Here, you can paddle through sites of national significance, from the Magna Carta at Runnymede and the military powerhouse of Portsmouth to some of the most important nature reserves in England – teeming with life, yet within touching distance of urban life and industry.

Medieval castles punctuate the landscape, while river trips through historic cities like Canterbury whisper tales of faith and pilgrimage. The intellectual legacy of Oxford and Cambridge is reflected in the gentle flows of the Cherwell and Cam, their waters winding past the spires and storied colleges. In London, the Thames threads its way through centuries of royal and cultural heritage, flanked by landmarks that define the city's identity. This region's waterways have inspired generations of creatives – John Constable and J.M.W. Turner immortalised their beauty on canvas, while influential writers like Geoffrey Chaucer, Virginia Woolf, and Ian Fleming wove their charm into enduring and popular works.

From the iconic White Cliffs of Dover to the rolling South Downs, the ancient New Forest, the serpentine Cuckmere Meanders, and the serene waters of the Medway and Beaulieu rivers, South East England is simply enchanting. Each route offers an adventure as diverse as the landscapes themselves, impossible to condense into just a few words. But come with me on a brief tour of this remarkable region, as I share the highlights of a year spent discovering these waterways.

Starting in Hampshire, the journey begins with the protected waters between Keyhaven and Henry VIII's Hurst Castle, framed by the Isle of Wight on the horizon. Nearby, the historic charm of Buckler's Hard offers an ideal base to paddle the Beaulieu River, winding through the ancient trees of the New Forest.

Calshot Lagoon provides a family-friendly haven, while adventurous paddlers can head along the coast to Lepe, where military history infuses the scenic shores. Inland, the Basingstoke Canal leads to the atmospheric ruins of Odiham Castle, while Hayling Island serves as the gateway to the tranquil beauty of Langstone and Chichester Harbours, where historic villages like Bosham and Dell Quay offer popular inns and idyllic paddles. For something uniquely Hampshire, paddle upriver on the Hamble to Botley and ring a bell for a beer, delivered straight to your paddleboard over the wall.

Canoe Pass, Tonbridge (42)

Sussex then has its own set of treasures. Glide past the soaring turrets of Arundel Castle or navigate the serene wetlands of Pagham Harbour, a sanctuary alive with birdlife and bordered by peaceful marshes. The tidal River Adur carries paddlers from Shoreham to Upper Beeding through the rolling contours of the South Downs, while Rye Harbour's nature reserve teems with life, sheltering thousands of species. Paddle through time at Bodiam Castle, where camping nearby under the stars adds an extra layer of magic. Other Sussex routes include the leafy Chichester Ship Canal or the Cuckmere River, which leads to the storybook village of Alfriston in one direction and the dramatic Seven Sisters cliffs in the other.

In Kent, an eclectic mix of waterways offer journeys like Ramsgate to Sandwich with a chance to spot seals basking on the sandbanks, while the marshlands of Oare to Faversham reveal a hidden inn perfect for a mid-trip pause. Paddle beneath the iconic White Cliffs for vistas that inspired some of James Bond's greatest adventures, or take on the multi-day River Medway Trail, with its canoe passes adding a touch of excitement. Margate's tidal pool brings a nostalgic seaside thrill, while Canterbury's waterways are a passage straight into the medieval world of Chaucer's *The Canterbury Tales*. Folkestone Harbour, with its bold art installations and vibrant beach scene, offers a modern contrast.

The pace shifts in Greater London and Surrey, where urban energy meets riverside peace. The stretch from Hampton Court to Kingston pairs Tudor grandeur with leafy pathways, while Hackney Wick's River Lea buzzes with street art and waterside breweries. Paddle to D'Oyly Carte Island for Victorian charm, or explore canal routes like Paddington to Horsenden Hill, where cityscapes give way to greenery, and Regent's Canal, alive with houseboats and Camden Market – oh, and wolves and monkeys if you know where to look. Reflective waters at the Isle of Dogs Millwall Dock mirror the city's towering skyline, while the Limehouse Cut loops around the Olympic Stadium. For thrill-seekers, the engineered rapids of the Lee Valley White Water Centre offer a thrilling backdrop, while secret rivers like the Abbey and Mole offer a peaceful retreat within miles of London's hum.

Essex, Cambridgeshire, and Hertfordshire bring a sense of wilderness and history. Sheppey Island launches you into the haunting marshlands of Deadman's Island, while the tranquil creeks of Tollesbury and West Mersea reveal fishing heritage and expansive estuary views. Wicken Fen, a National Trust treasure in Cambridgeshire, offers reed beds and rare wildlife in a pristine wetland setting. Paddle the River Stour through Constable's pastoral

Great Barford, Great River Ouse (85)

landscapes at Dedham and Flatford Mills, or explore the River Cam for a unique view of Grantchester and the College Backs of Cambridge. Adventurers can lose themselves in the Medway Islands, where military forts rise starkly from the water.

The journey concludes in Oxfordshire, Berkshire, Buckinghamshire, and Bedfordshire, where built grandeur and wild places coexist. Paddle through Blenheim Palace's parkland or along the Thames past Eton's spires, Windsor Castle, and the historic Magna Carta site at Runnymede. The stretch between Marlow and Maidenhead reveals idyllic riverside scenes, culminating in the elegance of Cliveden House perched above the water. Hidden backwaters like Hennington and St Patrick's Stream or the Jubilee River provide peace, while the River Cherwell through Oxford adds scenic detours with stories of academia and architecture. Returning finally to the Upper Thames at Lechlade and Buscot, I'm reminded of family picnics and childhood swims – simple joys that bring this journey full circle to a place of watery fun and lasting memories.

RESPECTING OUR ENVIRONMENT

Whatever our reason for paddling, South East England offers an extraordinary diversity of waters, many of which are highly popular with paddlers. While researching this book, I encountered many people whose passion for their local waterways inspired me to reflect on the impact of our activities on the natural world and our shared responsibility to minimise it. It's undeniable that the need to spend time outdoors, connecting with nature, has never been more critical – for both mental and physical wellbeing.

However, this growing exodus into the natural world is not without its challenges. With the rising popularity of paddleboarding and the desire to explore more waterways, the pressure on certain sites has become significant. This has led to a withdrawal of goodwill from some landowners. Meanwhile, others who were already interpreting access laws restrictively –particularly concerning rivers – have taken further steps to limit accessibility. It is disheartening to consider that of the UK's 42,700 miles of rivers, only 1,400 miles are recognised as having a clear and undisputed public right of access – just 3%.

Chichester Ship Canal (12)

Organisations like Paddle UK assert that historical evidence supports a public right of navigation under common law for all rivers capable of navigation. However, this position is firmly contested by opponents, making it all the more crucial to support the organisations that campaign for greater access rights.

We are also at a critical juncture regarding the health of our waterways. Inland water quality in England is rapidly declining under the weight of sewage discharge, agricultural runoff, and plastic pollution – so much so that only 16% of inland waters now achieve good ecological status. Oceans face similar threats, but they are now the focus of numerous campaigns for cleaner seas. Public awareness has grown regarding the alarming frequency of pollution incidents in British waters, which should, by any reasonable measure, be unlawful. Access to clean, high-quality blue spaces for everyone – not just a privileged few – is essential.

There is hope, however. The ever-expanding community of paddlers, swimmers, and water enthusiasts is joining the call for better protection and access to waterways. As Wallace J. Nichols beautifully said:

"Preserving, protecting, and restoring our waters are tasks for many lifetimes, and sometimes the effort can seem overwhelming. But as long as we stay connected with all of the many, many blessings that water provides, and continue to keep that love in the forefront of our minds and hearts, as long as we remind ourselves to hope, then our stories will help connect others to water and encourage them to do what they can to help care for this beautiful Blue Marble world."

I strive to embody this spirit, and invite you to do the same by respecting and enjoying the routes in this book. These routes have been carefully selected to avoid sensitive and fragile environments, and where such environments are encountered, clear guidance is provided on how paddlers should protect them. Many paddles can also be accessed via public transport. Where car use is necessary, only official parking spots with recognised water access are included, and carpooling is encouraged to reduce congestion and pollution.

In short, I wish you countless days of joyful paddling and encourage you to help preserve our precious blue spaces. Use this book as a source of inspiration, but don't forget to grab a map and explore independently. Water is never far away in the UK, and for that we are uniquely fortunate. Let's cherish and protect this gift together •

River Stour (76)

CHOOSING A BOARD, PADDLE AND FINS

TOP TIPS FOR CHOOSING A BOARD

• Always buy the best board you can afford (rather than the cheapest) for all-round better build quality.

• Go to a reputable SUP board supplier who will advise you on the best boards from their range based on your budget, your size and ability, and the environment you wish to paddle in. If possible, try them out on a demonstration day and find out whether a hard (solid) board or inflatable (iSUP) board will best suit your needs and space/transport availability. Most suppliers will also have a good range of buoyancy aids and will help you find the right fit.

• Don't choose a board that's too wide for you, otherwise you'll need to angle your paddle and create an arc with each stroke (meaning you swerve from side to side with each stroke), rather than running the paddle almost perpendicular and parallel to the edge (rail) of the board (to track in a straight line). If you are a larger paddler with broad shoulders, you may need a wider board. Always match your weight to the maximum weight recommended for the board, otherwise you will lose performance.

• Invest in a lesson from a qualified instructor to learn good stroke technique to help with stability, manoeuvrability, and speed – all necessary for overall enjoyment.

• An all-round board – usually 10–11ft long – is suitable for most of the routes in this book. It is wider than a touring board, will give better stability, and has a more rounded bow for easier manoeuvrability. On longer routes, however, a more advanced paddler may consider using a touring board – usually 12ft or more in length and narrower than the all-round board. It also has a slightly upturned pointed bow to track in a straight line, and with more options for attaching drybags and equipment.

• When choosing a board, always look out for well-placed carry handles, such as at the bow and stern on a long tourer. Alternatively, choose a board with built-in shoulder straps. We all end up carrying the board a lot, and these details make SUP life so much better.

• Finally, think ahead and aim for a board that will also be suitable when your paddling ability improves. Also, beware of retailers selling only one type and size of board, as that type may not be the best option for you.

TOP TIPS FOR CHOOSING FINS

• There are several different fin arrays, depending on the type and shape of your board. All help with tracking in a straight line, especially in windy conditions.

• Some boards have one removable large central fin towards the stern. The most versatile option is a detachable US Box Fin, which allows you to remove/change the fin depending on the paddling environment. With US Box Fins that enable you to choose the position of the fin within the box, slide the fin further towards the bow to improve manoeuvrability or further towards the stern for straighter tracking. Other boards may have two fixed smaller fins or three fins (one removable larger central fin and two fixed smaller side fins).

• For touring, a large vertical fin aids tracking, whereas a smaller curved fin can improve manoeuvrability. On many of the river trips in this book, you may need to replace a large central fin with a shorter fin that's suitable for shallower water, and for paddling over rocks or through summer weeds.

• Always carry a spare fin and screws/attachments.

TOP TIPS FOR CHOOSING A PADDLE

• If a paddle isn't included with the board purchase, a "touring"-style paddle will be suitable for all the trips in this book.

Dell Quay, Chichester Harbour (13)

• Shafts are usually made in one, two or three pieces and from a variety of materials. Choose one that is at least 15–25cm taller than you. A good rule of thumb is to stand straight, raise your arm up above you, and bend your hand down. The handle of the paddle should rest in the crook of your wrist.
• For very short journeys, the paddle material won't be an issue. If you plan to do long journeys, however, the weight becomes significant, so buy the lightest paddle you can afford – usually a carbon-fibre paddle with a foam-like core to the blade. Shaving just 50g off a paddle's weight means less effort is needed to lift it out of the water for every stroke. For example, with a paddling rate of 25 strokes per minute, over an hour-long journey you'll end up lifting 75kg less with a paddle that's 50g lighter •

ADVICE FOR BEGINNERS

• Always wear a buoyancy aid and waist leash.
• Always pump the paddleboard to the manufacturer's recommended pressure. If you can't achieve this with a manual pump, consider buying an electric pump.
• Find a qualified instructor to teach you the basics – someone who is accredited/affiliated to Paddle UK, Canoe Wales (CW), British Stand Up Paddleboarding Association (BSUPA), Academy of Surfing Instructors (ASI), or International Surfing Association (ISA).
• Know your limits.
• Find a local paddling group to build confidence on local waterways.
• Ensure you are a competent swimmer, through resources such as swimming.org/learntoswim/know-child-competent-swimmer/ or Swim Wales swimwales.org/learn-to-swim-wales/6-11-years-learn-to-swim/
• Learn about weather, wind, and water conditions using Surfline (surfline.com), Windy (windy.app), XC Weather (xcweather.co.uk), windguru (windguru.cz) and the Met Office (metoffice.gov.uk)
• Avoid paddling at mid-tide, especially on spring tides when flow is faster and may lead to more turbulent water.
• Wear clothing and take safety kit appropriate to the trip and the water temperature.
• Use PaddleLogger or a land-based contact so that someone knows where you are in an emergency.
• Have fun, go at your own pace, and enjoy exploring •

PLANNING A TRIP

Trip planning is key to safety and enjoyment. Use apps and online resources for information on tides, weather, and waterflows for your intended journey. Conditions can change quickly so always check the evening before, and again a few hours in advance of starting a paddle. Take a copy of the map of your route and mark your journey on it, plus wind direction and strength during the trip. If paddling along the coast or on an estuary, ensure you know the size and direction of the swell and the times of high and low tides. On river paddles, always check water levels. And if you get caught in thunder and lightning, exit the water as soon as possible and seek shelter at least 100m from the shoreline/water.

WIND

Wind is generally the top issue for paddlers and it's vital to understand its direction and strength when planning a trip. Use apps such as Windy, windy.app, which gives a visualisation of the wind and colour-codes its strength. Paddlers need to choose days and times when the wind is coloured blue. Other useful sites that forecast wind strength and direction over time are the Met Office, metoffice.gov.uk , and Surfline, surfline.com. Be aware, too, that valleys and estuaries often funnel wind up or down them. Even if the wind is forecast for one direction, you may find that this changes according to locality. Always check conditions on the day with local paddle schools or RNLI lifeguard stations.

In forecasts, **wind direction** is the direction the wind is coming from (not the direction it is heading). Paddling into a **headwind** (wind into your face) will significantly slow your progress, while a **crosswind** will affect your ability to paddle in a straight line and challenge your balance. One way to overcome such winds is to kneel down and paddle with hands closer together towards the blade of the paddle. In more extreme circumstances, lie on the board, use the arms to paddle – much like surfers do to reach a break – and return to shelter and safety if the wind has picked up while on the water. The best wind for paddlers is a **tailwind** (wind on your back), which will blow you in your desired direction of travel. **Wind speed** of up to 10 knots, or Beaufort scale 3, is classified as a gentle breeze and is probably the maximum strength for beginners.

Wind on the coast: Offshore winds are the most serious for safety as they can propel you further out to sea. They blow off the land to the sea and are the cause of most paddleboard RNLI rescues. Tall buildings and cliffs can offer shelter from offshore winds, but the winds can strengthen as you paddle further from the shoreline.

Clues for wind conditions can be gleaned from watching the surface of the water before you set out. If it's calm in the bay but there are ripples 100m beyond and the water is even choppier further out, this indicates that there might be an offshore wind that's hitting the water further out. **Wind over tide** means the direction of the wind is opposite to the flow direction of the water. This creates **wind chop**, when cresting waves are created by local wind conditions, which is bad news for the paddler. In this instance, if you are paddling with a tailwind the water often looks flat in your direction of travel as you are surfing over the wave crests. However, when you turn around and paddle into the wind, you hit the wave crests and your journey will be wetter and choppier. **Wind with tide** means wind and tide flow in the same direction. This can dampen down waves so is desirable when planning any estuary or coastal trip. Wind chop can also happen on any large expanse of water such as lakes and across estuaries, when waves suddenly pick up or drop as the wind changes

Bosham, Chichester Harbour (13)

strength. Early mornings and evenings are often the best time to paddle as the wind tends to drop naturally at these times.

SWELL

After wind, swell is the next big issue for the coastal paddler. When wind from a low- pressure system in the Atlantic transfers its energy to the ocean, ripples of water are created (known as swell). These move towards the UK, growing in size over days and breaking as waves on our shore. **Swell height,** the height from the wave's crest to the trough, greater than 0.3–0.6m (1–2 ft) will be challenging for most paddlers. **Swell direction** is the direction of travel. So, if a SW swell hits a SW-facing beach, the waves will break directly on the beach and may make launching/landing tricky. If a SW swell passes an E-facing beach, the waves are less likely to have an impact – making it potentially a safer or more comfortable spot to launch/land from. **Swell interval** can offer a good indication of conditions. An interval greater than 10 seconds between swells indicates that the swell is consistent and coming from the Atlantic. Intervals less than this – say of 5 seconds – indicate that local wind conditions are influencing the swell and may change over the day. The paddler, therefore, needs to track wind conditions to anticipate changes in swell and direction, especially when launching and landing. ***Clapotis*** is the name given to waves that rebound from vertical faces, such as cliffs and breakwaters, back into the incoming wave. This produces a jumbled, spikey effect on the water's surface, which can make balancing more difficult for the paddler. Paddling a distance away from these vertical features will help avoid the chaotic water.

TIDES

When planning a trip, always check tide tables for tide times and height, and whether it's a spring or neap in specific locations for any day of the year. Paper copies of local tide tables are often on sale in coastal villages and towns, and the BBC provides free online 5-day tide tables at bbc.co.uk/weather/coast-and-sea/tide-tables . Most places on the UK coast experience two **flood tides** resulting in **high tide/water** on a beach and two **ebb tides** resulting in **low tide/water** every day (or every 24hr 50min period, to be precise), and these times are shown in the tables. The period between high and low tide is around six hours. In some locations, where access to the water is only possible at certain stages of the tide, I've indicated the best time to paddle – e.g. "2hrs either side of high tide".

Tide tables also include symbols to represent moon phases, which affect tides. A full or new moon has the largest impact and generates a **spring tide**, resulting in water rising higher up the beach at high tide and ebbing further away at low tide. Paddling to the head of tidal creeks and estuaries is often only possible on spring tides. On **neap tides**, which occur at the first and third quarter of the monthly lunar cycle (represented by a crescent symbol on tide tables), the tide doesn't reach as high up the beach or ebb out as far. Considerably higher volumes of water move between high and low tides on spring tides compared to neaps. For this reason, neap tides are preferable for paddles along the coast or at the mouth of estuaries. Neap and spring tides also affect the **height of high and low water** (given in metres next to tide times in tables). For some paddles, a trip may only be feasible when the tide is deep enough at high water.

Technically speaking, a spring tide occurs on the day of the month when the tide is at its highest, which is often 1-2 days after a full and new moon. However, in this book "springs or neaps" refers to the period 2 days before and after a spring or neap tide when the paddler can maximise their benefits.

Xxxxxxxxx Xxxxxx, XX

For most paddles along the coastline of the South East, the water flows laterally west to east on the flood tide and reverses on the ebb. However, the tidal flows of the Thames estuary go from east to west; and on the Essex coastline they go from north to south. Understanding this **direction of flow** will assist you when choosing direction and timing. In the special notes section of each coastal paddle, the best tidal window for the route is given, as well as the suggested direction of travel for **tidal assistance** (paddling with the tide, not against it). Some locations, however, have their own peculiarities. For example, many of the Sussex and Kent rivers are tidal for up to 20-30 miles inland, so always seek local advice from a local SUP school or the RNLI.

The **speed of tidal flow** depends on the stage of the tidal cycle. At high tide and low tide, flows tend to be at their lowest – this period is often referred to as **slack water** and it's generally a good time to paddle. As the tide cycle shifts from high to low tide, the ebbing tide initially flows slowly and then builds up speed as it approaches the **mid-ebb** tide, which has the fastest flow. After this, the flow slows again towards low tide. The same is true for flood tides. For the beginner, the mid-ebb or mid-flood is one to avoid, especially around headlands or over reefs and ledges where turbulence and challenging conditions can occur. Mid-ebb and mid-flood tides on spring tides will be even more turbulent and challenging, compared to the same on neaps when less water is moving around. For a competent paddler, these mid-tides offer a key time to make good progress on the longer trips detailed in this book.

Rip currents: As waves break on a beach a rip current can form where water returns through a narrow stream. Rip currents are always very localised and mostly occur near river mouths, sandbars, and jetties that help funnel the returning water back out to sea. Generally, the bigger the waves, the stronger the rip current. From the shore, if you see a gap in the line of waves where the waves do not seem to break, it's most likely a rip current. For the experienced paddler, a rip current can be used to navigate through the breaking waves at the

St Margaret's Bay (32)

beginning/end of a paddle. Obviously, for a beach swimmer a rip current should always be avoided.

Tides and flows are complex. For in-depth information, refer www.marine-education.co.uk/free-tutorials/tide-tutorials/ and check with a local paddle instructor.

RIVERS

Be mindful of water flow on rivers and canals, as currents and fast-moving water may present significant hazards. Recent heavy rain as well as sluices, weirs, bridges, and locks en route can all increase **water flow speed**. Plan ahead, and once you get to the river, check for turbulence on the surface – a strong clue that the flow is quick. Anything over 4 knots (nearly 5mph/very brisk walking speed) is inadvisable to

Basingstoke Canal (10)

enter. A typical river will have large variations in flow depending on the shape of the riverbed (including obstacles), whether the river is getting deeper or shallower, and whether it is straight or meandering. Generally, the sections that move slower are near the bank, especially along the inside edge of a curve. When heading upstream, paddling will be easier closer to the bank. At the bank you are also likely to encounter eddy currents where the flow is generally upstream; this counter-flow can help the paddler. The fastest flow is generally on the surface in the middle of a river. Near the riverbed, water flow will be slowed by drag on sand and rocks, just as it is in the shallow water near the bank. This book is not intended to cover white-water sections of rivers; however, in certain low-water conditions, riffles – small rapids that often form across shallows – may be encountered.

Floodwater increases the speed of the flow and adds unexpected currents. Also, a multitude of dangers – from rocks and tree stumps to shopping trollies – can hide just under the surface, waiting to snag your fin. Always check online for water-depth information at riverlevels.uk or check-for-flooding.service.gov.uk/river-and-sea-levels and avoid the waterway if above normal levels. If water levels fall below 3ft (1m), always drop to your knees on the board to avoid falling into shallow water if you run aground. Increasingly, water boards discharge raw sewage into water courses during flood conditions, so check theriverstrust.org/sewage-map

Weirs, canal locks, and bridges on rivers can create specific flows. Plan ahead so you know where to exit weirs and canal locks en route and how to portage around them. When paddling beneath bridges with stanchions, you'll encounter faster flows and eddies, and when anywhere near boat moorings, always keep a look out for hidden hazards such as lines, chains, and ropes.

Portage or portaging is the practice of carrying your craft (board, kayak or canoe) over land, either around an obstacle in a river (such as a fallen tree), between two bodies of water, or around weirs and canal locks. There are many trips in this book where the local authority or Environment Agency have constructed excellent pontoons/launch points to enable the paddler to exit and enter the water safely. Some trips on the River Thames and River Cam, for example, have rollers enabling the paddler to bypass concrete weirs; others, like the River Medway, have canoe passes; and some have signs advising the paddler where to portage the obstruction. Note: kit can easily fall off and get wet when portaging, so ensure everything is safely stowed or removed from the board before making this manoeuvre. I'd also recommend carrying a long 3-metre loop tape and set of karabiners to attach to a D ring to assist with pulling the board up onto the bank (or over an obstacle in the waterway). Never use the leash as these are not strong enough for hauling •

Barcombe Mills, River Ouse (23)

SUP WITH YOUR PUP

Taking your dog out paddleboarding is a great adventure and with a little groundwork to get them used to the idea, you'll both enjoy the experience. Here are some tips:

- First, introduce your dog to the board so they can familiarise themselves with it. We inflated the board and kept it in the house and van for our spaniel to sniff. She soon realised it was a comfortable place to fall asleep We also gave her a few treats each time she sat on the board.
- Next, get your dog used to wearing a Personal Flotation Device (PFD) and choose one with robust grab handles and padding underneath so you can easily pull them out of the water. Attach the PFD when your dog has started to sit on the board so that they associate the two. With a well-trained dog you could also introduce a special command for getting on and off the board, particularly the latter – with tasty rewards of course.
- Once your dog knows how to sit and stay on the board (with the PFD), sit or stand on it yourself and spend some time together. Next, start to rock the board around a bit to get your dog used to motion.
- When it's time to put the training into practice, start on a stretch of quiet, shallow water. If all goes well, take your dog off on a short trip.
- On paddling trips, take a towel – dogs can't resist jumping in – and maybe something to keep your dog warm and dry when the water is cold •

WHAT TO PACK IN YOUR DRYBAG

BASIC KIT

• Buoyancy aid • Leash • Sun hat or beanie • Waterproof cagoule • Warm clothes • Summer/winter gloves • Sunscreen • Polarised sunglasses on floating leash • Mask and snorkel • Plenty of water, snacks, and a hot drink • Hand gel • Fully charged phone and waterproof case • Power bank if available • First aid/personal medication • Spare fin and screws • Bivi bag/foil sheet • Whistle • Torch for caves and canal tunnels • Emergency repair kit such as WRS Emergency Patch Field Repair Kit (the repair kits you get with your paddleboard purchase are only successful if applied in dry, clean conditions • Nano pump • Knife • Floating box for car keys • Cash/credit card • Karabiner and a 3-metre sling to attach drybag to bungees and board.

FOR MORE COMMITTED COASTAL JOURNEYS

In addition to the above, consider taking a tow line or tape and karabiners to attach to other paddlers; spare paddles; GPS device; physical map, compass and waterproof map case. Consider marking your route with the predicted weather, expected timings, landing/picnic spots and any potential issues on the map case with a chinagraph pencil. When relying on phones and other technology, be aware that the signal is often poor offshore.

SUSTAINABLE KIT

If you are keen to reduce your environmental and social footprint, choose brands that take this seriously, such as those that are BCorp-certified. Brands displaying the BCorp logo are audited and certified by a third party to meet extremely strict standards of social and environmental performance, accountability, and transparency. Our favourites are Starboard for boards, paddles and accessories – sup.star-board.com; for clothing we choose Alpkit, DryRobe, Finisterre, Vivobarefoot, and Patagonia among others.

Consider buying brands that are reducing the impacts of their raw materials and those that support environmental and social charities. For example, McConks, a family company, does its utmost to minimise the environmental impact of its products. Also choose brands that use recycled materials in their products. For example, OceanR removes plastics from the ocean and turns it into carbon-positive sustainable clothing. The company also undertakes impactful charitable work for the environment, and people too •

Jubilee River (103)

WHAT TO WEAR

CLOTHING

This will depend on the type of paddling, length of journey, seasons, and weather, along with individual skill levels and the likelihood of falling in. A general rule is to dress for the water temperature, not the air temperature, and wear layers.

Summer brings warm days with warm water temperatures, so paddle in swimwear, quick-drying leggings, a long-sleeve rash vest, and possibly a windproof outer layer for breezier days on the coast. Wear a sun hat for protection and polarised sunglasses on a lanyard.

Autumn is when water temperatures start to drop, so wear a wetsuit or waterproof top and trousers, with warmer spare layers, hats and gloves.

Winter is when we put on neoprene mitts and prefer a drysuit to prevent water directly contacting our body. Wear warm layers underneath, along with warm hats and gloves. Thicker wetsuits can be used but rapidly lose their warming benefits as soon as you exit the water. Alternatively, a split system of waterproof cagoule and trousers with seals around wrist, neck, waist, and ankles will do a similar job but won't keep you completely dry if you fall in.

Spring brings warmer air temperatures but water temperatures will still be cold, so wear similar clothing to autumn.

FOOTWEAR

This should be suitable for the terrain of the launching site and whether you are likely to have to portage around locks, weirs, shallows or obstacles in the water. We use wetsuit boots with hard soles, adding neoprene socks in the winter. In the summer we find that going barefoot offers the best balance and control of the board – but we always carry a pair of wet shoes for landing and portage •

USING THIS BOOK

There were quite literally hundreds more routes that we could have shared in this book but we've chosen those that are suitable for a range of abilities from beginner to intermediate, plus a couple of more challenging routes to aspire to/explore with a local guide. Most have recognised car parks and access routes to the water, toilets and facilities near the launch point, and refreshments along the way or at the destination (although these may be seasonal so always phone ahead).

THE ROUTES

Many of the routes in this book are covered by a local paddling provider, who can give advice or provide tours. They also offer alternatives to very popular locations to avoid further congestion/pollution. Most are unique and special for their natural beauty or cultural interest, and are worth adding to your bucket list. And we've deliberately excluded some "hidden" spots loved by local paddlers.

All of the routes are suited to SUP, canoe, or kayak trips. The choice of waters includes ocean, estuary, rivers, lakes, and canals. At many places you can simply enjoy being on the water or hone your paddling skills, while other routes entail longer journeys with timings dependent on the individual's technique, plus weather and tides. Routes range from those suitable for beginners to ideas for the more experienced paddler, and those looking for inspiration. Each route has a short description of the paddle and what you'll see, along with the start and end points, good places to eat and drink, parking, basic wind and tide advice for that location, and details of permits needed or access restrictions.

Oxford, River Thames (97)

DISTANCE AND TIMINGS

Distances are given for all routes, but timings are omitted because these depend on personal skills, as well as paddling environment and weather conditions. We have found that our average speed is generally around 3km/hour – this includes additional time for exploration.

CHOOSING THE RIGHT PADDLING ENVIRONMENT

Each route has a number assigned to describe the likely paddling environment, but this is just a guideline. It's up to you to judge your competency and experience in these environments. All routes should be undertaken only in the wind and tide conditions suggested for each route, and while adhering to the safety guidance given in this introduction •

Box, River Mole (50)

PADDLING ENVIRONMENTS

GRADE	LAKE	RIVER	CANAL	ESTUARY	COAST
1	Small area, protected, never far from bank	X	Stationary water	X	X
2	Larger area, larger waves, chop & exposure to wind	Some flow, maybe obstacles in water or from bank	Canal-river loop	X	Harbour with boats & obstructions
3	X	X	X	Tidal movements, wind direction	Predominantly sheltered bay
4	X	X	X	X	Coastal journey, some protected water
5	X	X	X	X	Coastal journey on more exposed water

Blenheim Palace Great Lake (98)

Best for

CASTLES & PALACES

- Keyhaven to Hurst Castle 1
- Portsmouth Harbour Explorer 6
- Basingstoke Canal Barley Mow to Odiham Castle 10
- River Arun Arundel to Black Rabbit 17
- River Rother Bodiam Castle 30
- River Thames Hampton Court to Kingston 55
- Blenheim Palace Great Lake 98
- River Thames Windsor to Staines 104

NATURE & WILDLIFE

- Beaulieu River Buckler's Hard to Beaulieu 2
- Basingstoke Canal Mytchett to Ash Lock 11
- Chichester Harbour 13
- River Rother Rye & Rye Harbour 27
- Pegwell Bay & River Stour Ramsgate to Sandwich 33
- Oare to Faversham 39
- Tollesbury Explorer 68
- Reach to Wicken Fen 80
- River Thames Tadpole Bridge to Newbridge 91

CAMPING & CAMPERVANNING

- Calshot Lagoon to Lepe 3
- River Hamble Swanwick to Botley 4
- Hayling Island Chichester Harbour 9
- Basingstoke Canal Mytchett to Ash Lock 11
- Bewl Water 20
- River Ouse Barcombe Mills & Isfield 23
- River Rother Bodiam Castle 30
- River Medway Trail 42 & 43
- River Great Ouse Houghton Mill 78
- River Lark Explorer 79

River Medway Forts (48)

Best for

MILITARY HISTORY

- Calshot Lagoon to Lepe 3
- Portsmouth Harbour Explorer 6
- Alverstoke Lake to Haslar 7
- Hayling Island Langstone Harbour 8
- River Rother Rye & Rye Harbour 27
- Royal Military Canal Hythe to West Hythe 28
- Sheppey Island Queenborough to Deadman's Island 45
- Sheppey Island Barton's Point Coastal Park Lake 46
- Chatham Docks 47
- Gillingham & Medway Islands 48

PUBS & CAFES

- River Hamble Swanwick to Botley 4
- Chichester Harbour Dell Quay to Bosham 13
- River Cuckmere Exceat to Alfriston 26
- Royal Military Canal Hythe to West Hythe 28
- River Rother Bodiam Castle 30
- Oare to Faversham 39
- Sheppey Island Queenborough to Deadman's Island 45
- Wey Navigation Weybridge to Desborough Island 54
- River Thames Richmond & Teddington 56
- Grand Union Canal Paddington to Horsenden Hill 57
- River Lea Tottenham Hale to Hackney Wick 62
- River Thames Tadpole Bridge to Newbridge 91
- Oxford Canal & River Thames Wolvercote Loop 95

Chichester Ship Canal (12)

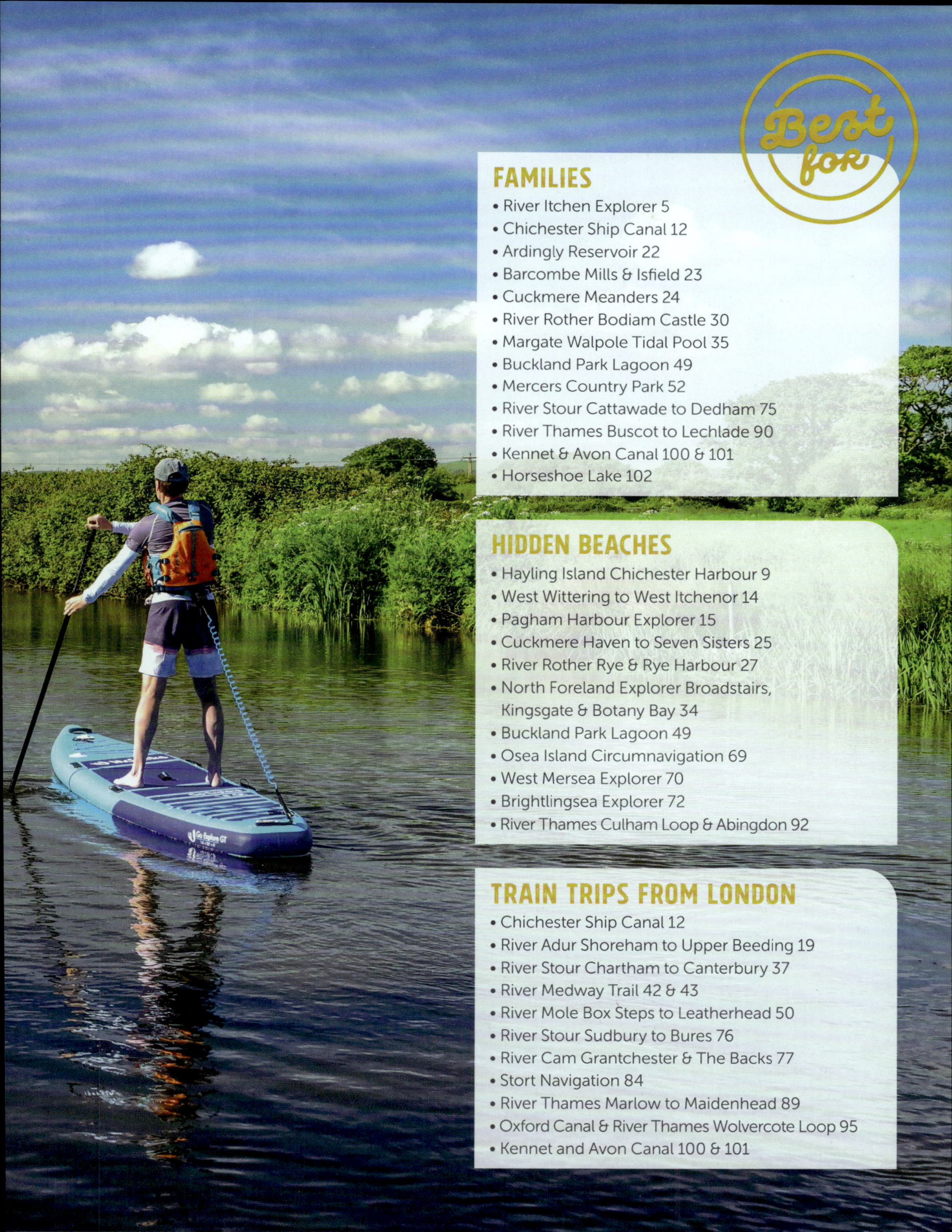

Best for

FAMILIES

- River Itchen Explorer 5
- Chichester Ship Canal 12
- Ardingly Reservoir 22
- Barcombe Mills & Isfield 23
- Cuckmere Meanders 24
- River Rother Bodiam Castle 30
- Margate Walpole Tidal Pool 35
- Buckland Park Lagoon 49
- Mercers Country Park 52
- River Stour Cattawade to Dedham 75
- River Thames Buscot to Lechlade 90
- Kennet & Avon Canal 100 & 101
- Horseshoe Lake 102

HIDDEN BEACHES

- Hayling Island Chichester Harbour 9
- West Wittering to West Itchenor 14
- Pagham Harbour Explorer 15
- Cuckmere Haven to Seven Sisters 25
- River Rother Rye & Rye Harbour 27
- North Foreland Explorer Broadstairs, Kingsgate & Botany Bay 34
- Buckland Park Lagoon 49
- Osea Island Circumnavigation 69
- West Mersea Explorer 70
- Brightlingsea Explorer 72
- River Thames Culham Loop & Abingdon 92

TRAIN TRIPS FROM LONDON

- Chichester Ship Canal 12
- River Adur Shoreham to Upper Beeding 19
- River Stour Chartham to Canterbury 37
- River Medway Trail 42 & 43
- River Mole Box Steps to Leatherhead 50
- River Stour Sudbury to Bures 76
- River Cam Grantchester & The Backs 77
- Stort Navigation 84
- River Thames Marlow to Maidenhead 89
- Oxford Canal & River Thames Wolvercote Loop 95
- Kennet and Avon Canal 100 & 101

Alfriston, Cuckmere River (26)

Best for

LAKES

GETTING AWAY FROM IT ALL

ART & CULTURE

St Margaret's Bay (32)

Best for

WILD SWIMMING

- Keyhaven to Hurst Castle 1
- Chichester Harbour Dell Quay to Bosham Quay 13
- River Stour Chartham to Canterbury 37
- Osea Island Circumnavigation 69
- River Stour Cattawade to Dedham 75
- River Stour Sudbury to Bures 76
- River Ivel Biggleswade to Tempsford 86
- River Thames Tadpole Bridge to Newbridge 91
- River Thames Culham Loop & Abingdon 92
- Oxford Canal & River Thames Wolvercote Loop 95

ADVENTUROUS JOURNEYS

- Pagham Harbour Explorer 15
- River Arun 16 & 17
- Cuckmere Haven to Seven Sisters 25
- River Stour & Pegwell Bay Ramsgate to Sandwich 33
- North Foreland Explorer Broadstairs, Kingsgate & Botany Bay 34
- Oare to Faversham 39
- River Medway Trail Tonbridge to Maidstone 42 & 43
- Gillingham & Medway Islands 48
- River Mole Box Steps to Leatherhead 50
- Abbey River & Penton Hook Island 53
- Grand Union Canal Paddington to Horsenden Hill 57
- Maldon Loop 66
- River Ivel Biggleswade to Tempsford 86

COASTAL ADVENTURES

- Calshot Lagoon to Lepe 3
- Pagham Harbour Explorer 15
- Southwick to Brighton 18
- Cuckmere Haven to Seven Sisters 25
- Folkestone Harbour Explorer 31
- St Margaret's Bay & the White Cliffs 32
- River Stour & Pegwell Bay Ramsgate to Sandwich 33
- North Foreland Explorer Broadstairs, Kingsgate & Botany Bay 34
- Minnis Bay to Margate 36
- Gillingham & Medway Islands 48

1

KEYHAVEN TO HURST CASTLE

ESTUARY · HAMPSHIRE

An estuary trip across Keyhaven Lake from Keyhaven to Hurst Castle. A tranquil haven on the Hampshire coast, this tidal lagoon offers a peaceful escape from nearby towns. Expansive skies and calm waters make it perfect for a gentle paddle, either staying close to Keyhaven Yacht Club or venturing to Hurst Castle.

Protected from the Solent by a shingle bar, these calm waters, fringed by salt marshes and reed beds in the north, are part of the Keyhaven and Pennington Marshes Nature Reserve. At low tide, the lagoon's saltings and mudflats dry out, leaving deeper channels that host lines of colourful moored boats. Within the lagoon, pools like Keyhaven Lake, Mount Lake, and Hawker's Lake attract birdwatchers with sightings of avocets, oystercatchers, and egrets.

For the circular route to Hurst Castle, start from Keyhaven slipway and head southwest along the shoreline, then turn southeast, following the shingle spit to reach the castle itself. Standing defiantly at the end of this windswept spit, Hurst Castle is a striking remnant of England's coastal defences. Built by Henry VIII to guard the Solent, the fortress has played roles from imprisoning Charles I to serving as a strategic point in World War II, with layers of history etched into its rugged stone walls. It is a fabulous place to explore (charges), as is the maze of waterways and salt marshes on the journey.

To return, follow the more direct northwest route of the summer ferry back to Keyhaven •

- **DISTANCE:** 5km return.
- **PADDLING ENVIRONMENT:** 4.
- **ROUTE MAP:** islandeering.com/paddleboarding-keyhaven-to-hurst-castle/
- **ACCESS RESTRICTIONS:** Launch and river use fee. https://www.newforest.gov.uk/article/1423/Keyhaven-River; queries to River Wardens on 01590 645695 or email keyhavenriverwarden@nfdc.gov.uk
- **OS MAP:** OS Explorer OL22 New Forest.
- **STARTING POINT:** Keyhaven slipway next to Keyhaven River Warden's Office. Grid ref. SZ 307 914; What3Words forecast.slicer.shifters.
- **PARKING:** Keyhaven Amenity Car Park (charges), Keyhaven, SO41 0TP. Launching: Slipway a short walk from car park.
- **PITSTOPS:** Good food and drinks in charming coastal pub The Gun, Keyhaven, tel. 01590 642391; delicious homemade cakes and stunning views, Hurst Castle Café, tel. 01590 642500.
- **GETTING THERE:** From Lymington, take the A337 south; L onto the B3058 towards Milford on Sea. Follow signs for Keyhaven, turning L at Keyhaven Road, which leads directly into the village and car park.
- **SPECIAL POINTS:** Best paddled 2hrs either side of HW. The shingle bank of Hurst beach offers some protection from SW wind and swell. Check Surfline surfline.com at Keyhaven for local conditions.
- **OFFSHORE WIND:** NW-W

AZTRON

2

BEAULIEU RIVER BUCKLER'S HARD TO BEAULIEU

TIDAL RIVER · HAMPSHIRE

Meander along the tranquil Beaulieu River from the timeless shipbuilding village of Buckler's Hard to the charming heart of Beaulieu on a tide-assisted paddle past salt marshes, ancient woodlands, and abundant wildlife in this peaceful New Forest haven. The Beaulieu River, one of the most picturesque in the south and part of the Beaulieu Estate, is a rare privately owned river that remains largely unspoiled, with diverse habitats rich in wildlife, flora, and fauna.

Start at Buckler's Hard, an atmospheric 18th-century shipbuilding village once renowned for constructing Royal Navy warships, including those that fought at Trafalgar. It later became a key base during World War II for building and repairing naval vessels and assembling parts of the Mulberry Harbours used in the D-Day landings. Launch from Buckler's Hard Marina, turn left upriver and pass moored boats with caution, avoiding the main channel.

The riverbanks, designated as a Site of Special Scientific Interest (SSSI), are lined with rich salt marshes and mudflats offering sightings of ospreys, curlews, redshanks, otters, and seals, along with specialised plants like sea lavender and marsh samphire. Small inlets, known locally as 'reaches', can be explored along the way. Magnificent secluded homes with private jetties dot the river, and the chimney of Bailey's Hard Brick Works can be seen on the left bank.

Arrival in Beaulieu reveals the village green and Beaulieu Palace on the right, with the weir ahead marking the end of the navigable river. Although landing here is not permitted, it is a peaceful spot for an onboard picnic while enjoying the serene surroundings before heading back.

The river can also be explored downstream from Buckler's Hard to Needs Ore Point, Gull Island, and the mouth of the river at the Solent. Confident paddlers can extend the journey further east to Lepe Beach, which is largely sheltered from the Solent •

- **DISTANCE:** 8.3km return.
- **PADDLING ENVIRONMENT:** 3.
- **ROUTE MAP:** islandeering.com/paddleboarding-bucklers-hard-to-beaulieu/
- **ACCESS RESTRICTIONS:** Launch fee £10, includes parking at Yacht Club, via online booking system, for a 2hr timeslot to launch (no restrictions on return time) beaulieuriver.co.uk/visiting/slipways-launch-fees/. No landing at Beaulieu, upstream or downstream of Buckler's Hard or Gull Island at the river mouth – all are important nature reserves.
- **OS MAP:** OS Explorer OL22 New Forest.
- **STARTING POINT:** Buckler's Hard Yacht Harbour, Dock Lane, Beaulieu, New Forest, Hampshire, SO42 7XB. Grid ref. SU 409 002; What3Words weeds.blockage.miles.
- **LAUNCHING:** Floating pontoon, 300m walk from car park.
- **PARKING:** Buckler's Hard Yacht Harbour (or in Buckler's Hard village car park).
- **PITSTOPS:** *Buckler's Hard* Good breakfasts, lunches, and afternoon teas, the Captain's Table, tel. 01590 616203; a cosy inn, hearty food, BBQs and great selection of beers, Henry's Bar, tel. 01590 616253; *Lepe* Fabulous views and good food, The Lookout Café 02380 899108
- **GETTING THERE:** J2 M27 onto A326 towards Fawley; B3054 to Beaulieu and follow signs to Buckler's Hard on the B3054. After Beaulieu Village, continue straight for approx. 2 miles until you reach Buckler's Hard Marina on the left.
- **SPECIAL POINTS:** Slipway available at all states of tide; best journey window 3hrs before HW to paddle upstream to Beaulieu. Use of buoyancy aids mandatory. No landing possible upstream in the National Nature Reserve. Check tide times at Harbour's live tide tracker beaulieuriver.co.uk/visiting/height-depth-atmospheric-live-data/. Note: 2hr delay on ebb during spring tides, meaning higher water for a longer period for the upstream trip; the ebb then has much higher flows to be aware of. Further information: beaulieuriver.co.uk/wp-content/uploads/2020/07/Beaulieu-River-Paddle-Sports-Guide-2020-WEB.pdf

3

CALSHOT LAGOON TO LEPE

ESTUARY/COAST · HAMPSHIRE

A wild mix of coastal beauty and history exploring Calshot Lagoon's sheltered waters, or a stunning Solent coastal adventure past hidden smugglers' tunnels and D-Day remnants around Lepe. For a gentle paddle, Calshot Lagoon, protected from The Solent by the 1.5 km-long shingle of Calshot Spit, is a haven of salt marsh and intertidal mudflats rich with native and migratory birds and wildlife.

For a more adventurous coastal trip to Lepe, start from Calshot Lagoon and head clockwise around the head of the spit into Southampton Water, passing the RNLI Lifeboat Station and Calshot Castle. Built by King Henry VIII, this low circular stone fortress was once armed with large guns to protect the vital harbour at Southampton from seaborne attacks by France or Spain. The large hangars of the Calshot Activity Centre, located on the Spit, were originally built as part of Calshot Naval Air Station for operating flying boats. In the early 1900s, it was also the venue for the prestigious Schneider Trophy, an international air race for seaplanes.

Head southwest alongside the shingle beach, initially passing colourful beach huts and then wooded coastline. Luttrell's Tower, a three-storey stuccoed yellow brick folly that's now a holiday home, looms above the trees. Built for Temple Simon Luttrell, a Member of Parliament and reputedly a smuggler, a 'smugglers tunnel' runs from the tower to the beach.

Towards Lepe Beach, the substantial visible remains of D-Day activities can be seen, including concrete ramps, slipways, and the distinctive dolphins – two metal structures in the water used to protect moored landing craft from the current. Head around Stansore Point, either around or over Horseshoe Spit depending on the tide, to reach Lepe Beach and its café. Return via the same route •

• **DISTANCE:** Free-range in Calshot Lagoon; or 13km return to Lepe Beach.

• **PADDLING ENVIRONMENT:** 3 in lagoon, 5 on coast.

• **ROUTE MAP:** islandeering.com/paddleboarding-calshot-lagoon-to-lepe/

• **ACCESS RESTRICTIONS:** No licence required.

• **OS MAP:** OS Explorer OL22 New Forest.

• **STARTING POINT:** Calshot Lagoon beach.

• **PARKING:** Calshot Activities Centre (charges), Jack Maynard Road, Fawley, SO45 1BR; Grid ref. SU 487 020; What3Words stability.fattest.either.

• **LAUNCHING:** Calshot Lagoon beach.

• **PITSTOPS:** Café with Solent views, The Lookout, Lepe Country Park, tel. 02380 899108.

• **CAMPING:** Stunning views over the Solent to the Isle of Wight and beachside camping with Calshot Activities Centre (annual Calshot Camping Access pass required for pitch booking – £35). hants.gov.uk/thingstodo/calshot/stay/camping

• **LESSONS AND HIRE:** The SUP Co. at Calshot Beach, thesupco.com

• **GETTING THERE:** J2 M27, then A326 south towards Fawley. Look out for the brown tourist signs for Calshot Activities Centre.

• **SPECIAL POINTS:** During spring tides a double high tide can occur, giving more time to explore within the lagoon. It's best to enter as soon as the mudbanks are covered, which can be up to 2.5hrs before high water (HW). Be mindful that the head of the lagoon empties quickly, and can catch paddlers out. It's recommended to exit 1hr after HW or stay within the deeper water around the end of the spit. The journey to Lepe is possible at most states of the tide, but several spits of land dry out at low water (LW). During spring high water the ebb is delayed, so timing the return to Calshot Spit is important. Aim to return anytime before 1.5hrs after HW to avoid stronger ebb currents.

• **OFFSHORE WIND:** NW

4

RIVER HAMBLE SWANWICK TO BOTLEY

TIDAL RIVER · HAMPSHIRE

Explore the tidal Upper River Hamble with plenty of great pitstops along the way. Bustling marinas, tranquil country parks, and a paddleboarders' gem, The Hidden Tap, offer perfect spots to pause and enjoy refreshments while staying afloat. Leave from the Swanwick slipway, turn left to reach the end of the mooring pontoons and head upriver along the left (west) bank, past the Jolly Sailor. Once under the A27 road bridge, keep to the middle of the channel to avoid the pontoons, then pass beneath the railway bridge. Stop off at Floaters Café, where service is available from their pontoon, just before reaching the M27 bridge. After the bridge, skirt to the left to avoid the pontoons at Eastlands Boatyard. From here, the river becomes peaceful, winding through the fields and woods of the River Hamble Country Park.

After 4.8 km, the river forks. Take the left fork to continue to Botley (the right fork leads to Curbridge). After a short distance, pass the grounds of YMCA Fairthorne Manor and continue up the ever-narrowing river through the wooded riverbanks and the outskirts of Botley. Once past the A334 road bridge, the old buildings of Botley Mills loom above. It's likely that grain milling has taken place here for well over a thousand years. Don't miss the invitation to 'ring the bell' here for excellent ales, ice cream, or pizza to be lowered down to you from the Botley Brewery's Hidden Tap. To see the Botley Waterfall, head upriver a little further before returning the same way, looking out for water voles, herons, and large grey mullet in the shallows •

• **DISTANCE:** 13.5km return.

• **PADDLING ENVIRONMENT:** 3.

• **ROUTE:** islandeering.com/paddleboarding-swanwick-to-botley/

• **ACCESS RESTRICTIONS**: No licence required.

• **OS MAP:** OS Explorer OL3 Meon Valley, Portsmouth, Gosport & Fareham.

• **STARTING POINT & PARKING:** Swanwick Shore Car Park (charges), Swanwick, Southampton, SO31 7EF. Grid ref. SU 495 092; What3Words twigs.fakes.result.

• **LAUNCHING:** Lower Swanwick slipway adjacent to car park.

• **PITSTOPS:** Goodies served from hatch of a boat to river-users, Floaters Café, floaterscafe.co.uk (check hours); great beers and vibe, The Hidden Tap, Botley, botleybreweryltd.com/hidden-tap ; Horse and Jockey, Curbridge mynewlocal.co.uk ; The Jolly Sailor, Old Bursledon, jollysailoroldbursledon.co.uk

• **LESSONS AND HIRE:** The Paddle Centre, Lower Swanwick, thepaddlecentre.co.uk ; self-launch and hire, YMCA Fairthorne Manor ymca-fg.org/fairthorne-manor/river-access/ (short paddle to Botley).

• **GETTING THERE:** *Car* Leave A27 onto Lower Shore Road, adjacent to Premier Marina and Boatyard; *Train* London (Waterloo) to Bursledon, change Southampton (2hr journey), and launch from Lands End Slipway near Jolly Sailor. southwesternrailway.com

• **CAMPING:** Large camping area, self-launch (charges) at YMCA Fairthorne Manor ymca-fg.org/fairthorne-manor/campsite/

• **SPECIAL POINTS:** Launch 2hrs before HW or as soon as the water covers the hard of the slipway. If visiting the pubs and cafés, check opening times align with your HW windows. Watch out for other water users as the water around Bursledon can be extremely busy. Once past all the moorings, keep to the right of the main channel upriver.

5

RIVER ITCHEN EXPLORER

RIVER · HAMPSHIRE

Experience the River Itchen's clear chalk stream waters near Winchester or enjoy a leisurely pub paddle near Swaythling – both ideal for beginners and families. The first route along the Itchen Navigation, fed by the River Itchen, offers clear chalk stream waters supporting rich wildlife, including water voles, otters, and the rare southern damselfly. This river also inspired Victorian writer John Keats during his time in Winchester. Start on the riverbank near the Handlebar Café at the base of St. Catherine's Hill, then head right toward Wharf Bridge (1.5 km round trip), the northernmost navigable section. The journey passes meadows, playing fields, and Winchester College Boat Club. Alternatively, the Itchen Navigation can be explored for just under a kilometre by heading left from the launch point.

The second route, downstream of Winchester and near where the Itchen flows into Southampton Water, follows a section of the River Itchen in Swaythling. Launch from the river beach near Woodmill Outdoor Activities Centre and paddle upstream to the White Swan pub (3 km round trip). This is a non-tidal stretch of the river, with the tidal section beginning downstream of Woodmill. The café at Woodmill, set in a picturesque 15th-century former flour mill overlooking the river, is ideal for post-paddle refreshments •

- **DISTANCE:** Free-range.
- **PADDLING ENVIRONMENT**: 2.
- **ROUTE MAP:** islandeering.com/paddleboarding-river-itchen-explorer/
- **ACCESS RESTRICTIONS:** No licence required.
- **OS MAP:** OS Explorer OL32 Winchester, New Alresford & East Meon; and OS Explorer OL22 New Forest.
- **STARTING POINT:** See parking and launching.
- **PARKING:** *Winchester* Garnier Road Car Park (free), Garnier Road, Winchester, SO23 9PA; Grid ref. SU 483 280; What3Words shipwreck.sleepers.view. *Swaythling* Riverside Car Park (free), Woodmill Lane, Hampton Park, Bitterne Park, Southampton, SO18 2JR. Grid ref. SU 440 151; What3Words total.loses.admire.
- **LAUNCHING:** *Winchester* Riverbank adjacent to car park; *Swaythling* Riverside adjacent to car park.
- **PITSTOPS:** *Winchester* Breakfasts and sourdough toasties, Handlebar Café, handlebar.cafe ; *Swaythling* Fabulous breakfast, brunch, lunch, and cake, Wood Mill Coffee Kitchen, tel. 02380 172419; carvery and grill, White Swan pub, tel. 023 8047 3322
- **LESSONS AND TOURS:** Woodmill Outdoor Activities Centre, tel. 02380 439185 activenation.org.uk/venues/woodmill/
- **GETTING THERE:** *Winchester* J10 off M3 towards Winchester; follow signs towards St Cross then along Garnier Road; CP on L. *Swaythling* J5 off M27 onto A335 towards Southampton; stay on main carriageway and follow signs for Swaythling (A335 veers left); L fork towards Portswood/City Centre along High Road, then at Swaythling Working Mens Club L onto Woodmill Lane and follow over river, CP on L.
- **SPECIAL POINTS:** Summer weed growth, use river fins.

The
Cafe

6

PORTSMOUTH HARBOUR EXPLORER

INLAND HARBOUR · HAMPSHIRE

The wilder side of Portsmouth Harbour, with an imposing castle, a wildlife island, and a quiet tidal creek. Portsmouth Harbour is a large tidal inlet, rich in natural habitats and iconic views. Sheltered by the bulk of Portsea Island and Gosport to the south, its northern shores are a haven of intertidal mudflats, tidal creeks, and salt marshes, supporting a diverse array of wildlife. From various vantage points along the north shore, sweeping views across the harbour reveal historic landmarks like the imposing walls of Portchester Castle, the sleek lines of the Spinnaker Tower, and the large warships of Portsmouth's naval dockyard.

Launching from Wicor beach offers a choice of two distinct trips to experience this captivating landscape. To explore Pewit Island and Portchester Castle, either head left to pass beneath the jetty or paddle around it, depending on the tide. Head southeast to circle the bird sanctuary of Pewit Island (landing is forbidden), then set a northeast course toward the imposing stone walls of Portchester Castle. It is possible to land here and explore further. Perched on the edge of Portsmouth Harbour, the castle was originally built as a Roman fort. The Norman keep, later transformed into a royal residence, adds grandeur to the site, while its history as a medieval prison adds further intrigue. Return to Wicor, paddling parallel to the shoreline, and stop at the Salt Café to enjoy some refreshments before completing the journey.

To explore the tidal Fareham Creek, leave Wicor and head right around Wicor Hard into the shallow Cams Bay. Find the main channel and continue north upstream along the creek. Pass the string of moorings at Fareham Sailing Club, or use the large slipway at Town Quay to exit for Tides Coffee Shop or Castle in the Air pub. Continue around the sharp right meander a short distance to Upper Fareham Lake, Cams Mill pub (once a large tidal mill), and the arches of the attractive red-bricked viaduct. Return the same way •

• DISTANCE: Wicor to Fareham 8km return; Wicor to Portchester Castle 7km return.

• PADDLING ENVIRONMENT: 4.

• ROUTE MAP: islandeering.com/paddleboarding-portsmouth-harbour-explorer/

• ACCESS RESTRICTIONS: No licence required.

• OS MAP: OS Explorer OL3 Meon Valley, Portsmouth, Gosport & Fareham.

• STARTING POINT: Wicor Lake (see parking)

• PARKING: Wicor Car Park (charges), Cranleigh Rd, Portchester, Fareham, PO16 9BY. Grid ref. SU 600 051; What3Words throat.dentures.best.

• LAUNCHING: Beach adjacent to car park.

• PITSTOPS: Hidden boatyard gem overlooking Wicor Lake and great spot for brunch or lunchtime pizza and cocktails, Salt Café, Wicor Marine Yacht Haven saltcafe.co.uk ; great home-made cakes and more, Tides Coffee Shop, facebook.com/tidescoffeeshop/ ; good food, Castle in the Air, Fareham, tel. 01329 280320.

• GETTING THERE: J11 off M27, then A27 towards Portchester. L onto White Hart Lane/Cranleigh Road. L onto Hoad's Hill and follow to Wicor Mill Lane. Car park on left opposite Wicor Recreation Ground.

• SPECIAL POINTS: Both trips are best on a rising tide 2hrs before HW to get to the halfway points around HW. The estuary is exposed to wind; check Surfline surfline.com at nearby Southsea for local conditions.

7

ALVERSTOKE LAKE TO HASLAR

TIDAL RIVER · HAMPSHIRE

Journey through three tidal lakes towards the iconic Spinnaker Tower and paddle underneath a submarine. Alverstoke Lake is a shallow, sheltered tidal lake surrounded by residential areas and green spaces, offering a peaceful spot for easy paddles in a sheltered environment. To take the trip to Haslar, exit Alverstoke Lake at its eastern edge and relaunch into the larger, more secluded Stoke Lake, which is flanked by Gosport Park and nature reserves. The mix of saltwater and freshwater habitats attracts a variety of birdlife, especially in winter when it becomes a haven for migratory species.

As the waterway widens into Haslar Lake, an area rich in naval history, look out for the nearby Royal Haslar Hospital, once a key military medical facility. The lake is surrounded by a blend of residential areas, green spaces, and remnants of maritime heritage. Paddle under Haslar Bridge and past the tall masts of the marina's sailing boats, keeping to the right around the large pontoons, to reach the Submarine Museum. No landing here, but you can paddle beneath the imposing metal hull of HMS Alliance, a restored Royal Navy submarine launched in 1945, which served during the Cold War and now stands as a striking exhibit of naval history. Return the same way •

• **DISTANCE:** Alverstoke Lake to Haslar 5km return.

• **PADDLING ENVIRONMENT:** 3.

• **ROUTE MAP:** islandeering.com/paddleboarding-alverstoke-lake-to-haslar/

• **ACCESS RESTRICTIONS:** No licence required.

• **OS MAP:** OS Explorer OL3 Meon Valley, Portsmouth, Gosport & Fareham.

• **STARTING POINT:** Alverstoke Lake, Little Anglesey Road, Gosport, PO12 2HS. Grid ref. SZ 603 987; What3Words couches.slope.dined.

• **PARKING:** Lakeside (free).

• **LAUNCHING:** Lakeside.

• **LESSONS AND HIRE:** GoSport Activity Centre, 07596 005613.

• **GETTING THERE:** J11 M27 for Gosport/Fareham. A32 S to Gosport then R onto B3333 and follow until it becomes Privett Road; L into Stokes Bay Road then L onto Clayhall Road to the lake.

• **SPECIAL POINTS:** Alverstoke Lake can be paddled at all states of the tide due to the dam at its eastern end, but route to Haslar Bridge best paddled 2hrs either side of HW to avoid the mudbanks and paddling against the main ebb tide. Watch out for other boat users around the marina.

8

HAYLING ISLAND LANGSTONE HARBOUR

ESTUARY · HAMPSHIRE

A tide-assisted trip through the hidden wilds of Langstone Harbour, where sweeping skies and wartime history merge with secret creeks and tranquil lagoons. Langstone Harbour is a haven for wildlife, with flocks of wading birds peppering the mudflats, busily foraging in the glistening shallows. The salt marshes buzz with life, and in summertime the air is filled with the cries of terns diving for fish. Lucky paddlers may even spot seals basking lazily on exposed mudflats. This is a secluded, wild corner of the south coast, hidden from the bustle of Portsmouth.

Leave from Sinah Beach and head north into Langstone Harbour, taking care to avoid the small ferry crossing to Portsea. Just north of the ferry jetty, the ruins of a Mulberry Harbour serve as a reminder of the area's significant military history. In World War I, it was a key mooring site for naval vessels, protected by fortifications guarding the naval hub of Portsmouth. In World War II, its importance grew further, with coastal defences and its role as a staging area for troops and landing craft ahead of the D-Day landings.

Round the head of the Sinah Peninsula to enter The Kench, home to a vibrant array of houseboats. Beyond, sweeping views span across the harbour, from Portsmouth's historic landmarks to the rolling hills of the South Downs National Park. Continue along Hayling Island's coastline, passing quiet inlets, small beaches, and reed-fringed creeks, to reach the lagoons of the West Hayling Nature Reserve. Once the site of the 1864 South of England Oyster Company, it is now a protected area for birds and wildlife (no landing permitted).

Pass through the clear gap in the remains of the defunct Hayling Billy rail bridge before continuing under the road bridge. Just north of the bridge, The Ship and the Royal Oak offer great pub options, with the quaint buildings of Langstone village and the picturesque mill providing a perfect backdrop. Return the same way •

- **DISTANCE:** 16km return (shorter options available).
- **PADDLING ENVIRONMENT**: 3.
- **ROUTE MAP:** islandeering.com/paddleboarding-hayling-island-langstone-harbour/
- **ACCESS RESTRICTIONS:** Langstone Harbour charges apply langstoneharbour.org.uk/pay-now
- **OS MAP:** OS Explorer OL8 Chichester, South Harting & Selsey.
- **STARTING POINT:** Sinah Beach, Ferry Road, Hayling Island, PO11 0DQ. Grid ref. SZ 688 998; What3Words alarm.invest.design.
- **PARKING:** Ferry Road Car Park (charges) adjacent to Sinah Beach.
- **LAUNCHING:** Sandy beach short walk from car park.
- **PITSTOPS:** Café fare with great views, Beach Café, Sinah Beach; pint overlooking the Solent, Ferryboat Inn, Sinah, tel. 02392 463459; popular pub on the quay, The Ship, Langstone, tel. 02392 471719; atmospheric waterside pub, The Royal Oak, Langstone, tel. 02392 483125.
- **GETTING THERE:** J12 off M27 onto A27 towards Havant/Emsworth; exit onto A3023 for Hayling Island and continue south through island, passing through Langstone and Northney. At roundabout near West Town, take third exit onto Ferry Road and continue to car park near Sinah Beach.
- **SPECIAL POINTS:** Best to paddle 2.5hrs before HW to gain access to the coastline and avoid jet skis, otherwise access will be limited to the main harbour channel. Southwest winds can sweep through the harbour. Check Surfline surfline.com at South Hayling Beach for local conditions. Return via the main channel for a faster journey, as egress at Sinah is accessible at all states of the tide. Strong currents can be encountered at the harbour mouth, whether on the flood or ebb tide.

9

HAYLING ISLAND CHICHESTER HARBOUR

ESTUARY · HAMPSHIRE

Explore the quiet tidal inlets of Chichester Harbour on the southeast coast of Hayling Island. This National Landscape is a wild mix of salt marshes, mudflats, and sand and shingle beaches, bursting with life and energy. It's internationally recognised for its biodiversity, with thousands of migratory birds making it their home, earning it both SSSI and Ramsar status. Renowned for sailing and watersports, its sheltered waters are a magnet for adventurers all year round.

To explore the southern reaches of Chichester Harbour, leave from Fishery Creek and head left along the tidal inlet. Once at its mouth, head northeast towards the masts of Sparkes Marina. Paddle around its moorings and then south into the tidal inlet to the west of Black Point at the eastern entrance to Chichester Harbour. Sandy and protected from the main water of the Solent, it is an idyllic place to paddle (although the beach itself is private and owned by the Hayling Island Sailing Club).

From Black Point, head north past Fishery Creek, Mengham Salterns, and the sailing club, into the tidal inlet of My Lord's Pond. Enjoy a peaceful paddle around the wooded creek before returning to Fishery Creek •

- **DISTANCE:** 6km return.
- **PADDLING ENVIRONMENT:** 3.
- **ROUTE MAP:** islandeering.com/paddleboarding-hayling-island-chichester-harbour/
- **ACCESS RESTRICTIONS:** Harbour dues required for Chichester Harbour conservancy.co.uk/on-the-water/paddlesports/. Contact the Harbour Office, tel. 01243 512301, or visit in Itchenor or Emsworth. Self-launch from Fishery Creek Touring Park – sign in at reception (£5 charge).
- **OS MAP:** OS Explorer OL8 Chichester, South Harting & Selsey.
- **STARTING POINT:** Fishery Creek Touring Park, Fishery Lane, Hayling Island, PO11 9NR; Grid ref. SZ 735 988; What3Words thrashed.scale.worry.
- **PARKING:** Car park (free) in campsite only if booked with Hayling Watersports.
- **LAUNCHING:** Campsite slipway.
- **CAMPING:** Great family creekside camping, Fishery Creek Touring Park, tel. 02392 462164.
- **LESSONS, HIRE AND TOURS:** Super-friendly and knowledgeable Simon at Hayling Watersports, Fishery Creek Touring Park, tel. 07539 449789.
- **GETTING THERE:** J12 off M27 onto A27 towards Havant/Chichester, then A3023 towards Hayling Island. Follow A3023 S onto Hayling Island. Take first R at Mill Rythe roundabout, following brown signs for Fishery Creek Touring Park.
- **SPECIAL POINTS:** Best paddled 2hrs either side of HW. Southwest winds can blow through Fishery Creek towards Chichester Harbour. Check Surfline surfline.com at nearby Hayling Island for local conditions.

10

BASINGSTOKE CANAL BARLEY MOW TO ODIHAM CASTLE

CANAL · HAMPSHIRE

Paddle a rural stretch of Basingstoke Canal to find the castle that played its part in changing British history. Start from at the Barley Mow car park and head right, passing beneath the historic brick-arched Barley Mow Bridge. Continue under several more arched bridges to reach Sandy Hill Bridge. Beyond this point, the canal takes a scenic route through Sandy Hill Cutting, shaded by tree canopies, offering a picturesque passage through rural Hampshire. Proceed past Broad Oak Bridge and the Odiham Bypass Bridge, and then arrive at the Galleon Marine boatyard and Colt Hill Wharf.

Continue beneath the canal bridge, passing the mooring spot for John Pinkerton boat trips and the Waterwitch Pub on the left. Pass open fields, then go under Lodge Bridge, with North Warnborough sluice visible further along. Travel beneath Swan Bridge in North Warnborough, then under the lift bridge to walk a short distance north to reach the ruins of Odiham Castle.

Locally known as 'King John's Castle', Odiham Castle stands near the canal. In the 13th century, King John set out from here to sign the Magna Carta at Runnymede, a pivotal event in British history. Signed in 1215, the Magna Carta established that even the king was subject to the law, shaping the foundation of the British judiciary and democracy. This historic act ensured the rule of law applied to all, emphasising that no one, not even royalty, was above the law. Return the same way •

- **DISTANCE:** 13.8km return.
- **PADDLING ENVIRONMENT:** 1.
- **ROUTE MAP:** islandeering.com/paddleboarding-barley-mow-to-odiham-castle/
- **ACCESS RESTRICTIONS:** Licence required, included in Paddle UK membership; or Basingstoke Canal Licence hants.gov.uk/thingstodo/basingstokecanal/onthewater/unpowered
- **OS MAP:** OS Explorer 144 Basingstoke, Alton & Whitchurch.
- **STARTING POINT:** Barley Mow, Winchfield (see parking).
- **PARKING:** Barley Mow Car Park (free), Spratts Hatch Lane, Winchfield, RG27 8DE. Grid ref. SU 777 537; What3Words supported.items.winks.
- **LAUNCHING:** Canalside or slipway adjacent to parking.
- **PITSTOPS:** Nice garden, The Barley Mow pub, Winchfield, tel. 01252 617490; food and drink at canalside pub in Colt Hill, The Waterwitch, tel. 01256 702778.
- **GETTING THERE:** Find Spratts Hatch Lane directly opposite the Barley Mow pub, following signs to Dogmersfield and Crookham. Car park almost immediately on left.
- **SPECIAL POINTS:** No locks/portages required. Please clean board before you enter the water to prevent spread of non-native plants and animal species.

11

BASINGSTOKE CANAL MYTCHETT TO ASH LOCK

CANAL · HAMPSHIRE

Family paddle along a wildlife-rich canal with several small lakes, including the wonderfully named Great Bottom Flash. The Basingstoke Canal was originally built to connect Basingstoke with the River Thames at Weybridge via the Wey Navigation, enabling boats to transport agricultural products from Hampshire to London. However, the canal was never commercially successful and gradually fell into disrepair until it was restored and re-opened in 1991.

Start from the Visitor Centre at Mytchett and turn left immediately to go under Mytchett Place Bridge. Beyond Mytchett Lake Bridge, look out for ducks, cormorants, and great crested grebes fishing in the large lake owned by the Ministry of Defence (MoD) on the left. Pass beneath Mytchett Lake railway bridge, then through a series of wider lake-like sections known as "flashes", where the canal crosses hollows in the natural landscape. Fringed by wetlands, they are great to explore away from the narrower confines of the canal. Continue under Deedman's footbridge, then Ash Vale railway bridge (station accessible from the right bank).

Great Bottom Flash is a stretch of open water with a couple of derelict canal barges now overtaken by nature. After Heath Vale Bridge, reach The Swan pub on the left. Continue under Ash Vale Bridge, then the rail bridge, passing the scenic high-sided Ash embankment with its colourful array of plant life. Pass the sluice and weir on the left, then continue over the aqueduct that spans the A331 and the Blackwater Valley. After a further railway bridge, arrive at Ash Lock.

Return the same way, keeping an eye out for the wealth of wildlife that can be spotted along this waterway, celebrated as the most botanically rich aquatic area in England. You might spot the nationally scarce hairlike pondweed and tasteless water-pepper, or a few of the 24 species of dragonfly here •

- **DISTANCE:** 10km return.
- **PADDLING ENVIRONMENT:** 1.
- **ROUTE MAP:** islandeering.com/paddleboarding-mytchett-to-ash-lock/
- **ACCESS RESTRICTIONS:** Licence required, included in Paddle UK membership; or Basingstoke Canal Licence hants.gov.uk/thingstodo/basingstokecanal/onthewater/unpowered
- **OS MAP:** OS Explorer 145 Guildford & Farnham.
- **STARTING POINT:** Canal Centre, Place Road, Mytchett, GU16 6DD. Grid ref. SU 893 550; What3Words fleet.cares.daisy.
- **PARKING:** Mytchett Canal Centre (free).
- **LAUNCHING:** Public slipway.
- **PITSTOPS:** Watch the canal boats with an all-day breakfast or cake, Canal Centre Café; popular canalside pub, The Swan, Ash Vale, tel. 01252 325212 (just beyond Heath Vale Bridge Road).
- **HIRE:** Canoe and kayak hire at Mytchett Canal Centre, tel. 01252 370073.
- **GETTING THERE:** *Car* J4 M3 then A3331, following signs towards Guildford; L following signs to Mytchett; at double roundabout follow signs towards Pirbright and brown canal sign; L following brown sign to Basingstoke Canal Visitor Centre; *Train* Ash Vale direct from London Waterloo, short walk to canal.
- **CAMPING:** Canalside camping next to Basingstoke Canal Centre (Easter–end September), tel. 01252 370073.
- **SPECIAL POINTS:** No locks/portages required. Please clean your board before you enter the water to prevent spread of non-native plants and animal species.

12

CHICHESTER SHIP CANAL

CANAL · WEST SUSSEX

A tranquil trip on a historic waterway where kingfishers dart, wildflowers brighten the banks, and the views of Chichester Cathedral are unmatched. The Chichester Ship Canal is a historic waterway, originally constructed in the 1820s as part of a broader plan to link Portsmouth and London via an inland route. The canal spans approximately 6.5 kilometres from Chichester to Chichester Harbour at Birdham, though only the section between the Canal Basin and Donnington remains navigable, with the stretch beyond serving as a protected nature reserve. While it was initially designed to accommodate larger ships, commercial use dwindled by the late 19th century. Today, the canal is a serene and picturesque destination that's especially popular with paddlers.

Starting from the Canal Basin in Chichester, a short distance ahead is the restored Poyntz Bridge, an original swing bridge that was relocated from further down the canal. Nearby, a charming butterfly sculpture perches above vibrant wildflowers clinging to the embankment.

Continue beyond the hum of the A27, a deep tranquillity settles over the canal with the canal banks teeming with hidden life. Kingfishers dart like bright jewels across the water's surface, while herons stand statuesque at the edge, waiting for their perfect catch. Listen for the melodious songs of robins, finches, and warblers, their notes weaving through the trees. Beneath the surface, perch and pike glide through shadowed depths, while dragonflies and damselflies dance above, their delicate wings flickering in the dappled sunlight.

After passing beneath the actual Poyntz Bridge, there is a public pontoon on a sharp bend in the canal at Hunston, an alternative launch point with a free car park nearby. Continue to Crosbie Bridge in Donnington, then return the same way to enjoy the stunning views of Chichester Cathedral rising above the meadows •

• **DISTANCE:** 4.2km (return).

• **PADDLING ENVIRONMENT:** 1.

• **ROUTE MAP:** islandeering/paddleboarding-chichester-ship-canal/

• **ACCESS RESTRICTIONS:** Chichester Canal Trust licence required, purchased from Canal Café during opening hours chichestercanal.org.uk/attractions/canoeing/

• **OS MAP:** OS Explorer OL8 Chichester, South Harting & Selsey.

• **STARTING POINT:** Canal Basin, Canal Wharf, Chichester, PO19 8DT. Grid ref. SU 859 041; What3Words weds.behave.chief.

• **PARKING:** Roadside (free) adjacent to Canal Basin.

• **LAUNCHING:** Pontoon close to parking.

• **PITSTOPS:** Good home-made cakes and local products, Canal Café, Canal Basin, tel. 01243 771363.

• **GETTING THERE:** *Car* J12 off M27 then A27 towards Chichester for 10 miles. Exit onto A259 Chichester/Bognor Regis. At the roundabout, take the first exit onto Stockbridge Road. Continue straight, then R onto Canal Wharf; *Rail* Frequent service from London Victoria to Chichester, 200m walk to canal basin www.southernrailway.com

• **SPECIAL POINTS:** Public liability insurance required (included in Paddle UK membership). Buoyancy aids mandatory. Please clean your board before you enter the water to prevent spread of non-native plants and animal species.

13

CHICHESTER HARBOUR DELL QUAY TO BOSHAM

TIDAL RIVER · WEST SUSSEX

Enjoy the timeless beauty of Chichester Harbour's waters, framed by quaint hamlets and inns, with sweeping views and abundant wildlife. A designated National Landscape, the harbour is a serene expanse of tidal creeks and salt marshes rich with birdlife, and ever-changing skies are reflected in tranquil waters.

Start from Dell Quay, a historic and picturesque spot on the harbour's eastern shore that was once a bustling medieval port that played a vital role in local trade. Launch from the public slipway, head around the quay, and paddle south past the lively pub lawn of the Crown and Anchor. As the moored boats fade behind, fields, woodlands, and salt marshes unfold, offering prime opportunities for wildlife spotting. Follow the north (right) bank towards Longmore Point, passing Birdham Pool Marina on the south bank, where the Chichester Canal ends. Continue west past jetties and West Itchenor on the south bank (with a lovely café), keeping an eye out for the summer ferry crossing from Itchenor Hard to Bosham Hoe.

Turn north into the Bosham Channel to find Bosham Quay on the right after 2 km. With picture-postcard charm, it's a favourite spot along Chichester Harbour. Here, gentle waters lap the quay's old stone walls, and colourful dinghies bob with the tide against a backdrop of traditional cottages and the spire of Holy Trinity Church, all reflected in the rippling shallows. The Anchor Bleu, with its harbourside terrace, offers hearty fare and sweeping views across the quay, while nearby village cafés provide a good place to find sustenance for the return journey •

- **DISTANCE:** 14km return.
- **PADDLING ENVIRONMENT:** 3.
- **ROUTE MAP:** islandeering.com/paddleboarding-chichester-harbour-dell-quay-to-bosham/
- **ACCESS RESTRICTIONS:** Harbour dues required for Chichester Harbour conservancy.co.uk/on-the-water/paddlesports/, call the Harbour Office on 01243 512301 or visit the Harbour Offices in Itchenor or Emsworth.
- **STARTING POINT:** Dell Quay, Dell Quay Road, Appledram, Chichester, PO20 7EE. Grid ref. SU 835 028; What3Words opposite.ranted.blatantly.
- **PARKING:** Roadside on Dell Quay Road (free).
- **LAUNCHING:** Public slipway.
- **PITSTOPS:** Popular waterside inn, The Crown and Anchor, Dell Quay, tel. 01243 781712; hearty food while watching the tides, The Anchor Bleu, Bosham, tel. 01243 573956; great coffee, delicious cakes, breakfasts, and lunches in the marina, The Quarter Deck Café, West Itchenor, quarterdeckcafe.co.uk
- **GETTING THERE:** J12 off M27 onto the A27 towards Chichester for 10 miles. L at roundabout onto A286 towards Chichester for 0.8 km then R onto Dell Quay Road for 2.4 km to quay.
- **SPECIAL POINTS:** Exposed to SW winds, best start 2hrs before HW (or as soon as water covers the mud below the slipway) to arrive in Bosham with time to explore before returning to Dell Quay. Bosham Quay is also a good starting point for a reverse trip. Be mindful of other boat users, especially around West Itchenor and its numerous swing moorings.

14

WEST WITTERING TO WEST ITCHENOR

ESTUARY · WEST SUSSEX

Escape the bustling beach crowds to explore the wilder parts of Chichester Harbour. West Wittering Beach offers the quintessential British seaside, with colourful beach huts lining wide sands that stretch out towards the sea. Launch from the beach to leave behind the family picnics, striped windbreaks, and fluttering kites. Head right past the groynes to enter Chichester Harbour, protected by the stunning unspoiled spit of sand and marram grass-topped dunes of East Head. Managed by the National Trust, this ever-shifting peninsula feels wonderfully remote. A beautiful beach at its northern tip offers a perfect spot for a swim before continuing north along Chichester Channel, exploring the eastern shore along the way. Keep right to reach West Itchenor, a lively hub with an excellent café in the marina. Return along the same route •

- **DISTANCE:** 11.7km return.
- **PADDLING ENVIRONMENT:** 3.
- **ROUTE MAP:** islandeering.com/paddleboarding-west-wittering-to-west-itchenor/
- **ACCESS RESTRICTIONS:** Harbour dues required for Chichester Harbour conservancy.co.uk/on-the-water/paddlesports/, call the Harbour Office on 01243 512301 or visit the Harbour Offices in Itchenor or Emsworth.
- **OS MAP:** OS Explorer 120 Chichester, South Harting & Selsey.
- **STARTING POINT:** West Wittering Beach closest to East Head (launch into lagoon east of East Head is not permitted).
- **PARKING:** West Wittering Beach (charges), West Wittering, Chichester, PO20 8GH. Grid ref. SZ 770 980; What3Words marsh.bought.efficient (note: park East Head side of parking area).
- **LAUNCHING:** Beach.
- **PITSTOPS:** Great coffee, delicious cakes, breakfasts, and lunches in the marina, The Quarter Deck Café, West Itchenor, quarterdeckcafe.co.uk.
- **GETTING THERE:** J12 off M27 onto A27 towards Chichester for 12 miles, then A286 exit towards The Witterings. Third exit at roundabout onto the A286 towards West Wittering for 5 miles, then R onto B2179 towards West Wittering. Continue through village, following signs for beach.
- **SPECIAL POINTS:** Start 2-3hrs before HW to travel into the harbour with the flood to arrive at West Itchenor, which has a full tide access launch point, and return on the ebb. Staying close to the shore helps avoid other boat traffic. Depending on the tide, the water can recede significantly across The Winner, exposing several sandbanks west of East Head, which you'll need to navigate around if outside the 2hr HW window. Be mindful of the groynes as you make your way back to the beach.
- **OFFSHORE WIND:** N-NE while on beach and in harbour entrance.

15

PAGHAM HARBOUR EXPLORER

COAST/TIDAL INLAND HARBOUR · WEST SUSSEX

Journey along the coastline into a wildlife-rich nature reserve, exploring tranquil creeks, spotting abundant birdlife, and visiting the historic Sidlesham Quay. Pagham Beach, east of Bognor Regis, is a quiet, pebbly stretch of coastline that's relaxed and unspoiled. Launch from the beach in front of the Pagham Yacht Club buildings and head right (southwest) along a gently sloping shoreline, backed by beach houses and bungalows. After a short distance, reach the entrance to Pagham Harbour. The waters at the mouth, sheltered by sand and shingle spits, offer a wonderful area to explore.

For a longer trip on a high spring tide, enter Pagham Harbour, a nature reserve teeming with birdlife, especially around the salt marshes and lagoons just behind the beach. Managed by the RSPB, this haven is vital for migratory birds, and in spring and summer it comes alive with warblers, terns, and skylarks. Head north on the main channel initially, then follow it west. On high spring tides, it's possible to reach historic Sidlesham – once a bustling quay for small boats transporting goods like salt and grain, now a charming village with a fabulous pub. On the return, enjoy sweeping views of Bognor Regis in the distance •

- **DISTANCE:** Pagham to Sidlesham 9km return.
- **PADDLING ENVIRONMENT:** 3.
- **ROUTE MAP:** islandeering.com/paddleboarding-pagham-harbour-explorer/
- **ACCESS RESTRICTIONS:** RSPB issues strict guidelines for no landing on the Harbour's islands and avoiding any disturbance to birds.
- **OS MAP:** OS Explorer OL8 Chichester, South Harting & Selsey.
- **STARTING POINT:** In front of Pagham Yacht Club, West Front Road, Pagham, PO21 4SY. Grid ref. SZ 891 972; What3Words warthog.siesta.umpires.
- **PARKING:** Pagham Beach Car Park (charges), Beach Road, Pagham, PO21 4SX. Grid ref. SZ 890 973; What3Words reworked.umpires.freshen.
- **LAUNCHING:** Beach 200m from car park.
- **PITSTOPS:** Fabulous upmarket pub in beautiful location, Crab & Lobster, Sidlesham Quay, tel. 01243 641233; seaside food, good breakfasts and more, Pagham Beach Café, tel. 01243 267433.
- **GETTING THERE:** J12 off M27 onto A27 to Chichester, then follow signs for the B2145 towards Selsey. Turn L at roundabout onto B2166 to Pagham, then L onto Sea Lane. At end of Sea Lane, go straight across junction to Pagham Beach Car Park.
- **SPECIAL POINTS:** Pagham Harbour only accessible 2hrs either side of HW. At mid-tide, the main channels are only accessible as mudbanks dominate the harbour, and water rushes in or out of the harbour entrance. This can be avoided by exiting the water, walking around the shingle banks, and re-entering where the water has begun to slow. Trips to Sidlesham Quay are best planned for high spring tides. Landing on the mudbanks or reed beds within the harbour is not permitted, as they are sensitive wildlife habitats.
- **OFFSHORE WIND:** NW while on coast.

Go Explore GT

16

RIVER ARUN PULBOROUGH TO STOPHAM BRIDGE

TIDAL RIVER · WEST SUSSEX

Family paddle along a gentle stretch of the River Arun through scenic countryside to a welcoming riverside inn. Pulborough, with its roots in Roman history, makes an ideal starting point, featuring ancient churches and traditional timber-framed buildings that set the tone for this serene trip. Leave from Pulborough's riverside, where the wide, slow-moving water makes it perfect for paddleboarders of all levels. Head upstream (right) beneath the 18th-century Old Swan Bridge, known for its charming arches and the time capsule embedded within its structure. Beyond the bridge, the river winds through open fields and farmland, with the South Downs gently rising in the distance. Reeds and willows line the banks, creating sheltered spots where herons, egrets, and the occasional kingfisher can be seen.

Further upstream, the river narrows slightly, leading to more secluded stretches. Approaching Stopham Bridge, its graceful medieval arches come into view. Just beyond, exit (on the right-hand side under the A283 road bridge) for a break at The White Hart Inn, or continue exploring upstream, where the tidal influence and changing vegetation offer varied paddling conditions. Return along the same route •

- **DISTANCE:** 4km return.
- **PADDLING ENVIRONMENT:** 2.
- **ROUTE MAP:** islandeering.com/paddleboarding-pulborough-to-stopham-bridge/
- **ACCESS RESTRICTIONS:** No licence required.
- **OS MAP:** OS Explorer OL10 Arundel & Pulborough.
- **STARTING POINT:** Slipway, Old Swan Bridge, off A29, Pulborough, RH20 2BJ. Grid ref. TQ 046 184; What3Words crispier.broom.unhappy.
- **PARKING:** Parking lay-by (free).
- **LAUNCHING:** Slipway short walk over bridge from parking or 500m walk from rail station.
- **PITSTOPS:** Lovely riverside terrace and historic inn, White Hart, Stoborough Bridge, 01798 874903.
- **LESSONS AND HIRE:** Hire at Stopham Bridge with Pulborough Paddles pulboroughpaddles.co.uk
- **GETTING THERE:** *Car* Lay-by just south of river at Pulborough on A29; *Train* Direct from London Victoria to Pulborough, Southern Railway southernrailway.com
- **SPECIAL POINTS:** At Pulborough high tide is 4hrs after Littlehampton. Although tidal all the way up to Pallingham, the flood and ebb flow is very gentle. Check flood alerts for Pulborough at check-for-flooding.service.gov.uk/location/pulborough-west-sussex

McConks

EVENTS

17

RIVER ARUN ARUNDEL TO BLACK RABBIT

TIDAL RIVER · WEST SUSSEX

Tide-assisted trip with stunning views of Arundel Castle's towering turrets, glimpses of kingfishers darting through wetlands, and the perfect riverside pub stop. The River Arun winds through a landscape rich in history and natural beauty. As one of England's fastest-flowing rivers, its tidal reach extends inland over 40 kilometres from the coast. Once a vital artery for transporting timber and chalk, the Arun also played a key role in the Wey and Arun Canal, linking London to the south coast in the 19th century. Today, it remains a haven for wildlife and a defining feature of Arundel's charm, flowing beneath the shadow of Arundel Castle and through the heart of the town.

Start at Arundel, launch from the pontoon and head upstream (left). As Arundel Castle rises into view, its towering turrets pierce the Sussex sky like a storybook fortress. Nearly a thousand years old, this castle is far more than a relic; it's a living narrative of England's history, woven with tales of Norman conquests, royal intrigues, and generations of the Dukes of Norfolk. Seen from the River Arun, the castle's imposing silhouette is at its most striking – a timeless sentinel standing watch over both river and town, its grandeur undiminished by the passage of time. Pass moored boats before a large left bend, where the conservation area managed by the Wildfowl and Wetlands Trust offers a peaceful oasis. This mosaic of reedbeds, lagoons, and wildflower meadows is a sanctuary for wildlife – keep an eye out for kingfishers darting between the willows or the elusive splash of water voles along the banks. A short distance upriver, The Black Rabbit pub makes an ideal spot to pause and wait for the tide to turn.

For a longer, linear 21 km journey from Arundel to Pulborough, continue past The Black Rabbit, take the left-hand stream, and paddle north through Amberley. Return to Arundel via Pulborough rail station, just a short walk from the Old Swan Bridge in Pulborough •

- **DISTANCE:** 6km to Black Rabbit return; 21km to Pulborough one way.

- **PADDLING ENVIRONMENT:** 3.

- **ROUTE MAP:** islandeering.com/paddleboarding-arundel-to-black-rabbit/

- **ACCESS RESTRICTIONS:** No licence required; pontoon access with permission of The Edible Sandwich Co. tel. 01903 885969 ediblesandwich.co.uk

- **OS MAP:** OS Explorer OL10 Arundel & Pulborough.

- **STARTING POINT:** Pontoon, High Street, Arundel, Arun, West Sussex, England, BN18 9AG. Grid ref. TQ 019 070; What3Words feels.required.streaking; slipway adjacent to Mill Road Car Park, Mill Road, Arundel, BN18 9PA; Grid ref. TQ 021 069; What3Words wordplay.smuggled.space.

- **PARKING:** Mill Road Car Park (charges).

- **LAUNCHING:** Pontoon at the Queens Road Bridge; slipway next to car park.

- **PITSTOPS:** Great place to pick up a sandwich, The Edible Sandwich Co., Arundel; popular riverside pub, The Black Rabbit, Arundel, tel. 01903 882638.

- **GETTING THERE:** Exit A27 towards Arundel town centre. R on to High Street, then first exit at roundabout onto Mill Road. Car park on R.

- **SPECIAL POINTS:** Start 2hrs before HW for trip to Black Rabbit. The trip to Pulborough is a 5-6hr+ trip for experienced paddlers, best in southerly winds to aid the paddler; tide assistance lessens as you travel north.

18

SOUTHWICK TO BRIGHTON

COAST · WEST SUSSEX

Adventurous coastal paddle that blends industrial history with Brighton's vibrant seaside charm and iconic landmarks. Launch from Southwick Beach and head left (east), where the coastline offers views of the port, Brighton's skyline, and the distant chalk cliffs. As the journey continues, the industrial backdrop gives way to the vibrant seafront of Hove, with its long stretch of colourful beach huts leading towards the King Alfred Leisure Centre, a 1930s landmark now home to a gym. Nearby, Marrocco's, a Hove institution, tempts with its legendary gelato.

Continue parallel to Hove Plinth, where contemporary sculptures stand against the backdrop of pastel beach huts. Further on, the ornate Brighton Beach Bandstand comes into view, a much-loved example of Victorian seafront architecture. Approaching central Brighton, the quirky Upside Down House stands out, its roof on the ground and furniture suspended from the ceiling – a playful addition to the seafront's eclectic character. Close by, the futuristic 162-metre i360 Tower rises skywards, its glass pod offering panoramic views that rival those from the water.

Approach the haunting remains of the West Pier, a skeletal silhouette left behind by fire and storms. Once a grand Victorian structure, its rusted frame now serves as a refuge for seabirds, and is a poignant relic of Brighton's seaside past. Continue paddling to the iconic Palace Pier, alive with the buzz of funfair rides, arcades, and food stalls. Nearby, look out for the remains of the sunken barge, visible on a low spring tide. The sounds of laughter and seaside nostalgia drift down, immersing paddlers in the timeless energy of Brighton.

Continuing east, paddle alongside the tracks of Volk's Electric Railway, the world's oldest operating electric railway, which has been charming passengers between the pier and the marina since 1883. Before reaching the marina, stop at Fika Sealanes, a stylish beachfront café near the Madeira Drive arches, known for its excellent coffee and brunches. Finish by pulling ashore on the beach just west of the marina – a fitting end to a paddle that captures the best of Brighton's seafront charm and character.

The full linear route is possible with two cars (one parked at either end) or a taxi return. Shorter options can start from either Southwick or Brighton Marina, depending on the prevailing wind. On a perfectly still day this is an amazing paddle at sunrise or sunset •

• **DISTANCE:** 10km one way.

• **PADDLING ENVIRONMENT:** 5.

• **ROUTE MAP:** islandeering.com/paddleboarding-southwick-to-brighton/

• **ACCESS RESTRICTIONS:** No licence required.

• **OS MAP:** OS Explorer OL11 Brighton & Hove.

• **STARTING POINT:** Southwick Beach.

• **PARKING:** *Southwick* Southwick Beach Car Park (charges), Southwick, BN41 1WD. Grid ref. TQ 244 047; What3Words venues.stem.deep; *Brighton Marina* Brighton Marina Car park (4hrs free), Marina Way, Brighton, BN2 5UT. Grid ref. TQ 335 031; What3Words scuba.grants.cities.

• **LAUNCHING:** *Southwick* Beach short walk from car park; or 600m walk from Southwick rail station on the walkway across the port lock gates (England Coast Path) accessed off the coast road just west of Station Road; *Brighton Marina* beach short walk west of marina.

• **PITSTOPS:** Great coffee, Port Kitchen, Southwick, tel. 01273 435263; great coffee and brunch on the beach west of the marina, Fika Sealanes, fikasussex.co.uk.

• **LESSONS:** Lagoon Watersports, Hove and Brighton Marina, tel. 01273 424842.

• **GETTING THERE:** *Car Southwick* From Brighton on A259 west towards Shoreham. Turn L onto Wharf Road and Hove Lagoon; L onto Basin Road S and car park; *Train* Southwick from London Victoria, change Hove southernrailway.com; *Brighton Marina* from Brighton city centre, head to seafront then L onto A259.

• **SPECIAL POINTS:** Only attempt in low wind/swell; check Surfline surfline.com and webcam at Brighton for local conditions. Ideally time trip to coincide with last few hours of flood tide for tide assistance, although a SW wind will give the most assistance. Underwater groynes/spikes throughout the route, especially near West Pier.

• **OFFSHORE WIND:** N.

19

RIVER ADUR SHOREHAM TO UPPER BEEDING

TIDAL RIVER · WEST SUSSEX

Tide-powered journey from harbour to pub, passing bird sanctuaries, rolling chalklands, and traces of industrial heritage. This former trading route offers a round trip from Shoreham to the Kings Head pub, or a linear route to Bines Bridge. Start at Shoreham near the RNLI station and head upriver through Shoreham Harbour's urban and industrial landscape, skirting several marinas.

Beyond the Adur Ferry Footbridge, the river opens into a vast waterway, part of an RSPB reserve and a designated Site of Special Scientific Interest, known for its tidal mudflats, salt marsh, and diverse birdlife. At high tide, look out for grey herons, snipe, redshanks, and linnets sheltering in the marsh. On the southern edge of this area lies a unique houseboat community that has thrived since the 1920s.

Pass beneath the A259, then the viaduct, and finally the beautifully restored, multi-stanchioned Old Shoreham Tollbridge, with the charming St. Nicholas Church at its eastern end. Continuing upstream, countryside views unfold, with the striking gothic Lancing College Chapel perched on the hillside to the left. Beyond the A27 road bridge, the river journey becomes notably more peaceful.

As the river narrows, it meanders through the open valley of the River Adur, flanked by gently rolling chalk downlands. On the east bank, the ruins of the Beeding Cement Works come into view, a reminder of the once-thriving industry active from the late 19th century until the 1990s, with its stark white chalk backdrop.

Further on, pass beneath the A283 before landing among reeds and grassy banks on the right (east) side near Beeding Bridge, close to the sign for the Kings Head pub. The pub's lawn is an ideal spot to relax and wait for the tide to turn for the return journey.

Alternatively, extend the trip by paddling from Upper Beeding to Bines Bridge. From the Kings Head, continue 8 km upstream, taking the left fork in the river. Reach Bines Bridge after another kilometre, where there is an access/egress point to the river (off the footpath northeast of the bridge accessed from the B2135) and a small car park (grid ref. TQ 190 175; What3Words nights.multiples.liked) in the lay-by east of the bridge on the B2135 south of Partridge Green •

• **DISTANCE:** 19km from Shoreham to Upper Beeding return; or 18.5km to Bines Bridge one way.

• **PADDLING ENVIRONMENT:** 3.

• **ROUTE MAP:** islandeering.com/paddleboarding-shoreham-to-upper-beeding/

• **ACCESS RESTRICTIONS:** No licence required.

• **OS MAP:** OS Explorer OL11 Brighton & Hove.

• **STARTING POINT & PARKING:** Kingston Beach car park (free), Brighton Road, BN43 6RG. Grid ref. TQ 233 048; What3Words drank.noted.trail.

• **LAUNCHING:** Beach west of RNLI Station adjacent to car park.

• **PITSTOPS:** Nice riverside garden, Kings Head, Upper Beeding, tel. 01903 812196.

• **GETTING THERE:** *Car* Exit A27 onto A283 to Shoreham-by-Sea. Left (first exit) at roundabout onto A259 towards Brighton. R at Kingston Lighthouse into car park; *Train* Southwick from London Victoria, change Hove southernrailway.com

• **SPECIAL POINTS:** The RSPB Adur Reserve is a delicate wetland habitat – avoid paddling into it or disturbing the wildlife. Wind can funnel N-S through the Steyning gap, so check Surfline surfline.com at Hot Pipe for local conditions and tides. Spring flood tides run fast upriver, helping your journey upstream, but may be too strong to paddle against if returning before the ebb. Start approximately 2hrs before HW at Shoreham to arrive at Upper Beeding (HW at Upper Beeding is +45 minutes after Shoreham) with ample time to visit the pub or explore the village before taking the ebb tide back to Shoreham. If continuing further north, choose a spring tide to aid the journey – the flood tide continues for up to 2hrs after HW at Shoreham.

20

BEWL WATER

LAKE · EAST SUSSEX

A scenic reservoir perfect for outdoor adventures, surrounded by diverse wildlife and picturesque landscapes. Bewl Water is a beautiful reservoir located in the High Weald National Landscape on the borders of Kent and East Sussex. Covering around 324 hectares, it's the largest stretch of open water in the southeast of England, created by damming the River Bewl and still serving as a reservoir for Southern Water.

Surrounded by woodlands, meadows, and farmland, it offers diverse habitats for a wide array of wildlife. Look out for great crested grebes, cormorants, herons, and various species of ducks, geese, and swans. During the spring and summer, kingfishers may dart along the water's edge, while the songs of warblers fill the nearby reeds and woodlands.

The lake is a hub for watersports and fishing, yet large enough for everyone to find their space. With camping options and a 13 km walk around the entire lake, there's plenty to see and do •

- **DISTANCE:** Free-range.
- **PADDLING ENVIRONMENT:** 1.
- **ROUTE MAP:** islandeering.com/paddleboarding-bewl-water/
- **ACCESS RESTRICTIONS:** Self-launch with permit purchased from Bewl Water Fishing Lodge on the lake's north shore next door to PTP Coaching/or book a day pass online ptpcoaching.co.uk/bewl-home . Buoyancy aid and insurance required, included in Paddle UK membership.
- **OS MAP:** OS Explorer 136 High Weald, Royal Tunbridge Wells, Cranbrook, Hawkhurst & Bewl Water.
- **PARKING:** Numerous onsite car parks (charges), Bewl Water, Bewlbridge Lane, Lamberhurst, TN3 6JH.
- **LAUNCHING:** Beach a short walk from parking. Grid ref. TQ 674 335; What3Words supposed.accented.eternity.
- **PITSTOPS:** Onsite, The Waterfront Café, tel. 01892 890000.
- **CAMPING:** Bewl Water Estate, bewlwater.co.uk/camping/
- **LESSONS AND HIRE:** Book with PTP Coaching, ptpcoaching.co.uk
- **GETTING THERE:** A21 S of Royal Tunbridge Wells past Lamberhurst, following brown signs for Bewl Water. Just beyond the Scotney Castle roundabout, turn R into Bewl Water Estate.
- **SPECIAL POINTS:** Please clean your board before you enter the water to prevent spread of non-native plants and animal species.

21

RIVER OUSE LEWES AND HAMSEY ISLAND CIRCUMNAVIGATION

TIDAL RIVER · EAST SUSSEX

Paddle through serene East Sussex countryside, past open fields and pastoral views, with a touch of history at every turn. Historic Lewes, a charming market town, is known for its rich history, medieval architecture, and a proud brewing tradition, embodied by the renowned Harvey's Brewery, the starting point of this route.

Start in Lewes and launch upstream of the brewery, passing Tesco and parkland, then head under the footbridge. Beyond this, the river is flanked by low chalk cliffs, pastureland, and gardens, soon opening up to vast countryside that feels delightfully remote. On a sharp right-hand bend, keep to the main channel (the smaller cut ahead will be your return route).

Now circumnavigating Hamsey Island – once a major Saxon port – take in views of St Peter's Church, perched on a mount at its centre. Continue to reach a small weir, which can be portaged on the left bank. Shortly after the weir, turn left into the smaller channel to rejoin the main river and return to Lewes.

For a longer adventure, continue paddling upriver towards Barcombe Mills 4.5 km away •

- **DISTANCE:** 8km return.
- **PADDLING ENVIRONMENT:** 3.
- **ROUTE MAP:** islandeering.com/paddleboarding-lewes-and-hamsey-island-loop
- **ACCESS RESTRICTIONS:** No licence required.
- **OS MAP:** OS Explorer OL11 Brighton & Hove.
- **STARTING POINT:** Phoenix Causeway Grid ref. TQ 419 103; What3Words drops.solving.upholding.
- **PARKING:** Phoenix Causeway Car Park (charges), Malling Street, Lewes, BN7 2JW. Grid ref. TQ 420 103; What3Words rehearsal.remembers.quail.
- **LAUNCHING:** River bank near Phoenix Causeway.
- **PITSTOPS:** Historic Harvey & Sons pub about 100 steps from the Bridge Wharf brewery, The Dorset, 01273 474823.
- **TOURS:** The Kayak Coach thekayakcoach.com/experiences-river-trips/river-ouse-lewes-hamsey
- **GETTING THERE:** *Car* Leave A27 for A26 towards Lewes town centre; first exit at roundabout onto A2029 towards town centre; first exit at roundabout (opposite Tesco) onto Malling St. R onto Harveys Way past Dorset pub to car park on R; *Train* Regular services from London Victoria to Lewes southernrailway.com ; 400m walk to riverside launch point.
- **SPECIAL POINTS:** Route possible at all states of tide, but leaving on a flooding tide helps with the flow upriver and makes launching easier as the water is higher up the muddy bank. HW at Hamsey is 1hr 45min after Newhaven. On some spring tides, the weir may be fully covered; otherwise, portage on the left. The cut is narrow with a few rapids at low water near the rejoining point and can be slightly overgrown in summer.

HARVEYS
BREWERY

22

ARDINGLY RESERVOIR

LAKE · EAST SUSSEX

A beautiful lake surrounded by ancient woodland, nestled in the stunning High Weald National Landscape. Located near Ardingly College, alma mater of notable figures including *Private Eye* editor Ian Hislop, Ardingly Reservoir is a haven for watersports and wildlife. Designated as a Local Nature Reserve, it's a prime spot for observing ospreys during their autumn migration from Scotland to West Africa.

Created in the 1970s to meet rising water demands, the reservoir's distinctive "forked stick" shape follows the paths of the former Shell and Ardingly Brooks. Near the slipways, the valve tower and overflow bell mouth quietly regulate the water flow, supplying communities from Crowborough to Hailsham and supporting the River Ouse's aquatic life during dry spells. The aerated water sustains fish and prevents algal blooms, while the overflow system helps manage flooding by channelling excess water into Shell Brook.

Paddle north along the right spur, where wildflower meadows burst with colour and wildlife, and Furzefield Wood, managed by Kew Gardens, shelters the elusive dormouse. Between the spurs, reedbeds planted to combat erosion provide sanctuary for reed warblers and harvest mice. In the left spur, Scrubs Shaw woods, once dominated by Austrian pine, have transitioned to ash, sycamore, and birch. Further along, ancient tree stumps from Great Burrow Wood emerge during dry spells, with Ardingly Sandstone outcrops revealing glimpses of the Cretaceous past. Here, a kingfisher might be seen, poised for its next catch.

The Ardingly Activity Centre offers watersports and refreshments at the Black Hut Kiosk, while anglers try their luck for carp, tench, and pike. A network of scenic paths around the lake offers plenty of opportunities for exploration •

- **DISTANCE:** Free-range.
- **PADDLING ENVIRONMENT:** 1.
- **ROUTE MAP:** islandeering.com/paddleboarding-ardingly-reservoir/
- **ACCESS RESTRICTIONS:** Private lake, self-launch (£10/day). Buoyancy aid mandatory; must have third-party liability insurance, ardinglyactivitycentre.co.uk/hiring/stand-up-paddle-boards/bringing-your-own-equipment-to-ardingly/, included in Paddle UK membership.
- **OS MAP:** OS Explorer 135 Ashdown Forest.
- **STARTING POINT & PARKING:** Car park (free), The Lodge, Ardingly Reservoir, Ardingly, RH17 6SQ. Grid ref. TQ 335 286; What3Words replied.dramatic.convinces.
- **LAUNCHING:** Lakeside pontoon short walk from car park.
- **PITSTOPS:** Lakeside drinks and snacks, The Black Hut Kiosk.
- **LESSONS AND HIRE:** Ardingly Activity Centre, tel. 01444 892549, ardinglyactivitycentre.co.uk
- **GETTING THERE:** J10 M23 onto A264 towards Crawley; third exit at roundabout onto B2028 towards Haywards Heath, follow to Ardingly village; R onto College Rd, following brown signs to Ardingly Reservoir; take second entrance to college and follow signs to reservoir.
- **SPECIAL POINTS:** Buoyancy aids mandatory. Lake exposed to N-S winds, but its shape ensures there will always be a sheltered spot. Clean your board before entering the water to prevent the spread of non-native plants and animal species.

23

RIVER OUSE BARCOMBE MILLS AND ISFIELD

RIVER · EAST SUSSEX

Journey through tranquil waters and past scenic countryside on the serene non-tidal section of the River Ouse. There are two options along this stretch – start at Barcombe Mills and paddle upriver to the weir just south of the Anchor Inn, or launch from the campsite near Isfield to explore further upstream.

Atmospheric Barcombe Mills, with its weir marking the end of the tidal influence, has a rich history. Once the site of several watermills, this popular spot now serves as a gateway to the peaceful upper reaches of the Ouse. From the launch at Barcombe Mills, head upriver (right). The Bevern Stream joins from the left, and the river then splits – taking the right fork is generally easier, though both are navigable. Further along, the Iron River merges from the right, and the weir ahead marks the turnaround point. Note that direct access to the Anchor Inn is not allowed by the current landlord, and portage on the right bank is discouraged by the farmer.

To explore further upstream, Boathouse Farm Camping offers an ideal base and starting point. From here, launch and paddle upstream to the White Bridge at Isfield, with the added bonus of visiting the excellent farm shop or pub before or after your trip •

- **DISTANCE:** Barcombe Mills to the Anchor weir, 3.6km return.
- **PADDLING ENVIRONMENT:** 2.
- **ROUTE MAP:** islandeering.com/paddleboarding-barcombe-mills-and-isfield/
- **ACCESS RESTRICTIONS:** No licence required.
- **OS MAP:** OS Explorer OL11 Brighton & Hove, Lewes & Burgess Hill.
- **STARTING POINT:** Riverside, Barcombe Mills. Grid ref. TQ 433 148; What3Words lorry.showrooms.chin.
- **PARKING:** Barcombe Mills Car Park (free), Barcombe Mills Road, Ringmer, BN8 5BX. Grid ref. TQ 434 146; What3Words widen.wire.modern.
- **LAUNCHING:** Riverbank. Exit car park at northeast end and turn R along small lane. Cross weir to find flat grass area on RH side of road on a LH bend.
- **PITSTOPS:** Popular Victorian village pub adjacent to the restored Lavender Line railway, Laughing Fish, Isfield, tel. 01825 750349; excellent picnic and BBQ fare, Isfield Farm Shop, tel. 01825 751271. At the time of writing, paddleboarders are not welcome to land/launch at the Anchor Inn.
- **CAMPING:** Rural camping beside the River Ouse, Boathouse Farm Camping, boathousefarm.co.uk
- **GETTING THERE:** A27 N of Lewes to Clayhill; L following sign to Barcombe. Car park on R just after Bridge Farm.
- **SPECIAL POINTS:** Check local river conditions at Anchor, Barcombe Mills, riverlevels.uk/east-sussex-barcombe-anchor-gates-rl

24

CUCKMERE MEANDERS

RIVER/LAKE · EAST SUSSEX

Family-friendly trip amid the stunning chalk cliff scenery of Seven Sisters Country Park. The Cuckmere Meanders, a breathtaking series of natural oxbow lakes and old river loops, wind through the lower reaches of the Cuckmere River, set against the beautiful backdrop of Seven Sisters Country Park. These meanders, tracing the original path of the Cuckmere River, were cut off from the main flow in 1847 when a straight channel was created to reduce flood risk. Today, they offer a scenic family-friendly paddle exploring the river's untamed past.

Start from the tiny hamlet of Exceat, a place steeped in history and once a bustling Saxon village recorded in the Domesday Book. Now more of a historical waypoint than a village, Exceat serves as a popular gateway to the South Downs National Park, with its rolling hills and stunning views.

From Exceat, paddle left along 1.5 kilometres of gentle, non-tidal water, free from the pull of the current. The meanders pass a landscape rich in wildlife – look out for herons, kingfishers, and wading birds, as well as the diverse plant life that thrives in the wetland conditions of the surrounding floodplain. This quiet stretch of water offers a rare glimpse into a beautifully preserved natural habitat •

- **DISTANCE:** 3km return.
- **PADDLING ENVIRONMENT:** 1.
- **ROUTE MAP:** islandeering.com/paddleboarding-cuckmere-meanders/
- **ACCESS RESTRICTIONS:** No licence required.
- **OS MAP:** OS Explorer OL25 Eastbourne & Beachy Head.
- **STARTING POINT & PARKING:** Seven Sisters Car Park (charges), East Dean Road, Cuckmere Valley, Exceat, BN25 4AD. Grid ref. TV 518 994; What3Words blanks.throat.converter.
- **LAUNCHING:** Riverside adjacent to car park.
- **PITSTOPS:** Café in charming historic 16th-century farmhouse, Saltmarsh Farmhouse and Café, opposite car park, saltmarshfarmhouse.co.uk; fabulous views for a pint, close to the Exceat Bridge, Cuckmere Inn, tel. 01323 892247.
- **LESSONS, HIRE AND TOURS:** Buzz Active in the Seven Sisters Car Park buzzactive.org.uk/locations/buzz-cuckmere/ , tel. 01323 463300.
- **GETTING THERE:** Exceat on A259 between Seaford and Eastbourne.

25

CUCKMERE HAVEN TO SEVEN SISTERS

ESTUARY/COAST · EAST SUSSEX

Adventurous trip along the tranquil Cuckmere River to its mouth and under the iconic chalk cliffs of the Seven Sisters. This advanced paddleboarding trip is ideal for those with strong technical and route-planning skills, offering a stunning journey to Sussex's only river mouth untouched by a port, and the opportunity to glide along one of England's most iconic coastlines.

Starting at Exceat, head right around a sharp left-hand bend to reach the embankment separating the Meanders from the main Cuckmere River. After a short portage, lower the board down a steep set of wooden steps into the main river. Paddle south along the straight section, with the chalk slopes of Exceat Hill on the left. As the river narrows, currents quicken, pulling you toward the sea.

At Cuckmere Haven, the much-photographed Coastguard Cottages appear on the right, while the Seven Sisters cliffs rise to the left like gleaming sentinels. Their stark white faces, etched by wind and wave, stand raw and elemental against the sky. Paddle 4 km beneath these towering cliffs, from the majestic Haven Brow to the progressively smaller "sisters" leading towards Birling Gap, where a steep set of stairs ascends to the National Trust café and car park. From there, either pick up a second car at the car park or catch the bus back to Exceat from East Dean (a 2 km walk from the café) •

• **DISTANCE:** To Cuckmere Haven 4.8km return; to Beachy Head 6.4km one way.

• **PADDLING ENVIRONMENT:** 3 on Cuckmere River, 5 on coast.

• **ROUTE MAP:** islandeering.com/paddleboarding-cuckmere-haven-to-seven-sisters/

• **ACCESS RESTRICTIONS:** No licence required.

• **OS MAP:** OS Explorer OL25 Eastbourne & Beachy Head.

• **STARTING POINT & PARKING:** Seven Sisters Car Park (charges), East Dean Road, Cuckmere Valley, Exceat, BN25 4AD. Grid ref. TV 518 994; What3Words blanks.throat.converter.

• **LAUNCHING:** Riverside adjacent to car park.

• **PITSTOPS:** Café in charming historic 16th-century farmhouse, Saltmarsh Farmhouse and Café, opposite car park, saltmarshfarmhouse.co.uk ; fabulous views for a pint, close to the Exceat Bridge, The Cuckmere Inn, tel. 01323 892247; National Trust café, Birling Gap, tel. 01323 423197; if returning via East Dean, stop at its 15th-century village pub, The Tiger Inn, tel. 01323 423209.

• **LESSONS, HIRE AND TOURS:** Buzz Active in the Seven Sisters Car Park buzzactive.org.uk/locations/buzz-cuckmere/ , tel. 01323 463300.

• **GETTING THERE:** Exceat on A259 between Seaford and Eastbourne; bus return from Birling Gap on Coaster X3 from East Dean to Exceat buses. co.uk/services/BH/13X

• **SPECIAL POINTS:** The wooden steps down to the river from the meander are in poor condition, so take care when using them. Below the steps, the mudbanks are only covered for 2-2.5hrs either side of HW. If on the one-way route to Beachy Head, aim to depart from Exceat around HW to take advantage of the slack or ebbing tide down the river, giving enough time to reach Birling Gap before mid-ebb. Check wind and swell conditions before setting off at Surfline surfline.com at Birling Gap for local conditions. Breaking waves may occur at Cuckmere Haven, but you can exit onto the LH shingle bank to avoid the surf at the river mouth.

26

CUCKMERE RIVER EXCEAT TO ALFRISTON

TIDAL RIVER · EAST SUSSEX

A picturesque family river journey through a landscape of rolling chalk hills and quaint villages with excellent pitstops. Starting at Exceat, head right towards the embankment that separates the Meanders from the main Cuckmere River. After a short portage, lower the board down a steep set of wooden steps into the river. Turn right and paddle upstream beneath Exceat Bridge, with views of the undulating chalklands of the South Downs unfolding ahead. To the right, Friston Forest blankets the hills, while the Litlington White Horse, etched into Hindover Hill, appears to gallop above the river.

As the journey continues upriver, reeds close in as the river narrows before reaching Litlington Bridge. Exit on the left bank, cross the bridge, and follow the signed village path to Litlington to explore the delightful café, brewery taproom, and pub.

Further north, the river narrows again to a small stream, leading towards the picturesque village of Alfriston. The spire of St. Andrew's Church, the so-called Cathedral of the Downs, rises above the meadows, beckoning paddlers onward. Access the village from the footbridge spanning the river to find a selection of historic pubs and charming cafes awaiting. Return the same way •

• **DISTANCE:** 12km return.

• **PADDLING ENVIRONMENT:** 2.

• **ROUTE MAP:** islandeering.com/paddleboarding-exceat-to-alfriston/

• **ACCESS RESTRICTIONS:** No licence required.

• **OS MAP:** OS Explorer OL25 Eastbourne & Beachy Head.

• **STARTING POINT & PARKING:** Seven Sisters Car Park (charges), East Dean Road, Cuckmere Valley, Exceat, BN25 4AD. Grid ref. TV 518 994; What3Words blanks.throat.converter.

• **LAUNCHING:** Riverside adjacent to car park.

• **PITSTOPS:** *Exceat* Café in charming historic 16th-century farmhouse, Saltmarsh Farmhouse and Café, opposite car park, saltmarshfarmhouse.co.uk ; fabulous views for a pint, close to the Exceat Bridge, The Cuckmere Inn, tel. 01323 892247; *Litlingdon* Cream tea in dappled sunlight in a friendly hidden gem of a café, Litlingdon Tea Gardens, tel. 01323 870222; refreshing beer in great location, Long Man Brewery, tel. 01323 871850; great food and garden in lovely 17th-century pub, The Plough and Harrow, tel. 01323 870632; *Alfriston* Lovely pub garden backing onto village green, Six Bells, tel. 01323 870811.

• **LESSONS, HIRE AND TOURS:** Buzz Active in the Seven Sisters Car Park buzzactive.org.uk/locations/buzz-cuckmere/, tel. 01323 463300.

• **GETTING THERE:** Exceat on A259 between Seaford and Eastbourne.

• **SPECIAL POINTS:** Timing is key to this tidal trip – start approx. 2.5hrs before HW, or as soon as the water reaches the wooden steps leading from the meander onto the river. This will give you plenty of time to visit the villages, relax and catch the ebb back to the steps without having to get caught in the mudbanks below the steps on your return.

ALFRISTON

27

RIVER ROTHER RYE AND HARBOUR EXPLORER

TIDAL RIVER/ESTUARY · EAST SUSSEX

Explore a medieval port, now surrounded by marshland and shifting shingle, where nature thrives alongside a rich seafaring and military history. The River Rother, once a vital trade route that brought ships into the heart of Rye, now flows quietly through the town, shaping the landscape of Rye Harbour. Its waters and the surrounding salt marshes create a haven for wildlife while maintaining the area's deep-rooted maritime heritage.

Start from Rye Harbour and, to make the most of higher water levels, head upstream (to the left) first, passing the long jetties and salt marshes of Rye Harbour. The industrial sites on the left soon give way to sweeping views of Rye's skyline. Dominated by the hilltop tower of the 12th-century St. Mary's Church, with its iconic weathervane, the town's medieval architecture rises proudly, while the crenellated parapets of Ypres Tower add a fortified character to this once-important Cinque Port.

The River Brede joins from the left, where houseboats and fishing boats are moored along a series of wooden jetties. Continue past the Rye Fish Market, along the wharf, and pass beneath the A259 and the viaduct. As the houses recede, the landscape opens up, revealing the inlet of Union Channel joining from the right. Not far beyond, the gates of Scott's Float come into view – a crucial part of the flood defence system, protecting agricultural lands and marshes from tidal surges while maintaining water levels for local wildlife.

Retrace the route and paddle downstream of Rye Harbour to explore the shingle banks and river mouth, teeming with life. The vast wetland to the west is one of England's largest and most important wildlife sanctuaries, home to over 4,355 species of plants and animals, including 300 that are rare or endangered. Breeding colonies of little, common, and sandwich terns thrive here, earning the area designations as a Site of Special Scientific Interest, a Special Protection Area, and a Special Area of Conservation. The modern timber and glass visitor centre, home to the Lime Kiln Café, stands above the marsh dotted with sea purslane, though it is inaccessible from the river.

For a quiet break, find a small patch of shingle-sand beach near the much-photographed Red Roofed Hut, once a storage space for shrimp nets – perfect for a picnic. Just a little further along, the silhouette of a World War II pillbox can be spotted on the west bank, while vast views of Camber Sands unfold to the east. Beyond, the river meets the English Channel. Return to Rye Harbour to complete the journey •

- **DISTANCE:** 7.5km return to Rye town and river mouth.
- **PADDLING ENVIRONMENT:** 3.
- **ROUTE MAP:** islandeering.com/paddleboarding-rye-harbour/
- **ACCESS RESTRICTIONS:** No licence required.
- **OS MAP:** OS Explorer 125 Romney Marsh, Rye & Winchelsea.
- **STARTING POINT:** Harbour Road, Rye Harbour, TN31 7TT. Grid ref. TQ 943 190; What3Words coolest.bangle.witty.
- **PARKING:** Rye Harbour Car Park, Tram Road, Rye Harbour, TN31 7TZ. Grid ref. TQ 941 189; What3Words emptied.divorcing.starter.
- **LAUNCHING:** Public slipway adjacent to RNLI station, 250m walk from car park.
- **PITSTOPS:** Local beers and harbour views, William the Conqueror, tel. 01797 223315; great breakfasts and more, Bosun's Bite, 07834 730528; cakes with fabulous views across the river and marshes, Lime Kiln Café in the Rye Harbour Discovery Centre, tel. 01797 360960.
- **GETTING THERE:** From Rye, head S on A259 towards Winchelsea for just under a kilometre. Turn R into Harbour Road to Rye Harbour village. Continue around R bend to reach car park on R.
- **SPECIAL POINTS:** The staff at the RNLI station are a font of knowledge on local conditions. Watch out for other water users, especially fishing boats and large stone/grain ships using the harbour on high spring tides. The upstream section is best paddled on a rising tide (ideally 2hrs before HW) to avoid the mud, then return on the ebb. Downstream there are fast flows in the canalised estuary at mid tide, so not for the inexperienced paddler. Wind can also funnel along this section. If paddling out of the river mouth towards Camber Sands avoid the west groynes during a flooding tide as eddies form inside the groyne. Check conditions and tides on Surfline surfline.com at nearby Camber Sands.
- **OFFSHORE WIND:** N-NW when outside the river mouth.

28

CAMBER NORTHPOINT WATER

LAKE · EAST SUSSEX

Family fun tucked away behind the bustling Camber Sands, this hidden gem just outside Rye features a peaceful freshwater lake with a lively, active atmosphere. Once a gravel pit, it has been transformed into a watersports haven with a mix of sand and shingle beach, and friendly, knowledgeable staff who ensure a welcoming experience.

Framed by good views – look one way to Rye's charming jumble of rooftops perched on a hill; glance over the embankment and the industrial landmarks along the River Rother near Rye Harbour can be spotted.

The real charm of North Point Water lies in its laid-back atmosphere, perfectly encapsulated by the café with its wooden decking overlooking the lake. Here, you can unwind with a coffee, watching the wildlife and soaking in the tranquility of a place that feels a world away from the hustle of Rye and Camber Sands •

- **DISTANCE:** Free-range.
- **PADDLING ENVIRONMENT:** 1.
- **ROUTE MAP:** islandeering.com/paddleboarding-northpoint-water/
- **ACCESS RESTRICTIONS:** Booking with Rye Watersports required, tel. 01797 225238.
- **OS MAP:** OS Explorer 125 Romney Marsh, Rye & Winchelsea.
- **STARTING POINT & PARKING:** Rye Watersports, Camber Road, Camber, Rye, TN31 7QS. Grid ref. TQ 936 201; What3Words shortens.saturate.guessing.
- **LAUNCHING:** Lakeside adjacent to car park.
- **PITSTOPS:** Great coffee, toasties and cakes on the lakeside, Hoolie Café, Rye Watersports, tel. 07857 538883.
- **LESSONS AND HIRE:** Rye Watersports, ryewatersports.co.uk
- **GETTING THERE:** From Rye, take A259 towards Folkestone; after Salts Farm Shop turn R onto Camber Road; after 1.4km turn R into car park.
- **SPECIAL POINTS:** Lake is exposed to wind so check Surfline surfline.com for local conditions at Camber Sands. Please clean your board before you enter the water to prevent spread of non-native plants and animal species.

29

ROYAL MILITARY CANAL HYTHE TO WEST HYTHE

CANAL · KENT

Easy trip through a serene waterway rich in military history and wildlife, to an excellent pitstop in West Hythe. Hythe offers lovely coastal paddling, but when the wind picks up this tranquil alternative offers a unique route through a historic landscape, teeming with wildlife and inviting pitstops.

The Royal Military Canal, a hidden gem in the Kent countryside, is a 45 km ribbon of water tracing the old cliff line along Romney Marsh. Built in the early 19th century as a defensive measure against Napoleon's forces, it stands as a testament to British ingenuity, despite never seeing action. The canal's distinctive zigzag bends were strategically designed to allow defenders to fire upon approaching enemies from multiple angles, making any attempted crossing a formidable challenge. Today, these historic defensive features, along with several pillboxes, serve as quiet reminders of the invasion fears that once haunted the nation. Now, the canal offers a peaceful escape, with tree-lined banks that provide a sanctuary for kingfishers, herons, dragonflies, and – with luck – the distinctive call of a marsh frog.

Start the journey at the canal's eastern terminus in Seabrook, passing beneath several footbridges en route to the Twiss Road Bridge, an alternative starting point with stunning upstream views. Here, the tree-lined banks and walkways invite locals and visitors alike to sit and watch the gentle activity on the water. Continuing, the route passes the Hythe Canal Bank Bandstand, with rows of moored rowboats ready for summertime hire just a little further on. The canal eventually leaves the town behind, opening up to fields along its northern bank, with the last stretch to West Hythe offering a serene rural experience with flotillas of pink water lilies blooming in season.

At the West Hythe Road bridge, exit the water on the left bank, where an excellent nearby café and bakery offer essential sustenance for the return journey •

• **DISTANCE:** 13km from Seabrook to Hythe return; 8km from Twiss Road Bridge to Hythe return.

• **PADDLING ENVIRONMENT:** 1.

• **ROUTE MAP:** islandeering.com/paddleboarding-royal-military-canal/

• **ACCESS RESTRICTIONS:** Between Seabrook Outfall and West Hythe a licence is required from Folkstone and Hythe District Council (£27.30/3 months, £35.40/year) folkestone-hythe.gov.uk/licensing/boat-paddle-board-canoe-licences . Along with this permit you also need public liability insurance, included in Paddle UK membership. No licence is required for a separate route from West Hythe Dam to East Rother.

• **OS MAP:** OS Explorer 138 Dover, Folkestone & Hythe.

• **STARTING POINT:** Seabrook Outfall, Seabrook Road, Hythe, CT21 5QT. Grid ref. TR 188 349; What3Words unsecured.scrapped.desktops; an alternative starting point for a shorter trip to West Hythe is at Twiss Road Bridge, Twiss Road, Hythe, CT21 5PD. Grid ref. TR 167 346; What3Words firepower.deduced.trendy.

• **PARKING:** *Hythe* Sea Point Car Park (charges), Princes Parade, Seabrook, Hythe, CT21 5FD. Grid ref. TR 187 348; What3Words spans.tidying.wolf; *Twiss Road Bridge* On-street parking (free); *West Hythe* West Hythe Car Park (charges), Royal Military Road, Hythe, CT21 4NT. Grid ref. TR 125 342; What3Words tuxedos.udder.skinning.

• **LAUNCHING:** Canalside in all locations, short walk from car parking.

• **PITSTOPS:** Brilliant alehouse (outlet for the Hopfuzz Brewery) and kitchen, Unit 1 Riverside, West Hythe, tel. 01303 265000.

• **LESSONS, HIRE AND TOURS:** Seapoint Canoe Centre, tel. 07909 517812.

• **GETTING THERE:** J11 off M20 onto A261 to Hythe, then L onto A259 towards Folkestone. Turn R into Twiss Road opposite the Bell Inn, follow L onto Prince's Parade on the seafront to car park on L near Seapoint Canoe Centre towards the end of the Parade.

• **SPECIAL POINTS:** Please clean your board before you enter the water to prevent spread of non-native plants and animal species.

30

RIVER ROTHER BODIAM CASTLE TO NEWENDEN BRIDGE

RIVER · KENT

A current-free trip through the High Weald with fabulous views of Bodiam Castle, great tearooms and fine camping options. Paddling along the River Rother from The Hub to Bodiam Boating Station is like stepping into a storybook, winding through the idyllic High Weald with views that capture the essence of England's pastoral charm. Setting off from The Hub near Bodiam, the river is very narrow up to Bodiam Bridge, where views then open up to reveal the majestic silhouette of Bodiam Castle. Rising from its wide moat, this 14th-century fortress was built by Sir Edward Dalyngrigge to defend against French invasion during the Hundred Years' War. The romantic ruins, managed by the National Trust, create a striking backdrop, though paddleboarders are asked not to land here to prevent bank erosion.

The river then meanders gently through a landscape of rolling hills and patchwork fields, running parallel to the Kent & East Sussex Railway line. In summer, the nostalgic puff of a steam train can often be seen as they chug through the countryside.

Past the confluence with the Kent Ditch, the river's meanders eventually lead under Newenden Bridge. Immediately after, the Bodiam Boating Station and café come into view. This is a perfect pitstop for refuelling before the return journey, which offers views of the castle from a different perspective.

This trip can start from either The Hub or Bodiam Boating Station, though starting at the latter requires turning around at Bodiam Castle, as paddling past Bodiam Bridge without permission from The Hub is not allowed •

- **DISTANCE:** 13km return.
- **PADDLING ENVIRONMENT:** 2.

ROUTE MAP: islandeering.com/bodiam-castle-to-newenden-bridge/

- **ACCESS RESTRICTIONS:** Self-launch £7 payable to the Hub Café (open 9-5, 7 days/week in season). Riparian rights west of Bodiam Bridge owned by The Hub, so this section of river can only be accessed with wristband issued by The Hub. Free launch and access to campers at The Hub.
- **OS MAP:** OS Explorer 136 High Weald, Royal Tunbridge Wells, Cranbrook, Hawkhurst & Bewl Water.
- **STARTING POINT:** The Hub, Quarry Farm, near Bodiam, TN32 5RA. Grid ref. TQ 779 248; What3Words scorch.lucky.unsightly.
- **PARKING:** The Hub (free).
- **LAUNCHING:** Riverside, short walk from parking and The Hub.
- **PITSTOPS:** Local food and great breakfasts in beautiful setting, The Hub, Quarry Farm, tel. 01580 830932; great vibes and food, Lime Wharf Café, Bodiam Boating Station, tel. 01797 330025.
- **CAMPING:** Eco-friendly camping and glamping at The Hub (no dogs), thehubquarryfarm.co.uk; family camping, Bodiam Boating Station, tel. 01797 330025 bodiamboatingstation.co.uk/camping/
- **LESSONS, HIRE AND TOURS:** Epic Life, The Hub, Quarry Farm, tel. 07377 184505.
- **GETTING THERE:** Head south on Main Road through Bodiam village to cross the river at Bodiam, then cross the heritage railway line. A little further on, turn R at sign for Quarry Farm.
- **SPECIAL POINTS:** This stretch of river has very little flow. Check local river conditions at riverlevels.uk/flood-warning-robertsbridge

31

FOLKESTONE HARBOUR EXPLORER

HARBOUR/COAST · KENT

A coastal journey blending history and contemporary art, with striking sculptures, vibrant installations, and panoramic seafront views. Launch from Folkestone's East Pier, where the Folkestone Mermaid, a striking sculpture by Cornelia Parker, watches over the waters. This is the first of many art installations on the journey. Glide past moored boats to spot the pink "Holiday Home" by Richard Woods, a commentary on the housing crisis and holiday homes in the Southeast.

Next, head towards the Grand Burstin Hotel, with its cruise ship-like silhouette, and paddle beneath the elegant arches of the Harbour Viaduct, an award-winning walkway that bridges Folkestone's industrial past with its creative present. Then exit the Inner Harbour to explore the restored Harbour Arm, once central to cross-channel travel, now featuring Antony Gormley's "Another Time XVIII", an iron figure that stands sentinel on its half-tide platform.

Further along, Patrick Tuttofuoco's vibrant "Folkestone" sculpture greets arrivals from the east, with each letter representing a country on the artist's journey from Istanbul. At the end of the Harbour Arm, the historic Folkestone Harbour Lighthouse, dating back to 1904, houses a chic champagne bar with panoramic views across the English Channel. The inscription by Ian Hamilton Finlay, "Weather is a third to place and time," serves as a reminder of the elements' influence on all seafarers.

If conditions allow, continue around the Harbour Arm to Folkestone Beach for more art installations. Once on the beach, follow the boardwalk toward the Lower Leas Coastal Park, to find "The Jelly Mould Pavilion" and "Out of Tune", a 16th-century tenor bell hanging between two tall steel beams. There are plenty of places for refreshments before returning to the Outer Harbour •

- **DISTANCE:** 3km return to Folkestone Beach.
- **PADDLING ENVIRONMENT:** 4 within harbour, 5 along coast.
- **ROUTE MAP:** islandeering.com/paddleboarding-folkestone-harbour/
- **ACCESS RESTRICTIONS:** No licence required.
- **OS MAP:** OS Explorer 138 Dover, Folkestone & Hythe.
- **STARTING POINT:** Sunny Sands end of Outer Harbour, The Stade, Folkstone. Grid ref. TR 235 361; What3Words pushes.sage.whirlwind.
- **PARKING:** Tram Road Car Park (charges), Tram Road, Folkstone, CT20 1QR. Grid ref. TR 232 360; What3Words grumbling.best.plays.
- **LAUNCHING:** Beach, 300m walk from car park.
- **PITSTOPS:** Fish and chips with harbour views, The Ship Inn, The Stade, tel. 01303 251114; famous crab soup, Bob's Seafood, The Stade, tel. 07768 402462.
- **LESSONS, HIRE AND TRIPS:** The SUP Hub, 07977 989965.
- **GETTING THERE:** J13 off M20, follow A259 then A260 to Folkestone Harbour, car park on R opposite brick arches.
- **SPECIAL POINTS:** Best at slack water or on very calm days, although there is generally good protection within Outer Harbour at HW. Watch out for other boat users and mooring lines. The W side of the outer harbour wall is exposed to SW winds and swell; clapotis can be experienced close to the outer wall at HW; and fishermen's lines need to be avoided. Check Surfline surfline.com at Folkestone for local conditions.

32

ST MARGARET'S BAY AND WHITE CLIFFS

COAST · KENT

Tucked beneath the White Cliffs, explore the hidden bay that inspired Ian Fleming - dramatic, secretive, and quintessentially British. St Margaret's Bay, at the base of a steeply winding road and reminiscent of a scene from Monaco, is a gem on the Kent coast. The iconic White Cliffs of Dover dramatically frame this shingle beach against the expansive English Channel. On a clear day, you can even catch a glimpse of France across the water.

Launch from the beach and the sheer beauty and grandeur of the White Cliffs become immediately apparent. These chalk formations, rising up to 107 metres high, have long symbolised England's strength and resilience, especially during times of war. The cliffs hold a rich history, serving as a crucial defensive site during World War II. Today, they continue to attract cross-Channel swimmers, with St Margaret's Bay often marking a starting or finishing point for those taking on the challenge.

Exploring the bay, a striking white house with green shutters catches the eye at the northern end of the beach – this is the famous "White Cliffs House". Originally owned by playwright Noel Coward, it served as a retreat for his circle of famous friends, including Katharine Hepburn, Spencer Tracy, and Gertrude Lawrence. Also among these visitors was Ian Fleming, the creator of James Bond, who fell in love with the house and its stunning location.

Fleming later purchased the house from Coward, using it as a weekend and holiday retreat. Nestled at the foot of the cliffs, overlooking the Channel, this was where Fleming wrote much of his James Bond series. The bay's tranquility and dramatic scenery inspired him, with St Margaret's Bay and nearby Deal featuring prominently in his novel *Moonraker*. In the book, Bond and Gala Brand recover at the former Granville Hotel (now residential flats) after their adventures. Paddling here, it's easy to imagine Fleming gazing at the passing ships, perhaps plotting another thrilling adventure for 007. The house, with its Art Deco design and prime beachfront location, remains one of the area's most iconic properties.

The Coastguard Inn, Britain's closest pub to France, is a perfect spot for post-paddle refreshments •

• **DISTANCE:** Free-range.

• **PADDLING ENVIRONMENT:** 5.

• **ROUTE MAP:** islandeering.com/paddleboarding-st-margarets-bay-and-white-cliffs/

• **ACCESS RESTRICTIONS:** No licence required.

• **OS MAP:** OS Explorer 138 Dover, Folkestone & Hythe.

• **STARTING POINT & PARKING:** St Margaret's Bay Car Park (charges), Bay Hill, St. Margaret's at Cliffe, Dover, CT15 6DX. Grid ref. TR 368 444; What3Words trackers.spits.game.

• **LAUNCHING:** Shingle beach short walk from car park.

• **PITSTOPS:** Good pub food and fabulous beach location, The Coastguard Pub, tel. 01304 853051; ice cream and snacks and super-friendly, St Margaret's Bay Kiosk on the beach; afternoon tea and cakes in wonderful gardens, The Pines Garden, Tea Room & Museum, tel. 01304 853173.

• **GETTING THERE:** A2 leaving Dover towards Deal; third exit at roundabout onto A258 for 2 km; turn R, following signs towards Pines Garden; in St Margarets, turn R at T-junction and continue through village, following road as it steeply descends to beach.

• **SPECIAL POINTS:** While the cliffs give some protection from the wind, this trip is best on a very calm/low swell day. Check Surfline surfline.com at nearby Folkestone for local conditions.

• **OFFSHORE WIND:** NW.

33

RIVER STOUR AND PEGWELL BAY RAMSGATE TO SANDWICH

COAST/TIDAL RIVER · KENT

Exhilarating coast and river trip with expansive seascapes and a nature reserve teeming with seals and birdlife. Launch from the beach and paddle southwest, leaving Ramsgate behind as the route heads towards the mouth of the River Stour. The coastline unfolds into the Sandwich and Pegwell Bay National Nature Reserve, a vast landscape of mudflats, salt marshes, and sand dunes. This reserve is internationally recognised for its vital role in supporting wading birds and wildfowl, serving as a key migratory stopover and wintering ground.

On the approach to the mouth of the Stour, watch for oystercatchers, terns, shelducks, dunlins, curlews, and seals bobbing in the water or basking on the sandy banks. Paddling upstream along the River Stour, more seals can often be seen lounging on the riverbanks. After passing a marina and a small industrial area, the river begins to meander more, leading past Stonar Lake and the moored boats of Sandwich Marina.

As the toll bridge of Sandwich comes into view, find the exit slipway on the left, just at the start of the quay and moorings. Nearby, the US Navy P22 Patrol Boat can be seen moored along the bank. Sandwich, one of the historic Cinque Ports, with its ancient buildings and rich maritime history, makes for a fascinating end to the paddle •

• **DISTANCE:** 11.5 km one way.

• **PADDLING ENVIRONMENT:** 3 in estuary; 4 in bay.

• **ROUTE MAP:** islandeering.com/paddleboarding-ramsgate-to-sandwich/

• **ACCESS RESTRICTIONS:** No licence required. No landing on the shores of the Pegwell Bay National Nature Reserve.

• **OS MAP:** OS Explorer 150 Canterbury & Isle of Thanet.

• **STARTING POINT:** Western Undercliff Beach, Royal Harbour Approach, West Cliff, Ramsgate, CT11 0EZ. Grid ref. TR 375 641; What3Words dent.stripped.germinate.

• **PARKING:** *Ramsgate* Roadside (free), Royal Harbour Approach Western Undercliff, Ramsgate, CT11 9PH; *Sandwich* Sandwich Quay Car Park (charges), The Quay, CT13 9DH. Grid ref. TR 333 582; What3Words trapdoor.leaves.chin.

• **LAUNCHING:** Beach short walk from parking.

• **PITSTOPS:** Riverside drinks at the Crispin Inn, Sandwich, tel. 01304 621943.

• **LESSONS AND TOURS:** Local guides to this trail, Canoe Wild, tel. 07947 835688.

• **GETTING THERE:** Follow A299 to Ramsgate Ferry Terminal. Once through tunnel, park towards the eastern end of Royal Harbour Approach.

• **SPECIAL POINTS:** Set off 2-3hrs before HW to take advantage of the flood tide flowing up the Stour. This timing will also ensure that the mud banks at the base of the slipway at Sandwich are covered. The trip can also be done in reverse by departing 1hr before HW at Sandwich (approximately +30 minutes HW Ramsgate) to ensure sufficient water in the bay for crossing and an easier exit at Ramsgate with a shorter beach walk. Landing on the seaward edge of the reserve at Pegwell Bay is prohibited year-round, but there's plenty of wildlife to observe from the water. Check Surfline surfline.com at Ramsgate Main Beach for local conditions before trip as the bay is prone to wind chop. Don't disturb seals in the water or resting on the estuary sandbanks. Give them a wide berth as they can be easily scared by humans, leading to injury and stress.

• **OFFSHORE WIND:** NW while in bay.

34

BROADSTAIRS TO BOTANY BAY

COAST · KENT

A coastal adventure to discover the seven bays between Dumpton Bay and Foreland Point, known as the jewels in Thanet's crown along a coastline that blends charming sandy beaches, dramatic chalk cliffs, and rich history. Leave the relatively peaceful beach of Dumpton Gap and head north along the low, grass-topped white cliffs to reach Louisa Bay, named after Queen Victoria's daughter. This charming bay offers a quiet café, an ideal spot to pause before continuing to Viking Bay, the heart of bustling Broadstairs, with its lively sandy beach, colourful beach huts, and Victorian charm that draws so many visitors.

Pass the jetty, often filled with diners, to reach a more tranquil atmosphere at Stone Bay, with its long stretch of sand backed by cliffs and a promenade. The 39 steps leading down to the beach here famously inspired the title of John Buchan's novel, part of which he wrote in this very spot.

Continuing north, the coast begins to curve towards the northwest as the area of North Foreland comes into view. Joss Bay offers a touch of historical fascination, named after the notorious 18th-century smuggler Joss Snelling. Beyond Joss Bay, the clifftop Kingsgate Castle marks the start of Kingsgate Bay, where dramatic white cliffs and small sea caves add to the bay's intrigue. The natural arch at its northern end is a fun challenge to paddle through on the way to Botany Bay.

Botany Bay is perhaps the most picturesque of the seven, renowned for its stunning chalk cliffs, two large chalk stacks that stand apart from the headland, and chalk caves in the cliffs. Despite its beauty, it has a darker history as the site of an 18th-century clash between revenue men and smugglers during the infamous Battle of Botany Bay. From here, the low chalk headland of Long Nose Spit stretches beyond Foreland Point. Return to Dumpton Gap along the same scenic route, retracing the journey through these lovely bays •

• **DISTANCE:** 11.5km return.

• **PADDLING ENVIRONMENT:** 5.

• **ROUTE MAP:** islandeering.com/paddleboarding-broadstairs-to-botany-bay/

• **ACCESS RESTRICTIONS:** No licence required.

• **OS MAP:** OS Explorer 150 Canterbury & Isle of Thanet.

• **STARTING POINT:** Dumpton Bay, Dumpton Gap, Broadstairs, CT10 1TD. Grid ref. TR 395 666; What3Words pillow.from.amount.

• **PARKING:** Roadside (free) close to beach.

• **LAUNCHING:** Beach.

• **PITSTOPS:** Worth the climb up the steps for refreshments with a view, Captain Digby, Kingsgate Bay, tel. 01843 867764.

• **LESSONS AND TOURS:** Kent Surf School, Broadstairs, tel. 07834 639679; Joss Bay Surf School, tel. 07719 902025.

• **GETTING THERE:** A255 from Ramsgate to Broadstairs. R after Ramsgate Garden Centre onto Montefiore Rd. L onto Dumpton Park Drive, then R onto Dumpton Gap Road to park near beach.

• **SPECIAL POINTS:** Suitable only on very calm seas. A flooding tide (which heads north) is best for exploring deeper into each bay, as they all reveal sandy beaches at low water. However, views are impressive at all states of the tide. Check wind, surf, and tide conditions on Surfline surfline.com at Joss Bay for up-to-date local information.

• **OFFSHORE WIND:** W to SW.

35

MARGATE WALPOLE TIDAL POOL

TIDAL POOL · KENT

Experience one of the largest and oldest tidal pools in the UK. Built in the 1930s, this seawater pool was designed to provide a safe and enjoyable swimming area, protected from the strong currents and waves of the open sea. The pool fills naturally with seawater during high tide and retains the water as the tide recedes, creating a unique and sheltered environment for paddlers and swimmers alike.

Walpole Tidal Pool is beloved by both locals and visitors for its retro charm and the sense of nostalgia it evokes. The pool offers stunning views of the coastline, and its expansive size means there's plenty of space for everyone to enjoy the water, even on busier days.

In recent years, the pool has seen a resurgence in popularity, partly due to the growing interest in wild swimming. It's also appreciated for its biodiversity, with various marine life species often visible in and around the pool, including lobsters, brittlestars, sea urchins, crabs, gobies, sponges, and more. It's also a good spot to watch the sunset •

- **DISTANCE:** Free-range.
- **PADDLING ENVIRONMENT:** 1.
- **ROUTE MAP:** islandeering.com/paddleboarding-walpole-tidal-pool/
- **ACCESS RESTRICTIONS:** No licence required.
- **OS MAP:** OS Explorer 150 Canterbury & Isle of Thanet.
- **STARTING POINT & PARKING:** Prince's Walk, Hodges Gap, Palm Bay, Cliftonville, Margate, CT9 3FD. Grid ref. TR 370 714; What3Words stone.salon.empire.
- **LAUNCHING:** Lido beach adjacent to car park.
- **GETTING THERE:** A28 Margate onto B2051 to Cliftonville. Pass Walpole Bay Hotel then, after sharp L bend and just before Woolls Pharmacy, head straight ahead (L off road) down narrow Hodges Gap to beach and parking.
- **SPECIAL POINTS:** At high tide waves can breach the pool's wall. Generally, calmest conditions 3hrs either side of LW when the tidal wall is exposed. Check surf, wind and tide at surfline.com at nearby Main Sands for local conditions.

36

MINNIS BAY TO MARGATE

COAST · KENT

Hidden bays, a historic harbour, a lively seaside town and an incredible sunset paddle along the Thanet coastline. Leave Minnis Bay, a peaceful stretch of sandy shoreline, and head east past the sea defences to Birchington Promenade, where the chalk cliffs start to rise a little higher. Look out for tunnels in the cliffs – these once provided private access to the beach for the houses above. Continue east to reach the small and secluded Epple Bay, then, a little further on, the popular family beach at Westgate Bay – with its colourful beach huts and bar – is a good place to stop for refreshments.

Round the headland to find St Mildred's Bay, a charming and sheltered bay with a picturesque promenade lined with cafés and beach huts, and a tidal swimming pool. Further along, at Westbrook Bay's long sandy beach, there are some great views of Margate's skyline. Closer to Margate Beach the vibe shifts to a bustling seaside resort. Margate is home to the largest and most lively beach on this route, with golden sands and a backdrop of the iconic Turner Contemporary art gallery and Dreamland's retro amusement park.

Head towards Margate Harbour past the Turner Contemporary, a striking modern art gallery that overlooks the sea. The harbour itself is home to a mix of fishing boats and pleasure craft, and the surrounding area boasts an array of quirky cafés, seafood restaurants, and independent shops. Return the same way or take the bus. For a shorter trip, start from Westgate Bay (3.7km one way) •

- **DISTANCE:** 8km one way; bus no. 32 return stagecoachbus.com
- **PADDLING ENVIRONMENT:** 5.
- **ROUTE MAP:** islandeering.com/paddleboarding-minnis-bay-to-margate/
- **ACCESS RESTRICTION:** No licence required.
- **OS MAP:** OS Explorer 150 Canterbury & Isle of Thanet.
- **STARTING POINT & PARKING:** Roadside, The Parade (free), Minnis Bay, CT7 9LX. Grid ref. TR 287 697; What3Words dollars.footpath.give.
- **LAUNCHING:** Beach short walk from parking.
- **PITSTOPS:** Post-paddle drink to watch the sunset, Minnis Bay Bar and Brasserie, tel. 01843 841844; hearty breakfasts and ice cream with a view, West Bay Café & Beach Bar, tel. 01843 831791.
- **LESSONS AND TOURS:** Margate Sup and Surf, tel. 07854 367033.
- **GETTING THERE:** A28 Canterbury towards Margate; in Birchington take first exit on roundabout and follow brown signs to Minnis Bay along Station Road/Minnis Road to The Parade.
- **SPECIAL POINTS:** The tide recedes significantly at LW. Start close to HW to take advantage of the slight ebb flow moving eastwards. Check wind, surf, and tide on Surfline surfline.com at Main Sands beach for local conditions.
- **OFFSHORE WIND:** S.

CRUISE

37

RIVER STOUR CHARTHAM TO CANTERBURY

RIVER · KENT

The timeless beauty of Canterbury from the beautiful waters of the Great Stour River, seeing centuries of history from a unique perspective. Canterbury owes its foundation and prosperity to the Great Stour River, which flows through a series of islands that form the land on which the city now stands. This strategic Roman crossing point on the route to London made the river essential, providing drinking water and food, and later powering Canterbury's milling and weaving industries. Today, the Stour, classified as a chalk stream for the length of this route, remains one of the cleanest rivers in the South East, its clear waters home to brown trout, eels, pike, and a variety of birdlife. Two paddling routes offer exploration of the city – a longer route from Chartham to Canterbury, and a shorter one from Toddler's Cove.

Launching at Chartham, pass through the peaceful Low Weald, glide beneath the A28, and see Hambrook Marshes full of birdlife. Beyond the viaduct, Whitehall Meadows Nature Reserve and Bingley Island, untouched by modern agriculture, host thriving plant species. Take the right fork around Bingley Island or, if starting from Toddler's Cove, head downstream a short way before taking a right fork. Pass under a small footbridge and then the A290, entering the historic heart of Canterbury. Pass by the Canterbury Punting Company, the 13th-century Franciscan chapel, King's Mill, and Cromwell's Iron Forge. Before King's Bridge, spot Eastbridge Hospital, which once housed poor pilgrims visiting St Thomas Becket's shrine and still serves Canterbury's elderly citizens.

Continue under King's Bridge, the middle section of which dates back to 1134, ducking to avoid beams originating from the Spanish Armada. Beyond, see the Old Weaver's House, a much-photographed 16th-century relic of Flemish and Huguenot weavers. Look out for the medieval witches' ducking stool nearby.

After Friar Bridge, pass the Marlowe Theatre, marked by the giant mask known as "Bulkhead". On the right stands the gothic Blackfriars Chapel, a surviving gem from the 13th century and one of the few remnants of the original Dominican friary. Beyond it, fabulous views open up to the right of the spire of Canterbury Cathedral, with its tower (known as Bell Harry) soaring into the sky with a graceful power. On the left, Abbots Mill Gardens marks the site of the former mill buildings, leading to Abbott's Mill Weir and the Millers Arms. From here, retrace your route to Toddler's Cove or exit the river for the rail return to Chartham •

• **DISTANCE:** From Chartham 5.5km one way; from Toddler's Cove 2.3km return.

• **PADDLING ENVIRONMENT:** 2.

• **ROUTE MAP:** islandeering.com/paddleboarding-chartham-to-canterbury/

• **ACCESS RESTRICTIONS:** No licence required.

• **OS MAP:** OS Explorer 150 Canterbury & Isle of Thanet.

• **STARTING POINT:** Great Stour Way footpath, Chartham. Grid ref. TR 110 551; What3Words romance.originals.format; or Great Stour Way footpath, Toddler's Cove. Grid ref. TR 142 576; What3Words closes.mash.player.

• **EGRESS:** *Abbott's Mill* Grass area on Millers Arms side of Abbott's Mill Weir, Mill Lane, The King's Mile, Canterbury, Kent, England, CT1 2AW. Grid ref. TR 149 581; What3Words flown.fines.allow.

• **PARKING:** *Chartham* Village Hall, Station Road, Chartham, CT4 7HZ. Grid ref. TR 107 550; What3Words lifeguard.rollers.tomb; *Toddler's Cove* Toddler's Cove Car Park (charges), Great Stour Way, Wincheap, Canterbury, CT2 8BG. Grid ref. TR 142 577; What3Words drum.enjoy.audit; *Canterbury* St Radigund's Car Park, St Radigund's Street, Canterbury, CT1 2AA. Grid ref. TR 149 582; What3Words dart.hill.walks.

• **LAUNCHING:** *Chartham* Walk to Great Stour Way from S corner of car park, launch downstream of weir; *Toddler's Cove* Short walk from car park to river.

• **PITSTOPS:** Ales, pies and roasts in historic country pub a short walk from river, The Artichoke, tel. 01227 738316.

• **GETTING THERE:** *Car* A28 Canterbury towards Ashford. Turn L to Chartham, then L into car park; *Train* Direct trains from St Pancras International to Chartham or Canterbury West southeasternrailway.co.uk

• **SPECIAL POINTS:** Check the river level before the trip riverlevels.uk/great-stour-chartham-horton-weir. Use river fins to minimise drag from summer weed growth. Once in the city you will be sharing the water with punters with varying levels of ability!

38

RIVER STOUR FORDWICH TO GROVE FERRY

TIDAL RIVER · KENT

The Great Stour, Kent's tidal river up to Fordwich, offers a peaceful and wildlife-rich journey between Fordwich and Grove Ferry. Launch at Fordwich, glide under the charming brick road bridge and past the marina moorings, then follow the river as it meanders through a mosaic of lakes, former gravel pits, and marshes toward Grove Ferry.

Westbere Marshes soon appear, a tranquil patchwork of reed beds teeming with life. Here, rare species like the elusive bittern, Desmoulin's whorl snail, and various fish and reptiles thrive within this crucial part of the Stodmarsh Site of Special Scientific Interest. These marshes are vital for preserving Kent's reedbed habitats, supporting a rich diversity of birdlife, amphibians, and insects. Beavers have even been spotted along this stretch.

Further along, the tidal lake offers a unique habitat where freshwater and brackish species coexist. Its fluctuating conditions support a diverse range of aquatic life, while the reed-lined shores shelter birds and small mammals. Nearby, Stodmarsh National Nature Reserve stands as one of the UK's premier wetland reserves, featuring reed beds, lagoons, wet meadows, and woodlands that support abundant wildlife, particularly bird species like bitterns, marsh harriers, and bearded tits.

Towards the journey's end, pass Port Farm Marina, a picturesque spot along the Great Stour lined with moored boats. Finally, reach Grove Ferry and exit the river on the left bank, next to the Grove Ferry Picnic Site and car park •

• **DISTANCE:** 7.7km one way.

• **PADDLING ENVIRONMENT:** 2.

• **ROUTE MAP:** islandeering.com/paddleboarding-fordwich-to-grove-ferry/

• **ACCESS RESTRICTIONS:** No licence required.

• **OS MAP:** OS Explorer 150 Canterbury & Isle of Thanet.

• **STARTING POINT:** Fordwich (see parking).

• **PARKING:** *Fordwich* Roadside (free), Marlow Meadows, Fordwich, CT2 0BF. Grid ref. TR 179 599; What3Words dressy.tagging.tissue; *Grove Ferry* Grove Ferry Picnic Site Car Park (charges), Grove Ferry Road, Canterbury, CT3 4BP. Grid ref. TR 236 631; What3Words exotic.activates.salads.

• **LAUNCHING:** Riverside opposite the George and Dragon pub.

• **PITSTOPS:** Lovely pub garden and food, The George and Dragon, Fordwich, 01227 710661; riverside beer garden, Grove Ferry Inn, Grove Ferry, tel. 01227 860302.

• **HIRE AND TOURS:** Canoe Wild, Grove Ferry and Fordwich, tel. 07947 835688.

• **GETTING THERE:** A28 Canterbury towards Margate, in Sturry turn R, following signs to Fordwich. Drop kit in car park of George & Dragon, then park in Marlow Meadows.

• **SPECIAL POINTS:** This river section is tidal, with the flood tide approximately 2hrs after HW at Ramsgate, providing assistance for paddling upstream, especially during spring tides. Be mindful of other boats, particularly around sharper bends, and keep to the right. Access to the tidal lake is not permitted. Check river levels before trip riverlevels.uk/great-stour-fordwich-river-level

39

OARE TO FAVERSHAM

TIDAL RIVER · KENT

A scenic trip through some of Kent's most beautiful waterways, from Oare Marshes Nature Reserve to Faversham Quay, with a stop at the historic Shipwright's Arms pub. Start at Oare Marshes, a haven for birdwatchers and nature lovers, featuring wide-open skies, salt marshes, and mudflats. Launch from the public slipway at the south end of the old Harty Ferry route; the southern shore of Sheppey Island's Isle of Harty lies just to the north. Paddle through the Swale National Nature Reserve, looking out for seasonal wildlife such as rare wading birds like avocets, redshanks and lapwings, as well as wintering wildfowl and marsh harriers.

After about 700 metres, the route turns right into the creek and continues toward the Shipwright's Arms. Tucked away at the confluence of the Oare and Faversham Creeks, this traditional pub provides a step back in time with its cosy atmosphere, wooden beams, and local ales. The location, surrounded by marshes and moored boats, is perfect for a relaxing stop with views across the water.

Continue along Faversham Creek (the creek on the left), where low grassy banks give way to occasional reed beds and the sounds of seabirds. The charming town of Faversham gradually comes into view, with boat moorings and centuries-old buildings reflecting its rich maritime history, including Oyster Bay House, a former warehouse for storing and processing oysters.

Faversham Quay is not only quaint but also steeped in history. The town's maritime heritage dates back to the medieval period, when it was an important port for exporting wool and other goods. Nearby, the Shepherd Neame brewery, Britain's oldest brewery, adds to the historical charm, and signs along the quay tell stories of the town's past. The quay serves as the ideal turning point for the return journey, with plenty of cafés and shops to enjoy nearby •

• **DISTANCE:** 12.5km return.

• **PADDLING ENVIRONMENT:** 3.

• **ROUTE MAP:** islandeering.com/paddleboarding-oare-to-faversham/

• **ACCESS RESTRICTIONS:** No licence required.

• **OS MAP:** OS Explorer 149 Sittingbourne & Faversham.

• **STARTING POINT & PARKING:** Oare Marshes Nature Reserve car park (free), Church Road, Oare, ME13 0QD. Grid ref. TR 013 647; What3Words tulip.cello.resort.

• **LAUNCHING:** Public slipway 200m walk north of parking.

• **PITSTOPS:** Step back in time at a 17th-century pub serving ales from the cask, The Shipwright's Arms, tel. 01795 590088

• **GETTING THERE:** From the A2 at Faversham, take Western Link Road towards Oare. Turn L at T-junction into Oare village. After Three Mariners pub, turn R onto Church Road and follow to end, with car park on R.

• **SPECIAL POINTS:** This is a tide-assisted trip, so leave Oare approx. 2.5hrs before HW. Check wind, tide and swell conditions before you start at nearby Herne Bay as the whole area is low lying and exposed to the wind www.surfline.com/surf-report/herne-bay/613bd4131e5772d9940e6dfa . If heading for the Shipwright's Arms, keep to the RHS when entering Faversham Creek, ignoring Oare Creek on your right, and land just beyond the large boat building shed on the grass bank.

40

ST ANDREWS LAKE

LAKE · KENT

A taste of the Mediterranean in Kent, with turquoise waters, sandy shores, and a range of watersports in a beautiful setting. Surrounded by rolling hills, woodland, and the cliffs of a former sand and gravel quarry, the lake feels both expansive and secluded despite being near urban areas. It's one of Kent's largest privately owned lakes, and ideal for both nature lovers and adventure seekers.

The vivid turquoise water is a striking feature and a result of the site's quarrying past, with chalky minerals giving the water its unique colour. On sunny days, it has a tropical appearance – rare for the UK. The clear waters are perfect for open-water swimming, paddleboarding, kayaking, and canoeing. Scuba diving is also available, featuring underwater attractions like submerged wrecks, while wakeboarding enthusiasts can enjoy designated zones for a thrilling experience.

Small sandy beaches around the lake give it a coastal atmosphere that's perfect for relaxing between activities. Luxury lodges on site allow for extended stays to appreciate the tranquil surroundings fully. The lake's rich ecosystem adds to its appeal, with plenty of wildlife to spot. Large shoals of fish swim below as you paddle, making the experience even more unique •

- **DISTANCE:** Free-range.
- **PADDLING ENVIRONMENT:** 1.
- **ROUTE MAP:** islandeering.com/paddleboarding-st-andrews-lake/
- **ACCESS RESTRICTIONS:** Self-launch, book with St Andrews Watersports (£15/3 hours May–Sept; £15/all day Oct–Apr).
- **OS MAP:** OS Explorer 163 Gravesend & Rochester.
- **PARKING:** St Andrews Lakes (free), Quarry Grove, Halling, Rochester, ME2 1BA. Grid ref. TQ 697 650; What3Words cling.fires.charmingly.
- **LAUNCHING:** Lakeside adjacent to car park; inflation station available.
- **PITSTOPS:** Onsite café.
- **LESSONS AND HIRE:** St Andrews Watersports, tel. 01634 926204.
- **GETTING THERE:** J2 off M2 onto A228 towards Gravesend; pass through Cuxton and North Halling. Take third exit from roundabout onto Limeburners Drive, following signs to St Andrews Lakes; then first exit at next roundabout onto Quarry Grove and follow to car park.
- **SPECIAL POINTS:** The lake gets very busy at peak times. Please clean your board before you enter the water to prevent spread of non-native plants and animal species.

41

LEYBOURNE LAKES

LAKE · KENT

Within Leybourne Country Park the largest lake, a former gravel pit, is ideal for paddleboarding, swimming and more. Surrounded by woodland, this friendly and relaxed lake is perfect for families and beginners, and has a lovely lakeside café where you can enjoy watching the antics of the geese, swans and other wildlife. Dogs are also welcome to paddle with you if you are bringing your own board •

- **DISTANCE:** Free-range.
- **PADDLING ENVIRONMENT:** 1.
- **ROUTE MAP:** islandeering.com/paddleboarding-leybourne-lakes/
- **ACCESS RESTRICTIONS:** Private lake, self-launch £15/4 hours, book with Leybourne Lake Watersports.
- **OS MAP:** OS Explorer 148 Maidstone & the Medway Towns.
- **PARKING:** Watersports Car Park (free with booking/sign car in), Leybourne Lakes Country Park, Larkfield, Aylesford ME20 6JA. Grid ref. TQ 696 603; What3Words typical.gushes.arise.
- **LAUNCHING:** Pontoon close to car park.
- **PITSTOPS:** Watch the lakeside action with coffee and cake, Refuel Café, tel. 01634 243397.
- **LESSONS AND HIRE:** Leybourne Lake Watersports Centre, tel. 01634 246006 (check opening times/restricted winter opening), leybournelakewatersports.co.uk
- **GETTING THERE:** J4 off M20 onto A228 towards Rochester; fourth exit off roundabout, following country park sign. At main car park continue to L to find watersports car park.
- **SPECIAL POINTS:** Buoyancy aids (including one for a dog) and leashes mandatory. Please clean your board before you enter the water to prevent spread of non-native plants and animal species.

42

RIVER MEDWAY TRAIL TONBRIDGE TO YALDING

RIVER · KENT

Experience the thrill of canoe passes, tranquil river sections, and some welcoming pitstops on the western half of the Medway Canoe Trail. Spanning 29 kilometres from Tonbridge to Allington Lock, just north of Maidstone, the trail offers a scenic adventure with many trip variations. Alongside Route 43, this option breaks the journey into two day trips, with the convenience of returning by train. Along the way, there are several excellent campsites, providing flexible options for those who prefer a multi-day trip or a slower pace on the water.

Launch and paddle alongside the playing fields of Racecourse Park before reaching the imposing walls of Tonbridge Castle. Perched above the River

- **DISTANCE:** 13.5km one way/rail return.
- **PADDLING ENVIRONMENT:** 2.
- **ROUTE MAP:** islandeering.com/paddleboarding-tonbridge-to-yalding/
- **ACCESS RESTRICTIONS:** Licence required, included in Paddle UK membership.
- **OS MAP:** OS Explorer 147 Sevenoaks & Tonbridge.
- **STARTING POINT & PARKING:** Lower Castle Field Car Park (charges), New Wharf Road, Brook Street, Tonbridge, TN9 1FS. Grid Ref. TQ 587 466; What3Words cure.having.helps; lay-by, Hampstead Lane, Yalding, ME18 6HJ. Grid ref. TQ 686 502; What3Words eyepieces.sugars.milder.
- **LAUNCHING:** Slipway adjacent to car park.
- **PITSTOPS:** Great hot and cold food on the riverside, Waterside Café at Branbridges, tel. 01622 391521; lovely riverside views, The Boathouse, Yalding, tel. 01622 814359.
- **CAMPING:** Hop Farm Campsite, 01622 872068; Banbridges Leisure, tel. 07803 335117; Riverview Camping, Yalding, tel. 07775 931430.
- **LESSONS AND TOURS:** Epic Life, Tonbridge, tel. 07377 184505; The Paddle Cabin, Branbridges Leisure, East Peckham, paddlecabin.co.uk
- **GETTING THERE:** *Car* Tonbridge exit off A21; at second roundabout take first exit following signs to rail station; continue on B2260 through Tonbridge. Cross river, then L onto Castle Street; L at T-junction onto Bank Street following signs to car park and swimming pool; L onto The Slade, following around to L into Lower Castlefield car park; *Train* Tonbridge (return via Yalding), regular services to Charing Cross southeastern.com , 600m walk to launch.
- **SPECIAL POINTS:** Always keep R when passing other river users. Before setting out, check local river levels for Tonbridge at riverlevels.uk/medway-tonbridge-town-lock . There are six locks along the route, with option to use canoe passes or portage. Tonbridge Town and Eldridges Locks offer a grade 1 easy canoe pass, while Porters has a grade 2 canoe pass (slightly more challenging). East Lock provides a standard portage. Oak Weir features a grade 2 canoe pass, and Old Sluice Weir has a grade 3 canoe pass, which is the most difficult and portage is recommended. River fins are required for the canoe passes, otherwise all locks can be portaged. More details in 'Paddling the River Medway' therivermedway.co.uk/media/s34lndaf/medwayrivertrail.pdf

Medway, it is a near-perfect slice of Norman history, with its 13th-century gatehouse standing proudly as one of England's finest. Once besieged during the Barons' Wars, when rebellious barons fought with the monarchy, peace reigns today.

Soon after, pass under the Tonbridge Town Bridge, where the iconic brick building with its clock tower, now a Pizza Express, can be seen. At Tonbridge Town Lock, there is a canoe pass on the left for easy navigation. Continue downstream, passing under Cannon Lane Bridge (A26), and head into the peaceful countryside of the Medway Valley. Over the next few kilometres, there are several locks to navigate, including Eldridges Lock, Porters Lock, East Lock, and Oak Weir Lock, before passing under Silstead Bridge and the striking metal Wagon Bridge. To locate the Hop Farm Campsite, keep an eye out for the wooden footbridge on the right and pass beneath it. The journey continues with Sluice Weir Lock before the village of East Peckham appears on the left. Branbridges Leisure offers a welcome spot for refreshments, and is home to Paddle Cabin, where paddleboards can be hired or lessons taken.

Pass beneath Branbridges Bridge, followed by the A228, to enter a peaceful stretch of water. Further along, the disused Stoneham Old Lock is passed, leading to one of the quirkier highlights of this route – Teapot Island, on the right. This is home to the UK's largest teapot collection and a relaxing riverside café.

Further along the route, The Boathouse pub comes into view on the left. Paddle beneath the low green bridge – there's a platform on the right for those wishing to stop and visit the pub. After a long straight stretch alongside the B2162, pass beneath the road bridge, reaching Hampstead Lock and portage to the right. After crossing the lock gates, Hampstead Lane and Yalding rail station are just a short distance away, offering an easy return journey by train to Tonbridge (with a 750m walk back to the car park) or London. Alternatively, park a second car at Yalding •

43

RIVER MEDWAY TRAIL YALDING TO MAIDSTONE

RIVER · KENT

Discover historic oast houses, orchards, and ancient bridges on the way to Maidstone's medieval centre on the eastern half of the Medway Canoe Trail. Launch from the lock and head left to join the main river, then, after a while, pass the boats moored at Wateringbury Marina and its quirky café. Enjoy the canoe pass at Teston Lock, where the trail runs alongside Teston Bridge Country Park. This park, with its grasslands and meadows, is perfect for a picnic and offers beautiful views of the oast houses on the hills to the east. Teston is also known as the historic home of high-quality leather cricket balls.

Beyond Teston, the river widens, and the scenery transforms into a charming patchwork of orchards, gardens, and wooded areas. As you pass under Barming Footbridge, take note of its local tradition: each year on May 1st, local Morris dancers called the "Kettle Bridge Clogs" perform a dance on the footbridge in a nod to ancient customs. A little further downstream is the village of East Farleigh, with its church spire visible from the river. Paddle beneath the arches of the historic East Farleigh Bridge, the site of the Battle of East Farleigh Bridge during the Second English Civil War in 1648.

Leaving behind the rural calm of East Farleigh, continue downstream towards Maidstone. Keep an eye out for the 14th-century Archbishop's Palace, once a key stopover for archbishops travelling between London and Canterbury. Exit the river on the east bank opposite the palace and take a short walk to Maidstone rail station for an easy return to Yalding by train.

To extend the adventure, continue paddling another 4km downstream towards Allington Lock. Along this stretch, pass Whatman Millennium Park and Allington Castle on the left.

Before reaching the lock, the Malta Inn – one of four named after British naval bases – is a riverside pub with origins dating back to the 18th century. Exit the river via the slipway on the left before Allington Lock •

• **DISTANCE:** 11km to Maidstone (rail return); 15km to Allington Lock (two-car return).

• **PADDLING ENVIRONMENT:** 2.

• **ROUTE MAP:** islandeering.com/paddleboarding-yalding-to-maidstone/

• **ACCESS RESTRICTIONS:** Licence required, included in Paddle UK membership.

• **OS MAP:** OS Explorer 147 Sevenoaks & Tonbridge.

• **STARTING POINT:** Hampstead Lock, Hampstead Lane, Yalding, ME18 6HH. Grid ref. TQ 686 503; What3Words ends.hikes.singles.

• **PARKING:** *Yalding* Lay-by, Hampstead Lane, Yalding, ME18 6HJ. Grid ref. TQ 686 502; What3Words eyepieces.sugars.milder; *Maidstone* Lockmeadow Car Park (charges), Barker Road, Maidstone, ME16 8LW. Grid ref. TQ 758 553; What3Words scary.focal.apron; *Allington Lock* Lock Keepers car park (charges), Allington Lock, Castle Road, Maidstone, ME16 0LU. Grid ref. TQ 747 581; What3Words straying.rhino.jigging. Pay duty lock keeper – charge includes use of slipway, toilets, and showers.

• **LAUNCHING:** Slipway close to parking/rail station.

• **PITSTOPS:** Friendly Ramblers Rest, Wateringbury, tel. 01622 960288; excellent cafe in historic narrowboat just downriver from the Archbishop's Palace, The Old Boat Café, Maidstone, facebook.com/theoldboatcafe/; al fresco coffee, cake and ice cream kiosk in miniature toll-house on its own island, The Little Old Toll House, Allington Lock, facebook.com/oldtollhouse

• **CAMPING:** River View Camping, Yalding, tel. 07775 931430; Allington Lock Camping, therivermedway.co.uk/allington-lock-camping-cabins/

• **LESSONS, TOURS AND HIRE:** The Paddle Cabin, Branbridges Leisure, East Peckham, tel. 07507 966098; River Medway Canoes, Wateringbury, tel. 07557 947592.

• **GETTING THERE:** Car Leave A26 between Tonbridge to Maidstone onto A228 towards Paddock Wood; first exit at roundabout onto B2015 towards Teapot Island; then R onto Hampstead Lane signed to Teapot Island. Pass Yalding rail station to parking lay-by just beyond on L; Train Regular services from London Charing Cross to Yalding; return via Maidstone southeastern.com, 100m walk to launch.

• **SPECIAL POINTS:** Keep to R when passing other river users. Check local river levels at Maidstone riverlevels.uk/medway-maidstone. Two locks to portage – Teston and East Farleigh. Teston lock has a canoe pass which is fun for experienced paddlers but can also be portaged if your paddleboard does not have river fins on. More details at 'Paddling the River Medway' therivermedway.co.uk/media/s34lndaf/medwayrivertrail.pdf

44

MOTE PARK LAKE

LAKE · KENT

A tranquil haven in Maidstone, this scenic river-fed gem is cherished by watersports enthusiasts and locals alike. The man-made lake is fed by the River Len as it flows from Lenham and Leeds Castle before joining the River Medway downstream. Renowned for its fishing, the lake hosts species like bream, roach, carp, pike, tench, and perch, many of which grow to impressive sizes. Birdwatchers can spot ducks, geese, and swans, while amphibians such as frogs and toads thrive along its shores. The lake is framed by a diverse landscape of more than 100 tree species, creating a perfect setting for *shinrin-yoku* (forest bathing) and quiet reflection while floating on a board.

A historic boathouse stands as a notable feature, connected to an underground water management system that directs flow toward Turkey Mill Pond. Though the lake offers various watersports, it retains its peaceful charm, and with its shallow depth (generally less than a metre), paddling and swimming are both accessible and safe •

- **DISTANCE:** Free-range.
- **PADDLING ENVIRONMENT:** 1.
- **ROUTE MAP:** islandeering.com/paddleboarding-mote-park/
- **ACCESS RESTRICTIONS:** Self-launch (£6/day with free parking); book with Mote Park Watersports.
- **OS MAP:** OS Explorer 148 Maidstone & the Medway Towns.
- **PARKING:** Mote Park Watersports Centre (free), Ashford Road, Maidstone, ME14 5DL. Grid ref. TQ 778 552; What3Words parts.listed.lately. Note: if not booked in with Mote Watersports Centre use main public car park (charges).
- **LAUNCHING:** Pontoon adjacent to parking.
- **PITSTOPS:** Friendly onsite café, Mote Park Café, tel. 01304 216179.
- **LESSONS AND HIRE:** Mote Park Watersports, tel. 07595 539555; moteparkwatersports.com
- **GETTING THERE:** A20 E of Maidstone towards Bearstead and M20; R at traffic lights onto Willington Street; then R into entrance of Park and Ride, and immediately R into Mote Park staff/members entrance. Follow estate lane to crossroads, turn R and follow to watersports centre. Park in field.
- **SPECIAL POINTS:** Please clean your board before you enter the water to prevent spread of non-native plants and animal species.

45

SHEPPEY ISLAND QUEENBOROUGH TO DEADMAN'S ISLAND

TIDAL RIVER · KENT

Naval history, wildlife, and a haunting past come together for paddlers exploring Queenborough on a free-range tour of its fascinating highlights. This short excursion passes through peaceful salt marshes and wetlands where wildlife thrives, and leads to the eerie legends of Deadman's Island, all set against the industrial backdrop of the Isle of Grain.

At the meeting point of the Swale and Medway Estuary before they flow into the North Sea, Queenborough offers a unique mix of natural beauty and historical intrigue. Once a key maritime hub during the Hundred Years' War, Queenborough was home to a castle that protected its thriving wool and chemical trade. Though the castle is long gone, the town's nautical heritage lives on, including its connection to Lord Nelson, whose body was brought ashore nearby after the Battle of Trafalgar. Today, Queenborough's peaceful harbour is filled with pleasure boats, diverse wildlife, and stunning sunsets.

Launch from the Hard and head 750m northwest to Deadman's Island. This uninhabited mudbank, rich in eerie folklore, has recently uncovered the remains of prisoners who perished on prison hulks moored offshore centuries ago. Now a protected bird sanctuary, the island is alive with oystercatchers, dunlins, and avocets, though its creeks and marshes are off-limits to land visitors in order to preserve the habitat.

After exploring the creeks and wetlands, return to The Hard and paddle past the historic boatyards of The Creek, rich with Queenborough's seafaring history. End the journey with a visit to one of the town's welcoming inns or cafés •

• **DISTANCE:** Free range.

• **PADDLING ENVIRONMENT:** 3.

• **ROUTE MAP:** islandeering.com/paddleboarding-sheppey-island-queenborough/

• **ACCESS RESTRICTIONS:** No licence required.

• **OS MAP:** OS Explorer 149 Sittingbourne & Faversham.

• **STARTING POINT:** Slipway, Crundell's Wharf, North Road, Queenborough, ME11 5AD. Grid ref. TQ 906 722; What3Words scaffold.truth.payer.

• **PARKING:** Park Road Car Park (charges), Park Road, ME11 5AA. Grid ref. TQ 907 722; What3Words steered.forest.roughest.

• **LAUNCHING:** Slipway, Queenborough Hard, short walk from car park.

• **PITSTOPS:** Quaint and friendly local with good roasts, The Old House at Home, tel. 01795 662463; huge array of beers, fabulous pizza, and great atmosphere, Admiral's Arm Micropub, tel. 01795 668598; tasty lunch and cakes, Bosuns, tel. 01795 669448.

• **GETTING THERE:** A249 onto B2007 to Queenborough; after rail bridge take second exit at roundabout towards town centre, then L onto High Street, follow through village then R onto Park Road to car park.

• **SPECIAL POINTS:** Best within 1.5hrs of HW to avoid the mudbanks below the Hard. The whole area is low lying and exposed to wind. Check wind and tides at metoffice.gov.uk at nearby Sheerness beach for local conditions.

• **OFFSHORE WIND:** S (if heading to Deadman's Island).

46

ISLE OF SHEPPEY BARTON'S POINT COASTAL PARK LAKE

LAKE · KENT

For a sheltered paddle or a family-friendly adventure, Queenborough's saltwater lake offers a good alternative to the open sea. Nestled within tranquil grassland and marshes, this 16-hectare lake is ideal for beginners or families looking for a peaceful day on the water. The lake is not only great for a relaxing paddle but also brimming with marine life, including crabs, making it a favourite spot for families to enjoy simple activities like crabbing or feeding the ducks and swans.

For those seeking a bit more history, the lake connects to the Queenborough Lines, a Scheduled Monument built between 1863 and 1868 to defend Sheerness Dockyard from land attacks. These fortified ditches, now water-filled and resembling canals, were further reinforced with air-raid shelters during World War II. Paddling along these waterways offers not only scenic beauty but also a glimpse into the area's rich military past, blending natural exploration with a touch of historical intrigue •

- **DISTANCE:** Free range.
- **PADDLING ENVIRONMENT:** 1.
- **ROUTE MAP:** islandeering.com/paddleboarding-sheppey-island-barton-point-coastal-park/
- **ACCESS RESTRICTIONS:** No licence required.
- **OS MAP:** OS Explorer 149 Sittingbourne & Faversham.
- **STARTING POINT & PARKING:** Barton's Point Coastal Park (free), Marine Parade, Sheerness, Isle of Sheppey, ME12 2BE. Grid ref. TQ 936 746; What3Words dentistry.layered.horns.
- **LAUNCHING:** Beach adjacent to car park.
- **PITSTOPS:** Lakeside café, Boathouse Café facebook.com/BartonsPointCafe/
- **GETTING THERE:** Follow Marine Parade from Sheerness towards Minster. At end of roadside seawall turn R into lane for coastal park.
- **SPECIAL POINTS:** A good spot to escape coastal winds, though the lake can still get choppy with wind, particularly from N-NE.

47

CHATHAM DOCKS

LAKE · KENT

A watersports haven within a regenerated dockyard, surrounded by the history that shaped Britain's maritime might. Chatham Docks, located on the River Medway, boasts a rich history dating back to the mid-16th century. Established in 1567, the dockyard quickly became one of the most important naval shipbuilding and repair centres for the Royal Navy, earning recognition as the birthplace of the British Navy. During its peak in the 18th and 19th centuries, Chatham was at the forefront of British naval power, constructing renowned warships such as HMS Victory, Admiral Nelson's flagship. The dockyard played a pivotal role in British military endeavours, particularly during the Napoleonic Wars and both World Wars. Before its closure in 1984 it refitted nuclear submarines. Today, much of the site has been preserved as a museum and heritage area, reflecting its maritime history and significant contributions to Britain's naval legacy.

In recent years, regeneration efforts have transformed the area, and Basin 2 is now a thriving watersports centre, surrounded by residential properties on St Mary's Island, along with industrial and heritage landscapes. This former naval dockyard spans 8 hectares and is around 9 metres deep, with saltwater supporting an array of marine life visible beneath the wooden walkways. The aeration of Basin 2 has resulted in significant wildlife coming back to the area. Watch out for cormorants catching an eel, or look at the marine life that attaches to the boardwalks and wooden struts.

After enjoying a paddle here, visitors can explore the historic dockyard buildings and take a scenic walk around St Mary's Island for stunning riverside views of the Medway •

- **DISTANCE:** Free range.
- **PADDLING ENVIRONMENT:** 1.
- **ROUTE MAP:** islandeering.com/paddleboarding-chatham-docks/
- **ACCESS RESTRICTIONS:** Self-launch, book with Chatham Maritime Watersports Centre chathammaritimewatersports.co.uk
- **OS MAP:** OS Explorer Map 163 Gravesend & Rochester.
- **PARKING:** Ship & Trades Car Park (2 hours free; limited parking also available by contacting Chatham Maritime Watersports), Maritime Way, Chatham, ME4 3ER. Grid ref. TQ 765 700; What3Words prone.worked.shots.
- **LAUNCHING:** Pontoon close to parking.
- **PITSTOPS:** Dockside café, Café Bueno, tel. 07469 701678.
- **LESSONS AND HIRE:** Chatham Maritime Watersports Centre, tel. 01634 891950.
- **GETTING THERE:** *Car* Leave A2 onto A289, then B2004 to Maritime Way, Ship & Trades car park on L before crossing to St Mary's Island; *Train/bus* Chatham rail station, regular service from London Victoria southeasternrailway.co.uk , then 140/141 bus to Dockside.
- **SPECIAL POINTS:** Buoyancy aids mandatory.

48

GILLINGHAM AND MEDWAY ISLANDS

ESTUARY · KENT

Explore two small islands in the River Medway, where the circular forts of Hoo and Darnet share a fascinating history. Built in 1872 to defend the Chatham Naval Dockyard from potential French invasion, these forts were armed with guns, and an underwater boom was stretched between them to trap enemy ships. Although they never saw combat, they served as observation posts during World War II, playing a key role in monitoring the skies and helping to fend off the German Luftwaffe, especially during the Battle of Britain. Now abandoned, their lower levels have been deliberately flooded to deter vandals, but they remain accessible to visitors arriving by paddleboard or kayak from The Strand in Gillingham at high tide.

To reach the forts, start from the slipway at The Strand, a popular area for swimmers and boaters. Paddle northeast towards Hoo Island, with the remaining flood current ferry-gliding you north to reach the island. Once out of the main channel, marked by red and green buoys, head east along the island's south shore to see the fort at its eastern tip. There is a small path leading from the shore east of the fort. From Fort Hoo, do not head directly towards Fort Darnet, but take a bearing due east to cross the main shipping channel at its narrowest point before then heading north to Fort Darnet. It is possible to land on a small beach here to investigate further (although not permitted March–July due to sensitive bird-nesting sites).

On the return, head southwest back towards the slipway, keeping to the left of the three red channel markers. Along the way, explore the Medway Cruising Club's boatyard, which played a key role during World War II, mooring numerous vessels. Nearby, several sunken concrete barges, originally used to shield the moorings from easterly winds, add historical interest. Continue along The Strand, tracing the shoreline of a cherished Victorian-era riverside resort once known for its natural swimming spots, boating activities, open-air pool, miniature railway, and lush green spaces •

• **DISTANCE:** 5.5km return.

• **PADDLING ENVIRONMENT:** 5 (for experienced paddlers only).

• **ROUTE MAP:** islandeering.com/paddleboarding-gillingham-to-medway-islands/

• **ACCESS RESTRICTIONS:** No licence required; but landing forbidden at both forts during bird nesting season (March–July).

• **OS MAP:** OS Explorer 163 Gravesend & Rochester.

• **STARTING POINT:** Strand Approach Road, Gillingham, ME7 1TT. Grid ref. TQ 784 694; What3Words hosts.drive.jazzy.

• **PARKING:** Roadside on Strand Approach Road (free).

LAUNCHING: Public slipway/beach close to parking.

• **GETTING THERE:** Leave A289 between Chatham and Medway Tunnel for The Strand; continue on Strand Approach Road between Leisure Park and Sailing Club.

• **SPECIAL POINTS:** Trip best started 1.5hrs before HW on a neap tide to gain the benefit of slack water at the forts. Only attempt on light/no wind days as the whole estuary is exposed, which creates wind chop. Take care crossing the main shipping channel, watching out for large boats. Lots of dangers walking within the forts including flooded floors; take a torch to explore. Check local flood conditions at riverlevels.uk/flood-warning-tidal-medway-medway-estuary-and-isle-of-grain

49

BUCKLAND PARK LAKE

LAKE · SURREY

A pristine lake and watersports lagoon set within a beautiful nature reserve, offering a serene Mediterranean vibe. Developed from a former sand quarry, it features clear turquoise waters surrounded by lush greenery and sandstone cliffs, providing a tranquil spot between Reigate and Dorking for nature lovers, swimmers, and paddlers. The shallow lagoon with its sandy beach is an excellent place for families or beginners to learn to paddleboard, while the more experienced can explore the large lake.

The Surrey Hills Adventure Company runs paddleboarding sessions and lessons and an open-water swimming club, and the surrounding park offers a range of activities for visitors, with a playground and paddling pool, woodland adventure tours and more. There are good trails around the lake reserve, allowing visitors to explore the scenic landscapes and enjoy panoramic views of the lagoon. The lagoon is a hotspot for birdwatching throughout the year, with waterfowl as well as migratory birds that find refuge in the lagoon's peaceful environment.

A lovely glass-fronted relaxed dining venue perched on a peninsula overlooking the lake offers great food in a lovely location, while a lakeside van offers hot drinks and food; both are perfect for a post-paddle treat •

- **DISTANCE:** Free range.
- **PADDLING ENVIRONMENT:** 1.
- **ROUTE MAP:** islandeering.com/paddleboarding-buckland-park-lagoon/
- **ACCESS RESTRICTIONS:** Self-launch (charges) booking via SHAC (must be able to demonstrate competency on water).
- **OS MAP:** OS Explorer 162 Maidstone & the Medway Towns.
- **PARKING:** Buckland Park Lake (free if booked in with SHAC), Park Lake Drive, Buckland, Betchworth, RH3 7FE. Grid ref. TQ 226 507; What3Words elder.sang.goats.
- **LAUNCHING:** Sand beach.
- **PITSTOPS:** Breakfast, lunch and dinner, The Reverie, tel. 01737 843023; lagoon-side food truck for burgers, baps and cakes, El Rocinante, tel. 07493 027131.
- **LESSONS AND HIRE:** The Surrey Hills Adventure Company (SHAC), theshac.co.uk
- **GETTING THERE:** West of Reigate on A25; turn L into park a short distance beyond The Pheasant at Buckland.
- **SPECIAL POINTS:** No dogs on site due to wildlife. Please clean your paddleboard before entering the water to prevent spread of non-native plant and animal species.

SEA LION

RESCUE

50

RIVER MOLE BOX STEPS TO LEATHERHEAD

RIVER · SURREY

An adventurous journey through one of the most picturesque areas of the North Downs passes through the Mole Gap, where the river carves through a striking chalk ridge, creating a lush green valley. Overlooking this scenic landscape is Box Hill, with the woodlands and farmland of Norbury Park stretching beyond.

Leave from the Stepping Stones to enter the swoosh of the river as it rounds the first bend and passes under a wooden footbridge. Pass beneath The Whites, the steep densely wooded chalk slope of Box Hill, to reach the gardens of the Burford Bridge Hotel. There is a small rapid beneath the noisy A24, but peace reigns again after the rail bridge as the river meanders through a wilderness that makes it hard to believe that this is only a short distance from London. Along the way, keep a lookout for water voles, kingfishers, herons, amphibians, and a variety of fish like brown trout and chub, along with dragonflies, butterflies, water lilies, reeds, and wildflowers.

After 3.5km, pass the wooded hillside of the Surrey Wildlife Trust-managed Norbury Park, and pass under Norbury Viaduct, leading directly into a tunnel historically engineered to protect the views from Norbury Park House. Pass beneath the A24 again; the weir further on can be portaged on either side. Continue through meadows to the outskirts of Leatherhead and its beautiful riverside gardens. After Thorncroft Bridge, as the river starts to split around numerous islands, keep to the right-hand channels. Just before the lovely red-brick arched Leatherhead Bridge, egress on the right bank, close to the Running Horse pub, to return to Box Hill & Westhumble station by train •

- **DISTANCE:** 8km one way; train return.
- **PADDLING ENVIRONMENT:** 2.
- **ROUTE MAP:** islandeering.com/paddleboarding/box-steps-to-leatherhead/
- **ACCESS RESTRICTIONS:** No licence required.
- **OS MAP:** OS Explorer 146 Dorking, Box Hill & Reigate.
- **STARTING POINT:** Riverbank adjacent to Box Hill Stepping Stones.
- **EGRESS:** Bridge Street, Leatherhead, KT22 9AD.
- **PARKING:** Box Hill Stepping Stone Car Park (charges), A24, Westhumble, RH5 6AE; Grid ref. TQ 170 513; What3Words closes.ozone.fantastic.
- **LAUNCHING:** Riverbank 100m walk from car park.
- **GETTING THERE:** *Car* A24 S Leatherhead to Dorking; 500m after Burford Bridge roundabout turn L into Box Hill Stepping Stone car park; *Train* Regular services from London Victoria to Box Hill & Westhumble, then 900m walk to Stepping Stones on River Mole; return from Leatherhead to Box Hill & Westhumble, southernrailway.com
- **SPECIAL POINTS:** One weir to portage. Use small river fins to minimise catching on the weeds and remove any leash while on the river. Take a sling with karabiners clipped to the front or rear D-rings on the board to help manoeuvre the board over obstacles. Water levels will be too low for this trip if the concrete plinths beneath the Stepping Stones are exposed, and too high if water is above Stepping Stones.

51

RIVER WEY NAVIGATION GODALMING TO GUILDFORD

RIVER · SURREY

Float downstream on the historic River Wey through lush water meadows, woodlands, and heath. As one of England's earliest navigable rivers, made so by a 1651 Act of Parliament, the Wey Navigation played a crucial role in the 18th and 19th centuries for transporting timber, coal, and produce. Now managed by the National Trust, it conserves its heritage buildings and wildlife. This one-way trip, with a return by rail, offers an idyllic and fascinating paddle.

Launch from Godalming Wharf, passing the meadows of Lammas Lands to reach Catteshall Lock and Farncombe Boathouse. Trees and pastureland stretch ahead to Unstead Lock, near Peasmarsh. Just beyond the iron-railed bridge a river junction on the right marks the Wey-Arun Canal Junction. Pass beneath the A248, then a rail bridge. Pass Riff Raff Weir (on the right, leading to one of the old river channels), then on to St Catherine's Lock Cottage. Continue north to St Catherine's Lock and portage on the right-hand side.

Meander around the base of St Catherine's Hill, with its chapel ruins. Guildford, originally a Saxon village, is thought to have derived its name from the golden sands and an old ford here. Continue through the outskirts of the town with the open fields of Shalford Park and Guildford Rowing Club on the right. Pass The Boathouse and continue to Millmead Lock. Portage on the left, continue past the theatre and exit the water adjacent to The White House pub just before the bridge (or continue through the town to reach Dapdune Wharf, with a visitor centre and café) •

• **DISTANCE:** 7km one way/train return.

• **PADDLING ENVIRONMENT:** 2.

• **ROUTE MAP:** islandeering.com/paddleboarding-godalming-to-guildford/

• **ACCESS RESTRICTIONS:** Visitor Pass required for River Wey and Godalming Navigations (£6.30 adult/24 hrs). Apply online: nationaltrust.org.uk/visit/surrey/river-wey-and-godalming-navigations-and-dapdune-wharf/river-wey-information-for-boat-users

• **OS MAP:** OS Explorer 145 Guildford & Farnham.

• **STARTING POINT:** Godalming Wharf, Godalming GU7 1LQ.

• **PARKING:** Sainsbury's Guildford (2hrs free, charges for longer, book at yourparkingspace.co.uk), Langham Park, Catteshall, Godalming, GU7 1NG. Grid ref. SU 976 440; What3Words apron.preoccupied.drama

• **LAUNCHING:** Short walk from car park to Godalming Wharf.

• **EGRESS:** Steps in front of The White House pub, Guildford. Grid ref. SU 994 493; What3Words jump.fees.ankle.

• **PITSTOPS:** Two riverside pubs in the heart of Guildford, The White House, tel. 01438 302006; and the Britannia, tel. 01438 572160.

• **LESSONS, HIRE AND TRIPS:** Roar Outdoors, Godalming, roaroutdoor.co.uk

• **GETTING THERE:** In Godalming, turn off A3100 following signs to 'Catteshall Business Area and Superstore'; access to river near entrance to car park. *Train* return 400m walk from White House pub to Guildford rail station for a regular service to Guildford, southwesternrailway.com

• **SPECIAL POINTS:** Check local river levels at riverlevels.uk/surrey-shalford-river-wey-at-unstead-sluice . There are four locks to portage along the route.

52

MERCERS COUNTRY PARK

LAKE · SURREY

A peaceful haven away from the hustle of urban life near Merstham, this former quarry is known for its beautiful blue waters. Surrounded by lush greenery and the rolling hills of the North Downs, it is especially beautiful at sunrise. Popular for watersports and diving, the lake boasts crystal-clear water with visibility often exceeding eight metres. The lake features an underwater forest teeming with various fish species, including perch, pike, bream, and giant carp.

Above water the lake is full of wildlife, with swans, ducks, herons, and kingfishers. There are well-maintained paths and trails around the lake that are perfect for walking, jogging, and cycling, with picnic areas and benches offering scenic views. Onsite facilities include a great café, a changing room and hot showers •

- **DISTANCE:** Free range.
- **PADDLING ENVIRONMENT:** 1.
- **ROUTE MAP:** islandeering.com/paddleboarding-mercers-country-park/
- **ACCESS RESTRICTIONS:** Self-launch, book with Aqua Sports. Non-member self-launch requires a minimum competency of Level 1/equivalent and third-party liability.
- **OS MAP:** OS Explorer 146 Dorking, Box Hill & Reigate.
- **PARKING:** Free parking at Mercers Country Park, Nutfield Marsh Road, Merstham, RH1 4EU. Grid ref. TQ 301 517; What3Words toys.once.jacket.
- **LAUNCHING:** Pontoon.
- **PITSTOPS:** Great coffee, hot and cold food with a lakeside view, Aqua Sports Café and Bar, tel. 01737 644288; good Sunday lunches overlooking Nutfield Marshes, The Inn on the Pond, Nutfield, tel. 01737 643000.
- **LESSONS AND HIRE:** Aqua Sports Mercers Lake, aquasports.co.uk
- **GETTING THERE:** *Car* Head east from Redhill on A25; after Patteson Court, turn L onto Cormongers Lane; at T-junction turn R onto Nutfield Marsh Road, then L following brown sign to country park; *Train/bus* Redhill rail services direct from London Victoria, then take bus 430 from Redhill bus station to Mill Lane in Merstham (opposite Watercolours Housing) for 12-minute walk around the lake to the centre metrobus.co.uk/services/MB/430
- **SPECIAL POINTS:** Please clean your board before you enter the water to prevent spread of non-native plants and animal species.

53

ABBEY RIVER AND PENTON HOOK ISLAND

RIVER · SURREY

Adventure along a hidden stream for a true Surrey safari, navigating limbo-worthy willow trees and a "Loch Ness monster", before rejoining the historic Thames. Launch onto the River Thames and turn left, going downstream to Chertsey Lock. Portage on the right using the steps just before the lock, cross the narrow tip of the island and exit immediately to the left of the weir. Do not cross the weir stream; instead, paddle towards the far bank where boats are moored and head upstream into the Abbey River.

Follow the line of moored boats to reach a small bridge with a roller-assisted portage through the main span. The Abbey River begins to narrow as it winds through farmland and willow scrub. Pass under a few low bridges, keeping an eye out for the 'Loch Ness monster' and a small step-over weir beneath one of the bridges.

In the summer, the next section can become overgrown, turning it into a reed-bashing adventure with an obstacle course of fallen willow trees. Despite appearances, there is always a way through this Surrey jungle. Hear the distant whoops and hollers from Thorpe Park while passing beneath the M3 bridge. The river then twists between two lakes before entering Penton Park Estate, where the route becomes easier, and soon rejoins the main River Thames.

Turn right and skirt around the southern tip of Penton Hook Island, a burial site for Great Plague victims and now a nature reserve popular with fishermen. Pass Penton Hook Lock on the left, and keep to the right along the Thames, back to the starting point at Laleham, passing luxurious houses and a historic boatyard along the way •

• **DISTANCE:** 7km return.

• **PADDLING ENVIRONMENT:** 2.

• **ROUTE MAP:** islandeering.com/paddleboarding-abbey-river/

• **ACCESS RESTRICTIONS:** Licence required, included in Paddle UK membership; or Unpowered Open Boat Licence from Environment Agency gov.uk/government/collections/river-thames-boat-registration-and-application-forms

• **OS MAP:** OS Explorer 160 Windsor, Weybridge & Bracknell.

• **STARTING POINT:** River Thames, opposite car park.

• **PARKING:** Laleham Park car park, Laleham, Surrey, TW18 1SS; Grid ref. TQ 051 677; What3Words natively.until.orchestra.

• **LAUNCHING:** Shallow river beach.

• **PITSTOPS:** Three great pubs in Laleham village.

• **CAMPING:** Riverside camping either at Chertsey Camping and Caravanning Club, tel. 01932 562405; or Laleham Camping Club, tel. 01932 564149.

• **GETTING THERE:** South of Staines on B376, pass through Laleham village to parking on left.

• **SPECIAL POINTS:** Keep to the right when passing other boat users on the Thames. To minimise catching on weeds, use small river fins, and ensure you remove any leash while on the Abbey River. Carry a sling with karabiners clipped to the front or rear D-rings of the board, to help manoeuvre over larger fallen branches. The Abbey River generally runs deep, with only a few shallow areas to navigate; be aware that the main channel can become overgrown with reeds during the summer months. For local conditions, check river levels ahead at riverlevels.uk/thames-chertsey-chertsey-lock

54

WEY NAVIGATION WEYBRIDGE TO DESBOROUGH ISLAND

RIVER · SURREY

A river adventure past historic mill sites, with an island circumnavigation and a café that oozes Victorian-era charm. Launch downstream of New Haw Lock, passing several buildings, and continue along a tree-lined stretch to the Millpond, developed for the iron mill built by Mr Cox. Coxes Mill and Coxes Lock (named before apostrophes were used in place names) feature old mill buildings now converted into apartments, with a heritage section remaining. Portage Coxes Lock on the left.

Continue past The Pelican to reach Town Lock, then portage left, cross Addlestone Road and turn right along the footpath. Turn left through a gate on the bridge and go down a ramp to re-enter the river. Head left under the A317, meandering past woodland and gardens to Thames Lock (portage left, cross the lock via a footbridge, and re-enter on the right bank). This is the entrance to the Wey Navigations. Whittet's Mill (now private homes) was a mill site for paper, iron, and oil seeds until 1963.

Enter the River Thames and head downstream past the cascading weir on the left. Just beyond, Shepperton Lock, also on the left, has a café. For the journey, take the right fork and pass beneath the ornate footbridge leading to D'Oyly Carte Island. Named after Richard D'Oyly Carte, a London theatre impresario who brought together dramatist WS Gilbert and composer Arthur Sullivan, the island once housed a crocodile kept to amuse guests. At the island's far end it's possible to land and enjoy crepes at the café, a re-created slice of Victorian magic.

From the café, continue downstream for approximately 100 metres, taking the left channel around Desborough Island, passing wooded banks and the Desborough Sailing Club, followed by houses and gardens. At the southeastern tip, turn right under the footbridge and head upstream, passing the café again. Look for the National Trust sign indicating the Navigation channel back up the River Wey to Thames Lock and retrace steps back to New Haw Lock •

- **DISTANCE:** 13.5km return.
- **PADDLING ENVIRONMENT:** 2.
- **ROUTE MAP:** islandeering.com/paddleboarding-weybridge-to-desborough-island/
- **ACCESS RESTRICTIONS:** National Trust licence required. nationaltrust.org.uk/visit/surrey/river-wey-and-godalming-navigations-and-dapdune-wharf/river-wey-information-for-canoeists
- **OS MAP:** OS Explorer 160 Windsor, Weybridge & Bracknell.
- **STARTING POINT:** From the parking area at New Haw Lock, cross the A318 and launch on the right bank downstream of the lock.
- **PARKING:** Off-road parking off A318, adjacent to New Haw Lock, KT15 3JQ. Grid ref. TQ 055 630; What3Words marked.manual.cope.
- **LAUNCHING:** Riverbank.
- **PITSTOPS:** Great vibes, crepes, cocktails and wine on tap, D'Oyly's, tel. 07850 686017; riverside garden between Coxes Lock and Town Lock, The Pelican, Addlestone, tel. 01932 847956; good food beyond Thames Lock, over the road from Weybridge Marine, The Minnow, tel. 01932 831672.
- **GETTING THERE:** Follow A318 south from New Haw village, pass the White Hart pub, cross the river bridge heading towards Byfleet, then turn R into the parking lane immediately after the bridge.
- **SPECIAL POINTS:** There are eight locks to portage during this journey (four each way). Be mindful of the wake from pleasure boats, particularly on the Thames. Stay close to the riverbanks to avoid the stronger currents found in the centre of the river. Check river levels ahead of the trip at riverlevels.uk/wey-weybridge, and on the Thames at Shepperton at riverlevels.uk/flood-warning-river-thames-at-shepperton-and-lower-halliford

55

RIVER THAMES HAMPTON COURT TO KINGSTON

RIVER · GREATER LONDON

Downstream exploration of Thames islands, luxurious houseboats, the grandeur of Hampton Court Palace, inns, and serene riverside landscapes stacked with royal history. Launch and float east, moving downstream past tiny Duck Eyot and then large Taggs Island and smaller Ash Island with their luxurious houseboats. Continue past East Molesey Cricket Club and café, then Molesey Boat Club, where a striking sculpture of a rowing boat rises 320 feet from the ground.

Approaching Molesey Lock, keep right and look for the 'portage' boat rollers on the left just before the lock gates. Slide the board down to the lower river level. A tearoom and gardens sit on the south bank. The river now widens, with The Mitre hotel standing prominently on the north bank. Navigate Hampton Court Bridge while keeping to the right, revealing majestic views of Hampton Court Palace on the left bank. This magnificent Tudor residence, tied to Henry VIII's tumultuous reign, is reflected beautifully in the water on a calm day.

Opposite Hampton Court, the River Ember offers a short detour for exploration. Further downstream, the palace's golden gates provide a glimpse of its formal gardens. Just beyond, The Albany is a good place to stop to meet local paddlers.

At the far end of Thames Ditton Island, after paddling along its quiet backwater, Ye Olde Swan makes for a pleasant pub stop before passing Swan Island and Boyle Farm Island. The journey continues around a large meander with Hampton Court Golf and Home Park on the left. Passing Kingston Island (Ravens Ait) and marinas, the river leads to Kingston Bridge with its elegant Portland Stone arches. Exit beyond the bridge at Kingston Turks Pier for a 650m walk to Kingston rail station, or continue downstream to Canbury Gardens to pick up a return car. Alternatively, extend the route to Richmond and return by rail from Richmond station to Hampton Court station •

- **DISTANCE:** 6km one way; rail return.
- **PADDLING ENVIRONMENT:** 2.
- **ROUTE MAP:** islandeering.com/paddleboarding-hampton-court-to-kingston/

ACCESS RESTRICTIONS: Licence required, included in Paddle UK membership.

- **OS MAP:** OS Explorer 161 London South.
- **STARTING POINT:** Hurst Park adjacent to car park: or beach to left of Hampton Court Bridge, 150m walk from Hampton Court rail station. Grid ref. TQ 152 685; What3Words voter.blend.ruled.
- **PARKING:** Sadlers Ride Car Park (free), West Molesey, KT8 9AZ. Grid ref. TQ 141 692; What3Words shiny.safely.book; return from Canbury Gardens, street parking on Lower Ham Road (charges), KT2 5UZ. Grid ref. TQ 179 699; What3Words copper.forum.mirror.
- **LAUNCHING:** Slipway adjacent to Hurst car park.
- **PITSTOPS:** Ice cream, cake, and toasties at Little H, Molesey Lock; popular paddlers' pub, The Albany, Thames Ditton, tel. 020 8972 9163; historic riverside inn, Ye Olde Swan, Thames Ditton, tel. 020 8398 1814; popular riverside pub, The Boaters Inn, Canbury Gardens, Kingston, tel. 020 8541 4672.
- **GETTING THERE:** *Car* A308 from Kingston towards Thames Ditton; first exit at Hampton Court roundabout towards Guildford, cross Hampton Court Bridge, then R onto A3050. Take third exit at roundabout signed to Riverside Open Space car park; *Train* Regular services from London Waterloo to Hampton Court (150m walk to launch from river beach just west of Hampton Court Bridge) and Kingston (650m walk from river) southwesternrailway.com
- **SPECIAL POINTS:** One lock with canoe rollers to portage. Check local river conditions at Thames Ditton riverlevels.uk/thames-long-ditton-thames-ditton-island

56

RIVER THAMES RICHMOND AND TEDDINGTON

TIDAL RIVER · GREATER LONDON

Explore two scenic paddle routes along the tidal Thames from Ham Street: one downriver to Richmond, passing iconic landmarks like Petersham Meadows and Glover's Island, and the other upriver to Teddington Lock, passing Eel Pie Island. For the downriver route to Richmond, turn right after leaving Ham Street car park. Pass the Hammerton Ferry, which links Ham House and Marble Hill, two famous houses visible from the river. Pass the wooded Glover's Island and Petersham Meadows, where cows often graze. This pasture is legally protected to preserve the iconic views from Richmond Hill, a scene immortalised by Turner and the only view in the UK safeguarded by an Act of Parliament. As Richmond Hill rises in the distance, crowned by the Star and Garter building, the number of rowers and boathouses increases. Take a break at Hollyhock Café or paddle under Richmond Bridge toward Corporation Island. For refreshments, stop at Tide Tables Café under the bridge or visit the White Cross pub opposite the island before returning the same way.

For the upriver route to Teddington Lock, turn left from Ham Street and cross to the Twickenham bank to reach the White Swan pub. From there, explore the tranquil backwater on the north side of Eel Pie Island, a place known for its rich musical history, having hosted legends like the Rolling Stones and The Who during the 1960s. Now the island houses a vibrant community, boatyards, and artists' studios, with nature reserves at both ends.

Continue upriver past Ham Lands Nature Reserve and the Radnor Gardens, where Swan Island is home to a floating community of houseboats and barges. On the right, Young Mariners Lock marks the entrance to a tidal lake, followed by the Teddington Obelisk, which signifies the end of the Port of London's jurisdiction. At Teddington Lock, the largest lock system on the Thames and the boundary between the tidal and non-tidal sections of the river, keep right to find the shingle beach at Angler's Ait for a picnic or visit The Anglers pub across the footbridge. Return the same way.

An alternative start point for this trip is Richmond •

- **DISTANCE:** 4km return to Richmond; 5.6km return to Teddington Lock.
- **PADDLING ENVIRONMENT:** 3.
- **ROUTE MAP:** islandeering.com/paddleboarding-richmond-to-teddington/
- **ACCESS RESTRICTIONS:** No licence required downstream of Teddington Lock.
- **OS MAP:** OS Explorer 161 London South.
- **STARTING POINT:** Ham Street Car Park.
- **PARKING:** Ham Street Car Park (free), Ham Street, Richmond, TW10 7RS. Grid ref. TQ 169 731; What3Words riding.broke.bucket.
- **LAUNCHING:** Riverside adjacent to Ham Street car park (or Richmond riverbank).
- **PITSTOPS:** Legendary riverside pub, White Cross, Richmond, tel. 020 8940 6844; delightful almost fairytale-like café with excellent food, Hollyhock Café, Terrace Gardens, Richmond, tel. 020 8948 6555; popular vegetarian café in arch of Richmond Bridge, Tide Tables Café, tel. 020 8948 8285; popular pub with riverside garden, The Anglers, Teddington, tel. 020 8977 7475.
- **LESSONS AND TOURS:** Active360 active360.co.uk
- **GETTING THERE:** *Car* From Richmond, take A3027 towards Kingston-on-Thames, turn R opposite the Hand and Flower pub along Ham Common, then Ham Street. Car park at end of road. *Train* Regular services from central London to Richmond southwesternrailway.com , short walk to Richmond Bridge; launch slipway/steps N of Richmond Bridge from N bank.
- **SPECIAL POINTS:** This section of the tidal Thames is managed by Richmond Half Lock, which maintains the water level between Richmond Lock and Teddington Lock at or above half-tide level. As a result, there is a noticeable tidal flow for approximately 2hrs either side of high water (HW). Outside of this window, there is a slight river current. Check the local river conditions at Teddington Lock before leaving riverlevels.uk/thames-teddington-teddington-lock.

57

GRAND UNION CANAL PADDINGTON TO HORSENDEN HILL

CANAL · GREATER LONDON

Explore the contrasting landscapes of the Paddington Arm, from the bustle of Merchant Square and the charm of Little Venice to the historic Kensal Green Cemetery, gritty industrial areas, and views of the Wembley Arch, before escaping to the green haven of Horsenden Hill and its community farm. Running from its junction with Regent's Canal at Little Venice to Bull's Bridge near Slough, the Paddington Arm of the Grand Union Canal offers a fascinating glimpse into the real London.

Start at Paddington Basin, passing beneath the Westway and the A404 as you head towards Little Venice, a picturesque junction where the Paddington Arm connects with Regent's Canal. To the right is Rembrandt Gardens; to the left, the impressive Warwick Crescent, followed by the charming Waterside Café barge. Continue left under the Westbourne Terrace Road bridge, paddling alongside Delamere Terrace and the tranquil community-run Meanwhile Gardens.

The landscape soon shifts, with views of tower blocks and housing estates as the canal leads beneath the A404 and skirts close to the Westway again, with the Union Tavern pub on the right beneath the Great

- **DISTANCE:** 12km one way.
- **PADDLING ENVIRONMENT:** 1.
- **ROUTE MAP:** islandeering.com/paddleboarding-paddington-to-horsenden-hill/
- **ACCESS RESTRICTIONS:** Licence required, included in Paddle UK membership.
- **OS MAP:** OS Explorer 173 London North.
- **STARTING POINT:** Merchant Square, Paddington Basin, outside Paddington Station. Grid ref. TQ 265 815; What3Words daily.much.moment; or Horsenden Farm, Greenford.
- **PARKING:** Horsenden Farm, Horsenden Lane, Greenford, UB6 7PQ. Grid ref. TQ 163 840; What3Words called.breath.cups.
- **LAUNCHING:** Canalside short walk from Paddington Station, or Horsenden Farm car park; 800m walk to Perivale tube station.
- **PITSTOPS:** Great pub with large canalside garden, Grand Junction Arms, Acton Lane, tel. 020 8161 0035; great food and atmosphere with wood-fired bakery, Perivale Brewery and farm shop, Horsenden Farm facebook.com/groups/friendsofhorsendenhill
- **LESSONS AND TOURS:** Active 360, Paddington Basin active360.co.uk/paddington-basin/
- **GETTING THERE:** *Paddington* Train or tube to Paddington station. *Horsenden by car* Take B456 off A40, following signs for Perivale; L onto Horsenden Lane; cross Ballot Box Bridge, then Horsenden Farm car park immediately on R; *Train* Perivale tube station 800m walk from Horsenden Farm.
- **SPECIAL POINTS:** Cross aqueduct on RHS. No locks to portage.

Western Road. After passing beneath the Ladbroke Grove bridge, enter the historically rich Kensal Green Cemetery, one of London's grand Victorian burial grounds. This area once received coffins by canal, with remnants like the Dissenters' Chapel and landing platforms still visible. The cemetery's tree-lined avenues and monumental tombstones create a serene and peaceful atmosphere. To the left, the sprawling Wormwood Scrubs Recreation Ground offers some green respite before the canal leads into the industrial areas of Old Oak Common, home to food production factories like Charlie Bigham's. Cooking aroma fill the air as the canal passes food production facilities, eventually reaching the Grand Junction Arms, a popular canalside pub.

Further along, the canal crosses the impressive aqueduct over the A406 North Circular, offering a view of the busy road below and a distant glimpse of the Wembley Arch. As the industrial scenery fades, the canal reaches Alperton and takes on a more serene atmosphere. Beyond Alperton Cemetery on the right, the canal is lined with well-tended gardens on the left and Sudbury Golf Course on the right. This stretch offers a peaceful escape surrounded by greenery, as the urban hustle and bustle gradually recedes.

Finally, the canal skirts the hilly parklands of Horsenden Hill, marking the transition into more rural scenery for the remainder of the trip. Exit the canal before Ballot Box Bridge to walk to Horsenden Farm, home to a great café and microbrewery •

58

REGENT'S CANAL PADDINGTON TO KINGS CROSS

CANAL · GREATER LONDON

Leave behind the glittering towers of modern businesses for a unique view of the capital's industrial heritage, green spaces, vibrant boating communities, and even the occasional monkey or wolf. This trip offers a seamless blend of the contemporary, historic, and wild.

Launch from the modern architecture and lively atmosphere of Merchant Square, passing under the Westway and the A404 into the charming Little Venice area with its Regency architecture and the Waterside Café floating on a barge. Keep right past Rembrandt Gardens and, after Warwick Bridge, exit the canal on the left bank for the Maida Hill Tunnel portage. Turn right onto Blomfield Road, cross the A5, and continue onto Aberdeen Place. At the sharp left bend near Crocker's Folly, take the alleyway straight ahead, then walk down the steps to relaunch on the canal at the north end of the tunnel.

Continue past the vibrant Lisson Grove moorings, under the rail bridges and alongside Park Road, where the canal winds through a scenic green stretch next to Regent's Park. Here, you'll pass

- **DISTANCE:** 5km paddle one way, plus 700m portage around Maida Hill Tunnel.
- **PADDLING ENVIRONMENT:** 1.
- **ROUTE MAP:** islandeering.com/paddleboarding-paddington-to-kings-cross/
- **ACCESS RESTRICTIONS:** Licence required, included in Paddle UK membership; paddling through the 251-metre Maida Hill Tunnel is not permitted.
- **OS MAP:** OS Explorer 173 London North.
- **STARTING POINT:** Merchant Square, Paddington Basin. Grid ref. TQ 265 815; What3Words daily.much.moment.
- **PARKING:** Randolph Road (charges), Paddington, London, W9 1AN. Grid ref. TQ 263 820; What3Words strain.tuck.string.
- **LAUNCHING:** Canalside adjacent to Paddington station.
- **PITSTOPS:** Brunch on a barge, Darcie & May Green, Merchant Square, tel. 020 3935 9045; tea and cake, The Waterside Café, Little Venice, tel. 020 7266 1066; 34-trader street market food, KERB, Camden Lock (gets hectic); pint by the canal, Ice Wharf Wetherspoons, tel. 020 7428 3770; classic boozer with lively waterside garden, Constitution pub, Camden Lock, tel. 020 7380 0767.
- **LESSONS AND TOURS:** Active360 active360.co.uk ; Paddleboarding London, Camden paddleboardinglondon.co.uk
- **GETTING THERE:** Paddington rail station.
- **SPECIAL POINTS:** Can leave pump and carry case in left luggage (charges apply) on Platform 12 at Paddington Station. There is one 700m portage to avoid Maida Hill Tunnel and three locks to portage. Some portages have tall banks, so bring a 3-metre tape and a karabiner attached to the board's bow or stern D-ring/grab handle to help pull the board out of the water.

tunning villas, including Hanover Lodge. The next andmark, Macclesfield Bridge, originally built in 1816, ained the nickname "Blow-up Bridge" after a tragic unpowder barge explosion in 1874. Jungle-like ounds may arise from Monkey Valley at London Zoo n the left, and wolves can occasionally be seen in heir enclosure on the right.

As the canal approaches a sharp left bend, the loating red pagoda of the Feng Shang Princess, a Chinese restaurant in Cumberland Basin, comes nto view, surrounded by houseboats floating on reen duckweed. Continue under two road bridges nd a rail bridge populated by pigeons to reach the irate Castle, a mock-castellated red-brick building sed by a community boating charity, surrounded by colourful rafts of kayaks. Beyond this point, the bustling energy of Camden Lock awaits, with its vibrant mix of shops, street food, and canalside bars. Pass under the road bridge with Camden Market on the left, and portage at Hawley Lock, also on the left.

After passing Kentish Town Lock and the road bridge, the atmosphere becomes calmer. On the right, after Camden Street bridge, is the utilitarian British Transport Police Headquarters. Continue beneath a network of road bridges before entering St Pancras Basin, where the large restored Victorian gasholder frames mark Gasholder Park, a popular green space for watching boats pass through St Pancras Lock. Exit the canal here and walk over the footbridge to reach King's Cross Station •

59

ISLE OF DOGS MILLWALL OUTER DOCK

LAKE · GREATER LONDON

Millwall Outer Dock, located in the heart of the Isle of Dogs, provides a unique and scenic spot for paddleboarding in East London. Once a bustling industrial hub in the 19th century, the dock has been transformed into a tranquil waterway surrounded by modern residential developments and green spaces. Paddleboarders can glide across the usually calm waters, enjoying views of the iconic dockside cranes – silent reminders of the area's industrial past. Once essential for loading cargo, these cranes now stand in striking contrast to the sleek, colourful skyscrapers of nearby Canary Wharf.

The dock's peaceful environment, coupled with its proximity to vibrant city life, makes it an ideal spot for both beginners and experienced paddleboarders. The Docklands Sailing and Watersports Centre, a local charity, serves as a lively hub for watersports enthusiasts, offering a variety of activities including paddleboarding, sailing, and kayaking in the heart of London's historic docklands •

- **DISTANCE:** Free-range.
- **PADDLING ENVIRONMENT:** 1.
- **ROUTE MAP:** islandeering.com/paddleboarding-millwall-outer-dock/
- **ACCESS RESTRICTIONS:** Self-launch booking via Docklands Sailing and Watersports Centre.
- **OS MAP:** OS Explorer Map 161 London South.
- **PARKING:** Docklands Sailing and Watersports Centre, 235A Westferry Road, London, E14 3QS; Grid ref. TQ 372 790; What3Words neon.brass.duck.
- **LAUNCHING:** Pontoon short walk from car park.
- **PITSTOPS:** Atmospheric café bar and arts centre in former Victorian chapel a short walk from the centre, The Space, tel. 020 7515 7799.
- **LESSONS AND HIRE:** Docklands Sailing and Watersports Centre, 020 7537 2626.
- **GETTING THERE:** Jubilee Line to Canary Wharf, then DLR to Crossharbour, with 10-min walk to centre along the dockside; or several buses from Canary Wharf to Westferry Road – use Crews Street bus stop close to watersports centre.
- **SPECIAL POINTS:** Please clean your board before you enter the water to prevent spread of non-native plants and animal species.

60

ROYAL VICTORIA DOCK

LAKE · GREATER LONDON

Beach vibes, overhead cable cars, roaring jets, and watersports fun all come together at Royal Victoria Dock, a lively waterfront spot full of history and modern attractions. Once the heart of London's global trade, the Royal Docks – covering Royal Victoria, Royal Albert, and King George V – have been transformed into a vibrant area with new homes, iconic buildings, and a hub for watersports, all set against the impressive Docklands skyline.

Royal Victoria Dock offers a fascinating blend of old and new landmarks. On the western end, cable cars glide overhead, linking the docks to the Greenwich Peninsula, while The Crystal, a modern glass building, showcases cutting-edge sustainability. Unique floating spots include the Oiler Bar, set in an old Royal Navy refueling barge, and the quirky Good Hotel, a social enterprise. A little further along is the luxurious Sunborn London Yacht Hotel, the UK's only superyacht hotel, with the massive ExCeL London convention centre towering in the background beyond the Royal Victoria Dock Footbridge.

On the southern shore, historic cranes stand as reminders of the area's industrial past. Just past the footbridge, an inlet leads to Silvertown, a former industrial hub that's now being redeveloped. Here, the derelict Millennium Mills and its towering chimney sit next to the Grade II-listed grain silo. Silverworks Island, once industrial, is now a thriving music venue and City Airport adds extra excitement, with jets roaring overhead as they take off •

- **DISTANCE:** Free-range.
- **PADDLING ENVIRONMENT:** 1.
- **ROUTE MAP:** islandeering.com/paddleboarding-royal-victoria-dock/
- **ACCESS RESTRICTIONS:** Self-launch, book with WakeUp Docklands (you must have a BSUPA Ready2Ride card; no under 18s); buoyancy aids and leashes must be worn.
- **OS MAP:** OS Explorer Map 161 London South.
- **STARTING POINT:** WakeUp Docklands, 1 Dock Road, London, E16 1AH. Grid ref. TQ 400 804; What3Words zealous.woke.holly.
- **PARKING:** Roadside parking (free) in Hanover Avenue adjacent to Western Beach Apartments, E16 1DZ; turn L off A1020 onto Britannia Gate, then first exit at small roundabout into residential area.
- **LAUNCHING:** Pontoon.
- **PITSTOPS:** Hawaiian-themed grass-roof hangout on the waterfront, Byrney's Beach Bar (part of WakeUp Docklands); fabulous floating beer garden with some decent local ales, The Oiler Bar, theoilerbar.com
- **LESSONS, YOGA, TOURS, & HIRE:** Super-friendly WakeUp Docklands, tel. 020 3950 3951, wakeupdocklands.com
- **GETTING THERE:** Located just a short distance from Canary Wharf and London City Airport, the Royal Docks are easily accessible via the DLR, and the cable car offers a unique way to reach the area while enjoying breathtaking views of the Thames and Docklands skyline.
- **SPECIAL POINTS:** Please clean your board before you enter the water to prevent spread of non-native plants and animal species.

HARBOUR
HELLES
WAVEHUNTER
HARBOUR
COLD IPA
ARCTIC SKY
CIDER
Life is good
AT THE BEACH

61

LIMEHOUSE CUT AND OLYMPIC STADIUM

RIVER · GREATER LONDON

A fascinating network of East London waterways starts on the city's oldest canal, where regenerated urban landscapes, striking graffiti, and historic sites lead to a unique circuit around the iconic Olympic Stadium. This route follows two waterways, beginning with the Limehouse Cut and winding through the Bow Back Rivers around the stadium.

The Limehouse Cut, a direct canal link between the River Lea and the Thames via Limehouse Basin, was built in 1766 to bypass the longer, tidal Bow Creek and improve commercial navigation. It holds the distinction of being London's oldest canal. The Bow Back Rivers, a network of mostly man-made channels around Stratford and Bow, were revitalised for the 2012 Olympics. Today, these waterways flow through Queen Elizabeth Olympic Park, blending East London's industrial past with its modern revival.

Start at Limehouse Basin, a colourful marina where Regent's Canal meets the Thames, and paddle along the basin's northern edge before crossing the mouth of a small inlet to enter the Limehouse Cut. The green expanse of Ropemakers Field lies to the right. After passing under the railway bridge, Kings Wharf Park appears on the right, with Rectory Gardens on the left. Continuing beneath the A13, the route follows a long straight section lined with modern apartments, warehouses, and bridges, leading toward the A12 bridge.

The canal then curves left toward Bow Locks, marked by a distinctive white footbridge. These locks link the tidal Bow Creek with the non-tidal Lea Navigation. Rather than passing through the locks, the route keeps left, continuing under the road and rail bridges and transitions into the River Lea Navigation. Passing Bow Free Wharf and continuing beneath the A118 bridge, St. Thomas' Creek appears on the right, indicating the return route. Here the surroundings shift from open spaces to industrial remnants and construction projects.

- **DISTANCE:** 10.5 km return.
- **PADDLING ENVIRONMENT:** 2.
- **ROUTE MAP:** islandeering.com/paddleboarding-limehouse-cut-and-olympic-stadium/
- **ACCESS RESTRICTIONS:** Licence required, included in Paddle UK membership.
- **OS MAP:** OS Explorer 162 Greenwich & Gravesend.
- **STARTING POINT:** Limehouse Basin, Pinnacle Way, Ratcliffe, Limehouse, E14 7PB. Grid ref. TQ 363 810; What3Words will.spits.life.
- **LAUNCHING:** North side of basin, off concrete platform beside the lock leading into Regent's Canal.
- **PITSTOPS:** Quirky café, great atmosphere and food, The Yurt Café, short walk from Limehouse Basin, tel. 0300 111 1147.
- **GETTING THERE:** Limehouse station on DLR, take Branch Road exit and turn left at the bottom of the stairs, then follow the rail arches to the canal (250m walk to launch).
- **SPECIAL POINTS:** In summer, floating invasive weeds can choke parts of the loop, making progress very slow. Be sure to wash your board and gear before entering another waterway to prevent the spread of non-native plants and animal species. No locks to portage on this route.

After passing beneath two rail bridges, the route approaches Old Ford Lock (Lock 19). Before reaching the lock, a right turn – going under a footbridge, pipes, and a road crossing – begins the loop around the London Stadium. The stadium dominates the right side of the waterway, with a right turn (ignoring Carpenter's Road Lock to the left) taking you under Diamond Bridge. This section, known as the City Mill River, was historically a branch of the Old River Lea.

Look out for the iconic ArcelorMittal Orbit, a twisting red steel structure from the 2012 Olympics, and the distinctive London Aquatics Centre – visible on the left. Continuing beneath road and rail bridges, the route passes City Mill Lock and enters the Bow Back Rivers, which were cleaned and revitalised as part of the Olympic Park redevelopment.

To complete the loop, go under St Thomas Creek footbridge (marked Number 1) and take a sharp left under the A118, rejoining the River Lea at Bow Free Wharf. From there, retrace the path along the River Lea and through the Limehouse Cut, returning to Limehouse Basin •

62

RIVER LEA TOTTENHAM HALE TO HACKNEY WICK

RIVER · GREATER LONDON

Paddling the River Lea between Tottenham Hale and Hackney Wick offers a unique mix of urban grit and natural beauty, where industrial and residential areas meet wild spaces. The river meanders past large reservoirs, marshes, and graffiti-covered warehouses, with sections where the city's hum mixes with the rustle of reeds and birdsong, creating a vibrant contrast of sounds and scenery.

Starting at Tottenham Hale and heading downstream (south), the River Lea flows alongside the Lea Valley reservoirs. On the right, houses line the water's edge, while on the left the green banks of the reservoirs stretch out, mostly hidden from view. As the river curves gently, the Lea Rowing Club comes into sight, followed by the green slopes of Springfield Park on the right. Across the river, Lee Valley Marina is home to narrowboats floating peacefully on the water. Soon, the river opens up into Walthamstow Marshes, one of the last untouched areas of London's ancient wetlands, offering a striking contrast to the surrounding urban sprawl. Further along, the Leaside Trust, a watersports charity, sits on the right.

- **DISTANCE:** 6.5km one way; train return.
- **PADDLING ENVIRONMENT:** 2.
- **ROUTE MAP:** islandeering.com/paddleboarding-tottenham-hale-to-hackney-wick/
- **ACCESS RESTRICTIONS:** Licence required, included in Paddle UK Membership.
- **OS MAP:** OS Explorer 174 Epping Forest & Lee Valley.
- **STARTING POINT:** Downstream of Tottenham Hale Lock, off Ferry Lane, Tottenham Hale, N17 9PY. Grid ref. TQ 347 894; What3Words could.sleepy.rarely.
- **EGRESS:** Hackney Wick (adjacent to Moo Canoes). Grid ref. TQ 373 844; What3Words skills.quite.burst.
- **LAUNCHING:** Canalside, 250m walk from Tottenham Hale rail station.
- **PITSTOPS:** Popular riverside pub renowned for its roasts, Princess of Wales, Lea Bridge, tel. 020 8533 3463; great beer and atmosphere, CRATE Brewery, Hackney Wick, tel. 07547 695841; burgers and hotdogs with a Latino twist, The Milk Float, Hackney Wick, themilkfloat.com
- **HIRE AND TRIPS:** Trips with Leaside Trust, Springfield Park, tel. 020 8806 6887; hire with Moo Canoes, Hackney Wick, tel. 07879 909423.
- **GETTING THERE:** *Start point* Tottenham Hale rail station to launch point, walk left onto Ferry Lane and follow to river bridge, take steps down to river, walk under bridge and launch south of bridge; *Egress point* Hackney Wick rail station, leave towpath by Moo Canoes, walk up 'slipway' to White Post Lane, then turn left and follow to station (320m walk).
- **SPECIAL POINTS:** Watch out for rowers on the river who may not see you as they pass by. Although water levels are managed by locks, check local conditions on the river before your trip at riverlevels.uk/flood-warning-lower-river-lee-at-hackney-and-walthamstow

The river bends right toward Lea Bridge, where the popular Princess of Wales pub sits on the right bank. Opposite, the Middlesex Filter Beds Weir marks the split of the River Lea: the Old River Lea follows its winding original course, while the more direct Lea Navigation, a Victorian canal, carries the main flow toward Hackney.

From here, the river passes between homes and the vast green space of Hackney Marshes, famous for its football pitches and natural beauty. After passing under Marshgate Bridge and the A12, the landscape shifts as the river approaches Hackney Wick. Here, industrial edges soften into an artistic neighbourhood, where old warehouses have become studios, their walls covered in vibrant street art. The river feels like part of a living gallery. Just past the rail bridge, Crate Brewery's riverside terrace buzzes with people enjoying craft beer in the sunshine.

Beyond the next road bridge, Moo Canoes and The Milk Float offer canoe and kayak rentals, reflecting Hackney Wick's creative, eco-friendly spirit. This stretch of the river pulses with energy. At the junction with the Hertford Union Canal, Old Ford Lock provides a natural turnaround point for those looking to soak up the Hackney Wick vibe before heading to the nearby rail station. For a longer trip, it's possible to continue from Old Ford Lock and complete the circuit around the Olympic Stadium (see route 61) •

63

LEE VALLEY WHITE WATER CENTRE

LAKE · GREATER LONDON

Combine the excitement of Olympic heritage with a dynamic water environment in a great destination for families and beginners. The Lee Valley White Water Centre, a world-class venue for watersports, was originally built for the London 2012 Olympic Games, where it hosted the canoe slalom events. Today, it remains one of the UK's top destinations for thrill-seekers and water enthusiasts, featuring two man-made courses: the 300-metre Olympic Standard Competition Course, with its powerful rapids and challenging turns, and the gentler 160-metre Legacy Loop, which has a calm area for paddleboarding off to the side.

A unique feature of the centre is its water supply, drawn from a borehole that taps into an underground aquifer. This ensures a steady flow of clean water, which is then chlorinated to leave sparkling clear water. The water is pumped into the centre's lakes and circulated through the rapids, allowing year-round operations with consistently high water quality and controlled flow.

The Terrace Bar & Café provides a comfortable spot to relax with panoramic views of the courses. Visitors can enjoy food and drinks while watching the action, making it an ideal place for spectators. Outdoor seating and picnic areas are also available – perfect for unwinding after a day on the water.

Part of the larger Lee Valley Regional Park, the White Water Centre is surrounded by 4,000 hectares of green spaces, lakes, and recreational areas, so there is plenty to see after your paddle •

- **DISTANCE:** Free-range.
- **PADDLING ENVIRONMENT:** 1.
- **ROUTE MAP:** islandeering.com/paddleboarding-lee-valley-white-water-centre/
- **ACCESS RESTRICTIONS:** Self-launch (charges), book with Lee Valley White Water Centre (before entering water you'll need to have a safety briefing and undertake a short competency assessment).
- **OS MAP:** OS Explorer 174 Epping Forest & Lee Valley.
- **PARKING:** Lee Valley White Water Centre (free with pre-booked activities/greater than £5 spend in café, but you must register your parking), Station Road, Waltham Cross, Hertfordshire, EN9 1AB. Grid ref. TL 372 005; What3Words surely.brings.watch.
- **PITSTOPS:** Onsite café great for people watching, Brew Street Kitchen and Bar.
- **LESSONS AND HIRE:** Lee Valley White Water Centre.
- **GETTING THERE:** *Car* J26 off M25 onto A121 towards Waltham Abbey. At T-junction (facing Royal Gunpowder Mills) turn left towards Waltham Cross along Highbridge Street, then R after 100m into car park; *Train* Waltham Cross rail station 800m walk along A121 to lake.
- **SPECIAL POINTS:** Must wear closed-toe shoes, shorts and t-shirt as minimum; min age 8+, and under-12s must be accompanied by an adult.

64

TWO TREE ISLAND LOOP

COAST · ESSEX

Take in the expansive Thames Estuary views and explore wildlife-rich salt marshes on a circumnavigation of Two Tree Island, near Leigh-on-Sea. This tidal island offers a picturesque paddle through creeks and mudflats. Once reclaimed for farmland in the 18th century, the island is now a vital wildlife reserve managed by the Essex Wildlife Trust. Spanning 259 hectares, its habitats support a wide variety of birdlife, including avocets, redshanks, and oystercatchers, making this an ideal route for nature enthusiasts.

Launch from the slipway and turn left (east) for an anti-clockwise paddle, to benefit from the natural flow. Follow the island's southern coast, skirting along an intricate network of salt marshes. Stay close to the marshes for excellent birdwatching opportunities and protection from stronger estuary currents. Continue paddling toward Leigh Marsh, located at the eastern tip of the island. This scenic area offers views ahead of Leigh-on-Sea with its waterside eateries and bars; look to the far right and you'll spot the distant skyline of Southend-on-Sea. If you have arrived by train, start from the Leigh-on-Sea foreshore and head southwest along the main channel towards the eastern tip of the island to join the rest of the route.

After rounding the eastern tip, follow Leigh Creek along the island's northern shore, passing moorings and a small boatyard. Enjoy stunning views of the marshes with seabirds foraging along the shores. After passing beneath the road bridge connecting the island to the mainland, the creek narrows, offering a peaceful experience as it winds through Hadleigh Marsh. At the western end of the island, re-enter Hadleigh Ray, turn left (east), and follow the southern shoreline back towards the slipway, or continue to Leigh-on-Sea as described •

• **DISTANCE:** 6.5km return.

• **PADDLING ENVIRONMENT:** 3.

• **ROUTE MAP:** islandeering.com/paddleboarding-two-tree-island-loop/

• **ACCESS RESTRICTIONS:** £5 slipway launch fee payable to Foreshore Officer located in the car park (on duty 1000-1600 Mon- Fri, May to October).

• **OS MAP:** OS Explorer 175 Southend-on-Sea & Basildon.

• **STARTING POINT:** Slipway adjacent to car park along southern foreshore of Two Tree Island.

• **PARKING:** Two Tree Island Car Park, Marine Parade, Leigh-on-Sea, SS9 2RF. Grid ref. TQ 822 848; What3Words bucket.holds.race.

• **LAUNCHING:** Slipway/beach adjacent to car park; if arriving by rail, launch from foreshore at base of Belton Bridge, 400m walk from station.

• **PITSTOPS:** Great seafood, Osborne Brothers, Leigh-on-Sea, tel. 01702 477233; a pint close to the action in Leigh-on-Sea, The Crooked Billet, 01702 480289 or Ye Olde Smack, 01702 476765.

• **GETTING THERE:** *Car* Exit A127 onto A129/A13 towards Leigh-on-Sea. Turn R onto Thames Drive; at traffic light cross Marine Parade onto Belton Way, turn immediately R after rail station and follow road to south shore of Two Tree Island for car park; *Train* Leigh-on-Sea station, then walk 400m to launch.

• **SPECIAL POINTS:** This trip is highly tide-dependent, with a small window for ideal conditions. The best time to start is 1.5-2hrs before HW, to take advantage of the remaining flood tide while paddling west along the northern shore channel. Aim to reach Hadleigh Ray near the end of slack water. On your return, the ebb tide will assist as you paddle east back to the jetty. If you start from Leigh-on-Sea, ensure you return no later than 2hrs after HW to land back on the hard and avoid the thick mudbanks. Watch out for jetskis in Hadleigh Ray and around the jetty. The area is quite exposed to E wind so check local weather, tide and surf conditions at surfline.com at Southend-on-Sea for local conditions.

• **OFFSHORE WIND:** NW while on southern shoreline.

65

CHELMER AND BLACKWATER NAVIGATION BEELEIGH FALLS TO PAPERMILL LOCK

RIVER · ESSEX

A hidden gem of a river that meanders past picturesque waterfalls, locks, and scenic countryside, offering a tranquil paddle rich with wildlife and leading to a popular boating spot and tearooms. Though the entire river flows from Chelmsford to the tidal estuary at Heybridge Basin, this section between Beeleigh and Papermill Lock is one of the best, marked by John Rennie's beautifully crafted red brick bridges and locks.

Launch upstream of Beeleigh Lock, where the River Chelmer joins from the left, and continue ahead on the Chelmer, past open fields and wooded stretches of peaceful Essex countryside. At the river split, stay right on the main navigation and portage around Rickett's Lock.

The river meanders through tranquil landscapes, passing beneath The Causeway bridge and on to a portage at Hoe Mill Lock. Further along, the moored boats of Willow Boat Hire line the riverbank, and the beautiful All Saints Church in Ulting comes into view, with its striking red brick and flint walls and bellcote perched along the right bank.

After passing Rushes Lock, the turnaround point lies ahead, just beyond Paper Mill Bridge, opening into the wide turning area at Paper Mill Lock in Little Baddow. This historic halfway stop for bargemen is now a popular spot for boaters and visitors. Paper Mill Lock, one of the oldest on the navigation, and its nearby tearoom offer a perfect riverside stop. After a refreshing break, retrace the journey to return •

- **DISTANCE:** 15.5km return.
- **PADDLING ENVIRONMENT:** 2.
- **ROUTE MAP:** islandeering.com/paddleboarding-beeleigh-falls-to-papermill-lock/
- **ACCESS RESTRICTIONS:** Licence required for Chelmer and Blackwater Navigation, £6/day essexwaterways.com/shop/paddleboard-licence-one-day
- **OS MAP:** OS Explorer 183 Chelmsford & The Rodings.
- **STARTING POINT:** Upstream of Beeleigh Lock.
- **PARKING:** Parking area (free), unmarked lane, Langford, CM9 6LL. Grid ref. TL 840 083; What3Words leafing.crusaders.canine.
- **LAUNCHING:** 250m walk from parking, over bridge, turn R along towpath past Beeleigh Falls to Beeleigh Lock (not the lock adjacent to the bridge).
- **PITSTOPS:** Large range of freshly made sandwiches, Paper Mill Lock Tearooms, Little Baddow, tel. 01245 225520.
- **CAMPING:** Hoe Mill Lock Caravan and Camping Club site (members only) campingandcaravanningclub.co.uk/campsites/uk/essex/maldon/hoemilllock/
- **GETTING THERE:** Leave Maldon and head towards Chelmsford on the B1019. In Langford turn L opposite Langford and Ulting Village Hall along a small lane, following signs to Maldon Golf Club. Before crossing the bridge over the River Blackwater, car parking area is on the L.
- **SPECIAL POINTS:** Six locks to portage (three each way). Check local river conditions at Ulting before your trip riverlevels.uk/essex-ulting-ulting-fgs-and-raingauge

66

MALDON LOOP

RIVER AND TIDAL ESTUARY · ESSEX

Tidal creeks, historic quays and salt marsh give way to the picturesque Beeleigh Falls and the quiet waters of the Chelmer and Blackwater Navigation. Launch from the café at Heybridge Basin and paddle left towards the charming Heybridge Basin Lock. Portage on the right side and relaunch onto the River Blackwater to the right of the lock gates. Turn right, paddling parallel to the shoreline, where you'll enjoy sweeping views of Northey Island. Look out for The Telegraph, an old wooden smack with tattered sails that looks like something straight out of *Pirates of the Caribbean*, resting in the still waters.

Keep right to continue up the Blackwater and soon the picturesque town of Maldon will come into view on the hill ahead. Cross over to the left bank, passing Maldon Yacht Club, and head toward the eastern tip of Maldon Promenade, marked by the imposing Statue of Byrhtnoth. This statue honours the earl who led the Anglo-Saxon forces in the Battle of Maldon on Northey Island in 991 AD. Paddle parallel to the promenade, between peaceful parkland and wide salt marshes, home to a variety of birdlife and coastal wildlife.

Next, the lively Maldon Quay comes into view, lined with historic Thames barges, moorings, and charming riverside inns and cafés – an iconic spot for both locals and visitors. After passing beneath Fullbridge, the scenery starts to change as the busy town fades into the quieter, greener spaces of the Chelmer Blackwater Reserve. The river flows calmly here, passing Maldon Golf Club. The hum of the A414 overhead briefly interrupts the peace, but beyond that the calm and serenity return.

At the far end of the golf course, keep right to reach Beeleigh Falls, a scenic spot where the River Chelmer meets the River Blackwater. This area's natural beauty is enhanced by the weirs and waterfalls, creating a unique riverscape. Portage to the left, follow the clear track up to the towpath, then turn right to cross over the weir. After passing the lock, relaunch onto the Chelmer and Blackwater Navigation and head southeast back towards Maldon.

Continue paddling through peaceful countryside, passing beneath the A414 twice, with Maldon Canoe Club located on a large river bend between the crossings. The river then winds through both industrial and residential areas before opening up to fields, eventually leading back to the café at Heybridge Basin

• **DISTANCE:** 9km return.

• **PADDLING ENVIRONMENT:** 2 on river and 3 in estuary.

• **ROUTE MAP:** islandeering.com/paddleboarding-maldon-loop/

• **ACCESS RESTRICTIONS:** Licence required for Chelmer and Blackwater Navigation (£6/day) https://essexwaterways.com/shop/paddleboard-licence-one-day

• **OS MAP:** OS Explorer 183 Chelmsford & The Rodings.

• **STARTING POINT:** Bargemasters Cabin, Daisy Meadow, Heybridge Basin, Maldon, CM9 4RR. Grid ref. TL 869 068; What3Words recall.files.unfit.

• **PARKING:** Daisy Meadow Car Park, Lock Hill, Heybridge Basin, Maldon, CM9 4RX. Grid ref. TL 870 069; What3Words community.dissolves.retraced.

• **LAUNCHING:** Pontoon short walk from car park.

• **PITSTOPS:** Coffee, breakfast rolls, homemade cakes, Bargemasters Cabin, Heybridge Basin, tel. 01621 880015; seafood, The Jolly Sailor, Heybridge Basin, tel. 01621 854210; a pint watching the waterside action, The Old Ship, Heybridge Basin, tel. 01621 854150; afternoon tea overlooking the River Blackwater, The Lock Tea Room, Heybridge Basin, tel. 01621 854466.

• **GETTING THERE:** Turn R off B1026 Maldon to Goldhanger road, following signs for Heybridge Basin. As Basin Road sweeps to L, turn R, following parking sign.

• **SPECIAL POINTS:** This is a tide-assisted paddle so aim to arrive at Heybridge Basin Lock 2hrs before HW. Check tides at bbc.co.uk/weather/coast-and-sea/tide-tables/1/123a at Osea for local conditions – alternatively, time your trip to leave Heybridge as soon as the water has covered the mudbanks below the lock gates (this might be earlier for spring tides). The first part of the estuary is exposed to east winds so check weather at metoffice.gov.uk at Maldon for local conditions. Once you start heading NW up the Blackwater, cross to the left bank and aim for the Statue of Byrhtnoth, on the tip of Maldon's promenade. Check water conditions for the area at riverlevels.uk/flood-warning-blackwater-north-bank to avoid fast flood water over Beeleigh Falls.

67

RIVER CROUCH HULLBRIDGE TO BATTLESBRIDGE

TIDAL RIVER · ESSEX

A scenic journey between two historic villages, following a tranquil waterway where remnants of a once-thriving trade and agricultural past still stand. A peaceful retreat for paddlers and sailors, the river's tidal estuary hosts a diverse blend of saltwater and freshwater habitats, making it an ideal destination for spotting wildlife.

Launch from the Hullbridge Slipway and head upstream, passing the wooded Kendal Park. Fenn Creek joins from the right and then, as the village fades, the river opens up with green banks and moored boats lining the way. The river meanders past a holiday park; beyond this, it begins to narrow as lush greenery closes in on both sides. The paddle becomes more sheltered on the approach to Hawk Hill Bridge, where the historic Battlesbridge Mill comes into view. Once the heart of the local grain trade, this iconic structure now houses a charming tearoom on its top floor, offering stunning views of the estuary.

To explore the antique stores or visit the tearooms and pubs, look for the metal steps and landing stage on the left, just before the bridge. To enter the mill pool, paddle under the bridge into a calm, sheltered stretch of water surrounded by the history of Battlesbridge. This part of the river once served as a key trade route between the mill and the local market. Be sure to time your return with the ebbing tide •

• **DISTANCE:** 8.5km return.

• **PADDLING ENVIRONMENT:** 3.

• **ROUTE MAP:** islandeering.com/paddleboarding-hullbridge-to-battlesbridge/

• **ACCESS RESTRICTIONS:** No licence required.

OS MAP: OS Explorer 175 Southend-on-Sea & Basildon.

• **STARTING POINT:** Slipway, Ferry Road, Hullbridge, SS5 6ND. Grid ref. TQ 809 955; What3Words saturate.acute.suitably.

• **PARKING:** Car park by Hullbridge Community Centre (free), Pooles Lane, Hullbridge, SS5 6ND. Grid ref. TQ 810 954; What3Words noun.backyards.apparatus.

• **LAUNCHING:** 100m walk along Ferry Road from car park to public slipway to left of The Anchor Riverside pub.

• **PITSTOPS:** Great river views from pub garden, The Anchor Riverside, Hullbridge, tel. 01702 230777; amazing views from the top of the antique centre, good cakes and lunches, The Hideaway Tearoom, Battlebridge, tel. 07305 764857; great beer and food in historic inn, The Barge Inn, Battlebridge, tel. 01268 732622.

• **GETTING THERE:** A130 S to Wickford and Woodham Ferrers; third exit at roundabout to Battlebridge; cross River Crouch on next sharp R bend and turn L onto Beeches Road/Watery Lane. Turn L at T-junction, straight over mini roundabout to Hullbridge, then L after the Co-op (first exit on mini roundabout), following signs to Hullbridge Riverside along Ferry Road. Car park on R.

• **SPECIAL POINTS:** This is a tide-assisted paddle so start 2hrs before HW (check times at bbc.co.uk/weather/coast-and-sea/tide-tables/1/122b) and leave Battlebridge within 1hr of HW as the water around the metal steps drains quickly, leaving deep mudbanks.

68

TOLLESBURY EXPLORER

ESTUARY · ESSEX

Enjoy a paddling adventure through the protected waters of Tollesbury Fleet's creeks, navigating atmospheric marshes, historic buildings, and salty boatyards, with the opportunity to circumnavigate two islands. This tranquil spur off the River Blackwater is accessed from Tollesbury Hard, next to the historic waterside granary that was once a trading store for barges. Launch from Tollesbury Hard and paddle up Woodrolfe Creek, passing the community of live-aboard boats and the striking red-and-white lightship Trinity. Upon entering Tollesbury Creek, turn right to explore the flat, uninhabited islands of Little Cob and Great Cob, with distant views of West Mersea's houses and sailing boat masts. Alternatively, turn left to explore the winding Old Hall Creek. Watch for wildlife along the way, especially the marsh harrier, a special species that's present all year round •

• **DISTANCE:** 5km to Great Cob Island return.

• **PADDLING ENVIRONMENT:** 3.

• **ROUTE MAP:** islandeering.com/paddleboarding-tollesbury/

• **ACCESS RESTRICTIONS:** No licence required.

• **OS MAP:** OS Explorer 184 Colchester, Harwich & Clacton-on-Sea.

• **STARTING POINT:** Tollesbury Hard, Tollesbury, CM9 8TB. Grid ref. TL 968 105; What3Words collide.snares.coil.

• **PARKING:** Woodrolfe Road Car Park (free), Woodrolfe Road, Tollesbury, Maldon, Essex, CM9 8SE. Grid ref. TL 963 106; What3Words protected.tweezers.officials.

• **LAUNCHING:** 600m walk to Tollesbury Hard (or drop off kit there before parking).

• **PITSTOPS:** Fabulous lunches and amazing cakes in characterful sail loft, The Loft, tel 01621 869063; tasty breakfasts and more, Tollesbury Café, tel. 01621 869980; relaxing drinks and great fish lunches and dinners overlooking marina, Harbour View Bistro and Bar, tel. 01621 869561.

• **GETTING THERE:** Follow B1023 through Tollesbury; turn left after the butcher's shop onto Woodrolfe Road. Car park on left after 450m (or continue to end of road to drop off kit).

• **SPECIAL POINTS:** Best paddled 2hrs either side of HW to avoid a muddy entrance/exit. The ebb tide drains out quickly, leaving muddy banks. Check wind, tide and swell conditions on Surfline surfline.com at nearby Walton-on-the-Naze.

• **OFFSHORE WIND:** NW when visiting Great Cob Island.

69

OSEA ISLAND CIRCUMNAVIGATION

ESTUARY · ESSEX

A trip that offers a rare glimpse into a secluded sanctuary, where private shores and hidden marshes guard a rich history that's usually reserved for only a few. Paddling around Osea Island, tucked away in the Blackwater Estuary, is a special experience. Its privacy is so closely guarded that it's normally only reachable by a tidal causeway or boat. This trip offers a rare peek into Osea's secret world – a peaceful retreat with a history as deep as the waters around it. There's a strong feeling of exclusivity, as though entering a place usually meant for the privileged looking for a quiet escape.

Start at the Stone slipway and follow the mainland shore to the west. Upon reaching the Marconi Sailing Club, head straight across to the sand spit at Osea Island's East Point. Paddle through the quiet marshes on the north side of the island to reach the tidal causeway at West Point. Continue around the island for views of lovely holiday homes in Edwardian and Arts and Crafts styles, then cross back to the mainland •

- **DISTANCE:** 11km return.
- **PADDLING ENVIRONMENT:** 3.
- **ROUTE MAP:** islandeering.com/ paddleboarding-osea-island-loop/
- **ACCESS RESTRICTIONS:** No licence required; public slipway.
- **OS MAP:** OS Explorer 176 Blackwater Estuary.
- **STARTING POINT:** Beach, The Stone, St. Lawrence, CM0 7NA. Grid ref. TL 951 061; What3Words jingles.slimming.lays.
- **PARKING:** Jubilee Field Car Park (free), St Lawrence, CM0 7LY. Grid ref. TL 954 054; What3Words unto. conjured.arrives. 700m walk to beach.
- **LAUNCHING:** At the terminus of Main Road steps lead down to beach.
- **PITSTOPS:** Indian food and seafood hut with great views, Stone Inn, St Lawrence, tel. 01621 778800.
- **GETTING THERE:** B1018 south of Maldon to Latchingdon, then follow brown signs to St Lawrence Caravan Park. Car park on the left just before the holiday park.
- **SPECIAL POINTS:** A tidal trip best started 2hrs before HW to give enough time to complete the circumnavigation and avoid mid-tide ebb currents and shoreline mudbanks on the return. The north of the island dries out, revealing thick mudbanks starting 1.5hrs after HW, or earlier on spring tides. Be mindful of other water users while crossing the main channel, and jetskis on your return. Landing on the island is not permitted.

70

WEST MERSEA EXPLORER

ESTUARY · ESSEX

A journey through tidal waters to an island rich in seafood history and a wilderness area full of hidden creeks. There is plenty to explore both downstream and upstream on the Strood Channel. Launch from the Town Hard and head downstream (left) through the lines of moored boats – ideally paddling between Middle Ooze and Thorn Fleet – soaking up the nautical atmosphere of West Mersea. Just offshore, Packing Shed Island remains a testament to the bustling 19th-century oyster industry, when Mersea Natives were prized across Europe. After an 800-metre paddle, land on the island's oyster-shell beach, where the restored Packing Shed still stands.

For a longer paddle, head upstream (right) from West Mersea Beach. Pass the weathered boathouses with their salt-worn facades, and enter the sheltered waters of Strood Channel. Along the shore, eerie remnants of historic oyster beds line the way, while the low-lying Ray Island rises just above the water on the left. After about 2.5 km, The Strood comes into view – this tidal causeway connects Mersea Island to the mainland and is often submerged at high tide. It becomes a lively spot during the Mersea Island Round the Island Race, when crews lift their boats over the causeway to continue.

Rich wildlife surrounds Ray Island, with sea lavender, golden samphire, oystercatchers, and shelducks in abundance. After the paddle, West Mersea offers plenty of seafood to enjoy as a post-paddle treat •

- **DISTANCE:** West Mersea to Packing Shed Island 1.6km return; West Mersea to The Strood 5.2km return.
- **PADDLING ENVIRONMENT:** 3.
- **ROUTE MAP:** islandeering.com/paddleboarding-west-mersea-to-the strood/
- **ACCESS RESTRICTIONS:** No licence required.
- **OS MAP:** OS Explorer 184 Colchester, Harwich & Clacton-on-Sea.
- **STARTING POINT:** Beach adjacent to Coast Road car park.
- **PARKING:** Coast Road car park (charges), Coast Road, West Mersea, CO5 8PB. Grid ref. TM 000 129; What3Words guesswork.precluded.silently.
- **LAUNCHING:** Town Hard opposite West Mersea Yacht Club.
- **PITSTOPS:** Seafood heaven, The Company Shed, West Mersea, (must book ahead, tel. 01206 382700); delicious food and great vibes, Waterfront Pizza, West Mersea, tel. 07493 184037.
- **LESSONS AND HIRE:** Mersea Island Watersports, tel. 01206 381859.
- **GETTING THERE:** Cross The Strood and follow B1025, then Coast Road to car park on L (in front of West Mersea Yacht Club).
- **SPECIAL POINTS:** Best paddled 2-3hrs either side of HW to avoid a muddy walk back up to the hard. The ebb tide drains quickly around The Strood, where the flow concentrates in the channels around mid-tide onwards. Check wind, tide and swell conditions on Surfline surfline.com at nearby Walton-on-the-Naze.
- **OFFSHORE WIND:** NW when visiting Packing Shed and Cobmarsh islands.

71

MERSEA BOATING LAKE

LAKE · ESSEX

A sheltered escape on Mersea Island, offering calm waters perfect for watersports beginners and families, all set against the backdrop of the stunning Blackwater Estuary. Created as a safe alternative to the unpredictable open sea, the saltwater lake taps into Mersea Island's deep maritime roots – fishing, boatbuilding, and coastal navigation – and brings these traditions into a modern space designed for paddleboarding, kayaking, and sailing. Though man-made and home to an adventurous aquapark, this relatively small lake feels at home in its natural surroundings, where the nearby salt marshes and estuaries create vital habitats for wildlife. Paddlers often spot herons, egrets, oystercatchers, and curlews, which thrive in this rich coastal environment.

Just a stone's throw from Mersea's beaches and the vibrant village of West Mersea, famed for its seafood and oysters, Mersea Island Vineyard adds to the island's charm – with award-winning wines, tours, and tastings there is plenty of sumptuous post-paddle refreshment •

- **DISTANCE:** Free range.
- **PADDLING ENVIRONMENT:** 1.
- **ROUTE MAP:** islandeering.com/ paddleboarding-mersea-boating-lake/
- **ACCESS RESTRICTIONS:** Self-launch, book with Mersea Boating Lake (£5/day).
- **OS MAP:** OS Explorer 184 Colchester, Harwich & Clacton-on-Sea.
- **STARTING POINT:** Mersea Boating Lake, Rewsalls Lane, Mersea Island, CO5 8SX. Grid ref. TM 042 134; What3Words underway.licks.limiting. Free parking on site.
- **LAUNCHING:** Pontoon short walk from parking
- **PITSTOPS:** Basic onsite café, Lake House Café, Mersea Boating Lake; sandwiches, toasties and jackets, The Vineyard Café (closed Mon & Tues), tel. 01206 384698.
- **HIRE AND LESSONS:** Mersea Boating Lake, tel. 07904 196238.
- **GETTING THERE:** Cross The Strood, turn L onto East Mersea Road, following signs to vineyard; turn R, signed to vineyard, then pass vineyard and car park for lake on left.
- **SPECIAL POINTS:** Perfect for beginners.

72

BRIGHTLINGSEA EXPLORER

ESTUARY · ESSEX

Scenic trips both upstream and downstream offer the perfect opportunity to explore low-lying islands, sandbars, and wide open views. Located at the mouth of the River Colne, Brightlingsea, with its rich maritime history and lively sailing club, makes an excellent base for exploration.

For the downstream trip, start at the harbour in front of Colne Valley Yacht Club and head west (right), passing the pontoon moorings. Paddle 500m towards the sandbar near Point Clear Ferry Landing. From here, there are some great views: to the north a colourful line of beach huts along the Promenade and Brightlingsea Beach, with Bateman's Tower standing out in the distance; to the southwest the sandy shores of East Mersea Landing on Mersea Island, with flat landscapes offering clear views across the island.

Ahead, the scene stretches along Pyefleet Channel and Geedon Creek as they meet the River Colne. More experienced paddlers can continue upstream to Wivenhoe, a 16km round trip with the help of the tide.

To explore Brightlingsea Creek's hidden waterways, turn left after launching. Paddle towards the salt marshes surrounding the low-lying Cindery Island. Nearby, the creek's north shore was once home to oyster pits, while the south bank's St. Osyth Creek leads to a jumble of boatyards near St Osyth. Continue upstream along Brightlingsea Creek, passing the tranquil Howlands Marsh Nature Reserve, where sea wormwood and golden samphire thrive in the salt marshes fringing the seawall •

- **DISTANCE:** Free-range.
- **PADDLING ENVIRONMENT:** 3.
- **ROUTE MAP:** islandeering.com/paddleboarding-brightlingsea/
- **ACCESS RESTRICTIONS:** No licence required.
- **STARTING POINT:** Brightlingsea Harbour or Ferry Landing Pontoon. Grid ref. TM 085 161; What3Words helpful.highlight.blurred.
- **OS MAP:** OS Explorer 184 Colchester, Harwich & Clacton-on-Sea.
- **PARKING:** Tower Street car park (charges), Copperas Road, Brightlingsea, CO7 0AW. Grid ref. TM 086 162; What3Words system.lyricism.talents.
- **LAUNCHING:** 100m walk from car park along Copperas Road to shore.
- **PITSTOPS:** Pick up seafood, continental meats and cheeses for a picnic, Waterside Deli, Brightlingsea, tel. 01206 304200; good food and real ales, Yachtsmans Arms, Brightlingsea, tel. 01206 302342.
- **GETTING THERE:** A133 S of Colchester, turn R onto B1028, then L onto B1027, then B1029 to Brightlingsea. After The Sun, turn L onto New Street and follow to car park on L.
- **SPECIAL POINTS:** The main channel is accessible on all states of the tide, but the creeks do dry out so are best explored on a flooding tide. Look out for boats when using the pontoon, especially when ferries are operating. Do not leave any boards/kit unattended on the pontoon, and move away as soon as you have landed to allow access for other users. Check local tide, swell and wind conditions for Walton-on-the-Naze at surfline.com before entering the main estuary.
- **OFFSHORE WIND:** S when out in the main estuary.

73

ST OSYTH MILL DAM LAKE

LAKE · ESSEX

An ideal spot for beginners and families, especially when windy conditions make coastal paddling difficult. With plenty of other watersports available, it's perfect for a fun day out. The lake is located on the edge of St. Osyth, a village rich in legend and history near the Essex coast. It once served as the mill pond for the historic St. Osyth Tide Mill, originally powered by tidal waters from St. Osyth Creek, a tributary of Brightlingsea Creek.

Today, a small stream feeds the lake at the eastern end, where calm waters and reeds provide a peaceful haven for wildlife. It's a great place for nature lovers, with herons, kingfishers, and dragonflies frequently spotted. In contrast, the western end of the lake is more energetic – it's home to the Wake Park, where people enjoy activities like wakeboarding and create a lively atmosphere.

Nearby, the ancient St. Osyth Priory offers an interesting place to explore after a session on the lake. Once a grand Augustinian abbey, the priory is now a relic of medieval England, with its weathered stones and vast grounds. Wandering through the ruins, you can sense the deep history of the place, from monks to martyrs, all set against the backdrop of the village's marshlands and coastal winds •

- **DISTANCE:** Free range.
- **PADDLING ENVIRONMENT:** 1.
- **ROUTE MAP:** islandeering.com/paddleboarding-st-osyth/
- **ACCESS RESTRICTIONS:** Self-launch, book via Curve Watersports (£6/day).
- **OS MAP:** OS Explorer 184 Colchester, Harwich & Clacton-on-Sea.
- **STARTING POINT:** Curve Watersports, Mill Dam Lake, St Osyth, CO16 8EW. Grid ref. TM 116 153; What3Words weeds.brushing.appear.
- **PARKING:** Free onsite car park.
- **LAUNCHING:** Pontoon 150m walk from parking.
- **PITSTOPS:** Watch the fun from the lake's decked terrace, Mill Street Lake Café, tel. 01255 821915.
- **LESSONS AND HIRE:** Curve Watersports, tel. 01255 821915, www.curvewatersports.co.uk
- **GETTING THERE:** Turn L off the Colchester to Clacton road (B1027) onto Colchester Road and follow it into the heart of St. Osyth village. Just after passing The Kings Arms, turn R onto The Bury/Mill Street. As the road curves, you'll spot Curve Watersports on your L. Parking is located over the bridge on the R.
- **SPECIAL POINTS:** Please clean your board before you enter the water to prevent spread of non-native plants and animal species.

74

RIVER COLNE EXPLORER

TIDAL RIVER · ESSEX

From a village steeped in maritime history, paddle upstream through reed-lined banks and bird-rich marshes to uncover relics of an industrial past at The Hythe, once Colchester's thriving port. Alternatively, head downstream to explore the hidden beauty of the little-known Roman River.

Launch from the Rowhedge Slipway on the south bank of the River Colne and head left, upstream, along the historic waterfront of Rowhedge, a charming village with deep maritime history. Paddle past The Anchor pub and soon Wivenhoe Wood appears on the right, its dense greenery contrasting with the open Hythe Marshes on the left, a haven for birdlife. This peaceful stretch of water feels wonderfully secluded, with views of reed-fringed banks occasionally interrupted by passing trains just beyond the reeds on the right. As the journey continues, the buildings and tower blocks of the University of Essex campus appear on the right, signaling the approach to the outskirts of Colchester. On the left, King Edward Quay comes into view, with houseboats gently bobbing at their moorings. Just beyond the large pylon, the King Edward Quay Pontoon can be spotted on the left – a perfect place to stop for a rest or picnic. Nearby, the distinctive Colchester Sea Cadets Lightship adds a splash of colour to the riverscape.

To continue, paddle under the A134 Colne Causeway. This part of the river passes through a redeveloped area lined with residential flats, and then under a white pedestrian bridge. Beyond that, the older buildings of the old Hythe port come into view – one a tall industrial relic with corrugated tin structures and ivy-covered walls. Once a busy port, this is now a derelict yet captivating site, where remnants of old warehouses and docks stand amid the overgrowth. Just beyond the Hythe Station Road bridge, the river narrows considerably. In the distance, Colchester Town Hall can be seen rising above the reed beds before it's time to turn back and retrace the route.

An alternative trip explores the Roman River. Head downstream from Rowhedge a short way, then, opposite Wivenhoe, turn right into the narrow creek fringed with wild meadows – it's tidal up to the imposing Fingringhoe Mill.

These trips can also start from the north bank of the river at Wivenhoe using the public jetty, with car park and rail station close by. After launching, head upstream past Rowhedge and continue the trip as described •

• DISTANCE: 8.5km return to Hythe; 3.5km return to Fingringhoe Mill.

• PADDLING ENVIRONMENT: 3.

• ROUTE MAP: islandeering.com/paddleboarding-rowhedge-to-colchester/

• ACCESS RESTRICTIONS: No licence required.

• OS MAP: OS Explorer 184 Colchester, Harwich & Clacton-on-Sea.

• STARTING POINT: *Rowhedge* Public slipway, Waterfront Promenade, Rowhedge, CO5 7BB. Grid ref. TM 033 214; What3Words scuba.once.discrepancy; *Wivenhoe* Public slipway, south of Cooks Yard car park.

• PARKING: *Rowhedge* Roadside parking (free), High Street, Rowhedge, CO5 7ES. Grid ref. TM 032 215; What3Words relay.evenly.stores. *Wivenhoe* Cooks Yard car park (charges), Walter Radcliffe Road, Wivenhoe, CO7 9FF; Grid ref. TM 041 213; What3Words lobby.debater.greed.

• LAUNCHING: Rowhedge Slipway 200m walk along High Street; Wivenhoe Slipway 20m from car park.

• PITSTOPS: Tasty pub classics and lovely riverside garden, The Anchor, Rowhedge, tel. 01206 728382; excellent cakes, The Hut (Rowhedge Coastal Rowing Club), weekends Mar to Nov, tel. 07775 687531.

• GETTING THERE: *Car* Head SE on the A134 from Colchester centre; turn L onto B1025 (Mersea Road). Pass through Fingringhoe, then turn L following signs to Rowhedge and High Street parking; *Train* London Liverpool Street to Wivenhoe, then 600m walk to public slipway.

• SPECIAL POINTS: Start 2hrs before HW at Brightlingsea – check bbc.co.uk/weather/coast-and-sea/tide-tables/1/126 – or as soon as the water has reached the base of the public slipway. Look out for boats and the ferry as you head north.

75

RIVER STOUR CATTAWADE TO DEDHAM

RIVER · ESSEX

Experience some of the most idyllic countryside in East Anglia as you pass Flatford Mill, made famous by Constable's paintings, and take in nature reserves, open farmland, and wide open skies. Launch from Cattawade, a picturesque spot at the head of the River Stour. Turn right and, after a few hundred metres, pass an industrial estate and paddle through a disused lock pool, a reminder of the river's industrial past. After 3km, pass Judas Gap Weir. Further upstream, the river meanders sharply to the right through a wooded area where kingfishers, herons, and other wildlife are often spotted.

Approach Flatford Mill – famous for being the setting of John Constable's painting The Hay Wain – where the river heads through the Flatford Mill Lock. Follow the portage signs for approximately 100 metres upstream to rejoin the river in front of the National Trust tearooms. Bridge Cottage, adjacent to the bridge, is a 16th-century thatched house that's now a National Trust property showcasing exhibits on John Constable and local history. This charming area, rich in history, is perfect for a short break or a visit to Flatford Mill and its scenic surroundings.

Pass under the wooden footbridge and continue upstream, past tranquil meadows with overhanging willows, to the well-known Boathouse Café with its rows of colourful rowing boats – a lovely spot to pause or grab refreshments if needed. Pass under the B1029 road bridge, which marks the turning point for this route.

On the return journey, keep an eye out for fish darting through the clear waters and the various bird species that inhabit this peaceful environment. The journey from Cattawade to Dedham takes you through some of the most idyllic countryside in East Anglia, offering a perfect blend of natural beauty, cultural heritage, and wildlife spotting •

- **DISTANCE:** 12km return.
- **PADDLING ENVIRONMENT:** 2.
- **ROUTE MAP:** islandeering.com/paddleboarding-cattawade-to-dedham/
- **ACCESS RESTRICTIONS:** Licence required, included in Paddle UK membership.
- **OS MAP:** OS Explorer 196 Sudbury, Hadleigh & Dedham Vale.
- **STARTING POINT & PARKING:** *Cattawade* Cattawade Picnic Site car park (free), Bergholt Road, Brantham, CO11 1QW. Grid ref. TM 100 331; What3Words dove.often.dugouts; *Dedham* Dedham Riverside car park (charges), Dedham Road, Dedham, CO7 6DH. Grid ref. TM 057 335; What3Words cupboards.darling.cheerful.
- **LAUNCHING:** *Cattawade* Riverside adjacent to parking; *Dedham* Short walk to riverside from parking.
- **PITSTOPS:** Beautifully located National Trust tearoom, Flatford Mill, tel. 01206 297201; riverside seating, The Boatyard, Dedham, tel. 01206 323153.
- **GETTING THERE:** A137 to Brantham, at roundabout follow signs for Flatford along B1070, then first R onto Darwin Close and follow to the end for car park.
- **SPECIAL POINTS:** One lock to portage twice. Check local river conditions at Dedham, riverlevels.uk/flood-warning-the-river-stour-upstream-of-cattawade-

76

RIVER STOUR SUDBURY TO BURES

RIVER · ESSEX

Peaceful trip along the Essex-Suffolk border, taking in the beauty of the Stour Valley's farmland, historic towns, and unspoiled landscapes, with a classic pub stop along the way. Launch from Sudbury, a historic market town linked to artist Thomas Gainsborough, and turn left to follow the main river downstream. Surrounded by ancient grazing lands, Sudbury offers a first glimpse of the traditional rural landscape of Dedham Vale with its wide open meadows.

After a long right-hand bend, keep left to reach Great Cornard Lock. Portage at the lock, then continue past Mill Tye, a brick-built mill that reflects the area's industrial heritage. After 3.5 km reach The Henny Swan, a popular riverside pub with riverside gardens. Portage left of the weir and relaunch at the designated spot. Beyond the pub, the river winds through lush green meadows and pastures. In summer, cattle graze along the banks, while willow trees arch over the river, forming shaded green tunnels. This peaceful stretch feels very calm and secluded.

Next, portage at Pitmire Weir and continue downstream through a landscape of rolling fields, valley sides, lush meadows on the valley floor, and patches of ancient woodland. Portage again at Lamarsh Weir then, as the river approaches Bures, pass under the B1508 bridge, with the medieval church on the left making a characterful landmark. To the right, a landing spot in the parkland provides an easy exit, or continue a little further to exit on the left if parked in Wharf Lane. The village of Bures, nestled along the riverbanks, is a peaceful place to end the journey for a car shuttle or rail return to Sudbury •

• **DISTANCE:** 11 km one way; car or train return.

• **PADDLING ENVIRONMENT:** 2.

• **ROUTE MAP:** islandeering.com/paddleboarding-sudbury-to-bures/

• **ACCESS RESTRICTIONS:** Licence required, included in Paddle UK membership.

• **OS MAP:** OS Explorer 196 Sudbury, Hadleigh & Dedham Vale.

• **STARTING POINT:** *Sudbury* Riverside at end of Quay Road parking, grid ref. TL 872 407; What3Words birthdays.impulses.obliging; *Bures* Riverside in front of the Community Centre parking or, if arriving by train, the riverbank adjacent to the green space off Bridge Street south of the B1508 bridge, grid ref. TL 906 339; What3Words erupt.newer.indirect.

• **PARKING:** *Sudbury* End of Quay Lane, Sudbury, CO10 2AN. Grid ref. TL 871 407; What3Words dairy.wealth.passports; *Bures* Bures Community Centre (free), Nayland Road, Bures, CO8 5BX. Grid ref. TL 908 339; What3Words types.prancing.flotation.

• **LAUNCHING:** *Sudbury* Footpath at south end of Quay Road, turn L, walk over bridge then turn R under trees to follow east bank of small tributary and pontoon; *Bures* Short walk across sports field from Community Centre parking to river.

• **PITSTOPS:** Pub grub and local ales, Eight Bells, Bures, tel. 01787 227354; very popular gastropub on riverside, The Henny Swan, Henny Street, tel. 01787 267953.

• **HIRE AND TOURS:** The Paddle Company, The Henny Swan, tel. 07508 420104.

• **GETTING THERE:** *Car* Once in Sudbury, look out for the brown theatre mask signs to find Quay Lane parking next to the Quay Theatre; *Rail* Bures and Sudbury have rail stations close to the river, with regular services from London Liverpool Street, greateranglia.co.uk

• **SPECIAL POINTS:** One lock and three weirs to portage on this trip. Check local river conditions before the trip at Sudbury riverlevels.uk/flood-warning-river-stour-from-sudbury. Summer weed growth can choke quieter parts of the river.

77

RIVER CAM GRANTCHESTER AND THE BACKS

RIVER · CAMBRIDGESHIRE

From Lammas Land, there are options either to explore the famous colleges of the Backs, to drift through beautiful Grantchester meadows to its historic tearoom, or to combine both into a longer trip. To explore the Backs, launch at Lammas Land, a large green space in the heart of Cambridge, and turn left (downstream), passing the trees and open parkland. Head under The Fen Causeway, followed by Crusoe Bridge and Robinson Crusoe Island, almost invisible as it runs alongside Coe Fen.

Portage around Scudamore's punting station by exiting the river opposite the Graduate Hotel and using the rollers to re-enter near Darwin College's balconied library. Stay left and pass under Silver Street Bridge. Continue past Queen's College and its iconic Mathematical Bridge, originally designed without nails. The river then flows under King's College Bridge, with the majestic Gothic spires of King's College Chapel rising on the right, dominating the skyline and providing an impressive backdrop as the journey continues.

Next, Clare College's elegant stone bridge – the oldest on the river – comes into view, with the college's lush gardens stretching to the water's edge. Following this is Trinity Hall, known for its peaceful riverside lawns, leading to the grandeur of Trinity College. From the river, you can spot Trinity's Wren Library, an architectural gem housing rare books. Further along, St John's College appears, starting with Kitchen Bridge and then the stunning Bridge of Sighs, a covered structure reminiscent of its Venetian counterpart. The expansive grounds and ornate buildings of St John's evoke a regal, timeless atmosphere.

Under Bridge Street lies Magdalene College, the last college along this stretch. Its charming historic brick buildings sit close to the riverbank, offering a quieter, more modest contrast to its grander neighbours. The turning point is near Jesus Green Lock, with the return journey providing a different perspective on the colleges.

Alternatively, paddle upstream to Grantchester by heading right (upstream) from Lammas Land. After approximately 2.8 km, the cricket pitch appears on the right; in its far corner is the entrance to the Orchard Tea Garden, a historic spot that's been serving visitors since 1897. This peaceful garden, once frequented by notable figures like Virginia Woolf and Rupert Brooke, offers a serene setting beneath apple trees. Traditional cream teas with freshly baked scones, clotted cream, and jam can be enjoyed before returning to the river and Lammas Land •

- **DISTANCE:** 5.6km return to Grantchester; 4km return to The Backs.
- **PADDLING ENVIRONMENT:** 2.
- **ROUTE MAP:** islandeering.com/paddleboarding-cambridge-backs-and-grantchester/
- **ACCESS RESTRICTIONS:** Licence required, included in Paddle UK Membership. Otherwise purchase a licence from Conservators of the River Cam (must have own third-party insurance). All vessels must have their unique registration number clearly displayed.
- **OS MAP:** OS Explorer 209 Cambridge.
- **STARTING POINT:** Lammas Land, grid ref. TL 447 573; What3Words pack.that.slide.
- **PARKING:** Lammas Land car park (charges), Driftway, Cambridge, CB3 9PA. Grid ref. TL 446 573; What3Words ties.stages.slot.
- **LAUNCHING:** 200m walk, leave via the north exit of the car park and cross bridge over narrow tributary to reach the main River Cam. Plenty of launch options on either bank.
- **PITSTOPS:** A Cambridge classic for cake and tea, The Orchard Tea Garden, Grantchester, 01223 840230; watch the punting antics with a riverside pint, The Anchor, Silver Street, tel. 01223 353554.
- **LESSONS AND TOURS:** SUP Cambridge, tel. 07790 776541.
- **GETTING THERE:** *Car* M11 exit 12 onto A603 towards Cambridge; continue for 2.5 km, at sharp left bend turn R onto Driftway, then car park on R; *Train* Regular services to Cambridge from London Kings Cross greatnorthernrail.com , 2km walk to Lammas Land.
- **SPECIAL POINTS:** The River Cam is extremely popular with punters of all levels of experience so The Backs are best paddled early morning to avoid the crowds. Check water levels before you paddle at Cambridge Jesus Lock riverlevels.uk/river-cam-cambridge-cambridge-jesus-lock

78

RIVER GREAT OUSE HOUGHTON MILL AND COOK'S STREAM LOOP

RIVER · CAMBRIDGESHIRE

From a historic flour mill through the tranquil countryside of the Ouse Valley, exploring one of the Great Ouse's quiet backwaters. Launch upstream of Houghton Mill Lock, close to the idyllic setting of the National Trust's Houghton Mill, a historic watermill nestled on the banks of the River Great Ouse. Paddle past Hemingford Meadow, an expansive grassland that lines the river, offering stunning views of the surrounding countryside.

Continue along the river, keeping an eye out for Wyton Marina on the right and a weir on the left. Pass Hartford Marina and on the left is the entrance to Cook's Stream, which will be used later for the return journey. For now, follow the main river towards the historic town of Huntingdon. As Huntingdon approaches, pass the scenic All Saints' Church and Riverside Park. Shortly after, go under the stone road bridge and the Godmanchester footbridge, with Riverside Mill's impressive buildings enhancing the historic atmosphere. After the A1307 road bridge, take the left fork to follow the main navigation channel. Stay close to the left bank, passing Huntingdon Boathaven marina, and then take the left fork into the narrower Cook's Stream. This peaceful waterway meanders through open countryside, offering a slower pace. Pass under the B1044 and A1307 bridges as traffic sounds fade into the quiet of Westside Common.

Cook's Stream reconnects with the River Great Ouse in front of Hartford Marina. From here, complete the loop, enjoying the final stretch back to Houghton Mill for refreshments •

• **DISTANCE:** 9.5km return.

• **PADDLING ENVIRONMENT:** 2.

• **ROUTE MAP:** islandeering.com/paddleboarding-houghton-mill-and-cooks-stream/

• **ACCESS RESTRICTIONS:** Licence required, included in Paddle UK membership.

• **OS MAP:** OS Explorer 208 Bedford & St Neots.

• **STARTING POINT:** Upstream of Houghton Mill Lock, grid ref. TL 280 719; What3Words acrobat.marketing.garden.

• **PARKING:** Houghton Mill (NT members free; 3 hours max.), Mill Street, Houghton, PE28 2AZ. Grid ref. TL 282 720; What3Words chosen.inherits.printer; or roadside parking in Houghton village.

• **LAUNCHING:** From Houghton Mill car park walk underneath the walkway through the mill across the river from the car park. Pass Houghton Boats and follow the path round to Houghton Mill Lock. Launch just in front of the boat rollers.

• **PITSTOPS:** Perfect scones and more, Houghton Mill Café (National Trust), 01480 301494; good food and beer, Three Jolly Butchers, Houghton, tel. 01480 463228; excellent village café, Houghton Tea Rooms, tel. 07894 950151.

• **CAMPING:** Excellent waterside camping, Waterclose Meadows Campsite, Houghton Mill, PE28 2AZ nationaltrust.org.uk/holidays/cambridgeshire/waterclose-meadows-campsite

• **HIRE:** Canoe hire, Houghton Boats, tel. 07759 316260.

• **GETTING THERE:** J14 A1(M) onto A1307, then A141 to Huntingdon; onto A1123, then turn R to Houghton, following the National Trust signs to the car park.

• **SPECIAL POINTS:** Check local conditions before you paddle at Hemmingford riverlevels.uk/river-ouse-hemingford-grey-hemingford; Cook's Stream can get choked with floating weed in mid-summer, making progress slow.

79

RIVER LARK EXPLORER

RIVER · CAMBRIDGESHIRE

Paddling the River Lark offers a peaceful journey through flat fenland landscapes where wildlife thrives and centuries of drainage work have transformed marshy land into fertile farmland. Two routes from Isleham take paddlers through this secluded waterway, each offering a glimpse into the area's history.

The first route heads upstream to Judes Ferry, a historic riverside pub. Launch from Isleham Marina, paddle north and then turn right onto the main river, immediately portaging the lock to its left. This peaceful stretch of the original river offers open countryside views, making Judes Ferry an ideal rest stop before the return trip.

Alternatively, paddle downstream to Prickwillow, a village tied to the transformation of the Fens and offering a unique opportunity to explore the region's engineering history. Starting from Isleham, turn left at the River Lark and follow the fairly straight Roman-era artificial cut, with numerous pumping stations lining the route. Just as you reach Prickwillow, the Prickwillow Engine Museum provides a fascinating look at the steam and diesel engines that drained the Fens and reshaped the land. Egress on the left before the B1382 road bridge to visit the museum, then enjoy a leisurely return to Isleham •

• **DISTANCE:** Isleham to Judes Ferry 8km return; Isleham to Prickwillow 18km return.

• **PADDLING ENVIRONMENT:** 2.

• **ROUTE MAP:** islandeering.com/paddleboarding-river-lark/

• **ACCESS RESTRICTIONS:** Licence required, included in Paddle UK membership (or Environment Agency licence).

• **OS MAP:** OS Explorer 226 Ely & Newmarket.

• **STARTING POINT:** Riverbank at Isleham Marina (see parking).

• **PARKING:** Lay-by just outside of Riverside Island Marina, Isleham, CB7 5SL. Grid ref. TL 648 757; What3Words fists.tone.vent.

• **LAUNCHING:** Use the slipway across the lane from parking.

• **PITSTOPS:** Good food and lovely riverside location, Judes Ferry, West Row, tel. 01638 354595; hot and cold drinks, light snacks and ice cream, Prickwillow Engine Museum café, tel. 01353 688360; friendly pub great roasts, The Rising Sun, Isleham, tel. 01638 780471.

• **CAMPING:** Rustic and peaceful, Karma Farm Eco Campsite, Isleham, tel. 07900 961217.

• **GETTING THERE:** B1104 to Isleham village. Turn L at Griffin pub onto Church Street, then after church turn L onto Sun Street. Turn L onto Waterside/Fen Bank then R to the entrance of Riverside Island Marina with parking on right before bridge.

• **SPECIAL POINTS:** This paddle is exposed to the wind so check conditions at Prickwillow before you start at metoffice.gov.uk

80

REACH TO WICKEN FEN

RIVER · CAMBRIDGESHIRE

Navigate two unique Cambridgeshire Lodes to reach the National Trust's oldest nature reserve and England's most famous Fen. Start in the village of Reach, once a thriving medieval port. Launch and head right along the small tributary, then merge onto the main Lode. The unique experience here is floating above the fields, as the fens have dried out and sunk over time. After 3.5km, the Burwell Lode joins from the right – stay left to pass through Adventurers' Fen. Continue for 600m before turning right onto Wicken Lode. Alternatively, as a detour, continue straight on Reach Lode to Reach Lode Lock, then keep right for a stop at the Five Miles From Anywhere No Hurry Inn at Upware.

Continue under the footbridge and along Wicken Lode. After 1.9 km the river forks, with Monk Lode joining from the right. Egress at the clearing in the reeds between the two forks. Avoid landing on the pontoon on the left fork, as it is reserved for National Trust boat trips, and don't paddle up the left fork, as it is closed to paddlers. A short walk northeast will take you to the Wicken Fen visitor centre and café. Return the same way to Reach and enjoy its hidden gem of a pub overlooking the village green •

- **DISTANCE:** 12km return.
- **PADDLING ENVIRONMENT:** 2.
- **ROUTE MAP:** islandeering.com/paddleboarding-wicken-fen/
- **ACCESS RESTRICTIONS:** Licence required, included in Paddle UK membership (or Environmental Agency Licence required).
- **OS MAP:** OS Explorer 226 Ely & Newmarket.
- **STARTING POINT:** Head of navigation on Reach Lode, The Hythe, Reach. Grid ref. TL 565 664; What3Words jogged.qualifier.jacket.
- **PARKING:** Roadside, The Hythe, Reach, CB25 0JQ. Grid ref. TL 565 662; What3Words revision.torches.stiffly.

LAUNCHING: Short walk from parking on The Hythe to riverbank adjacent to pumping station.

- **PITSTOPS:** Great beer and food in friendly local pub, The Dyke's End, Reach, tel. 01638 743816; Docky Hutt café, Wicken Fen, tel. 01353 720274; riverside garden, Five Miles From Anywhere No Hurry Inn, Upware, tel. 01353 721654.
- **GETTING THERE:** Leave A14 Cambridge to Newmarket at J35; B1102 to Swaffham Prior then left onto minor road, following signs to Upware. Continue through Reach village and at far end, where road rounds a tight left bend, continue ahead onto The Hythe.
- **SPECIAL POINTS:** Check wind conditions on metoffice.gov.uk at Reach as this paddle can be exposed to wind.

Go Explore GT

DYKE'S END
Free House

81

GRAND UNION CANAL KINGS LANGLEY TO BATCHWORTH

CANAL · HERTFORDSHIRE

Explore a peaceful stretch of the Grand Union Canal, where historic locks, a hidden waterfall, and lush parklands run alongside the River Gade. In this scenic section, the canal and river often intertwine, with the canal following the natural course of the Gade in places. This area is known as The Three Rivers (after the Chess, Colne, and Gade rivers) and is home to charming towns like Rickmansworth and Croxley Green. Here, wide green spaces and historic sites reflect the region's industrial heritage, including milling and paper production.

Launch at Kings Langley and turn right (south). Soon, paddle beneath the M25 Gade Valley Viaduct to enter a quiet stretch where the canal runs alongside the River Gade, bordered by green fields. Further along, pass under Hunton Bridge (Bridge 162). From here, a short walk along Bridge Road leads to the charming Kings Head pub.

Ahead of the A41 bridge, the South West Herts Narrowboat Trust appears on the left, offering a glimpse into the area's boating history. Further along is the historic Lady Capel's Lock (74), named after a 17th-century aristocrat with local connections. The route continues past the parklands of The Grove Hotel, once home to the Earl of Clarendon, and Clarendon Park Farm on the right. Paddling under the graceful span of Grove Bridge and Grove Mill Lane, the canal flows into a wooded section just before reaching Cassiobury Park, a vast public green space with history dating back to the Saxon era.

A series of moorings leads to Batchworth Lock, where the River Chess meets the canal near the Batchworth Lock Canal Centre and cafés. Exit here for a short walk to the nearby rail station, or continue a bit further to reach Rickmansworth Aquadrome, a convenient spot to end the trip and collect the car shuttle •

• **DISTANCE:** 11km one way; car or train return.

• **PADDLING ENVIRONMENT:** 1.

• **ROUTE MAP:** islandeering.com/paddleboarding-kings-langley-to-batchworth/

• **ACCESS RESTRICTIONS:** Licence required, included in UK Paddle membership.

• **OS MAP:** OS Explorer 182 St Albans & Hatfield.

• **STARTING POINT:** Canalside adjacent to parking in Kings Langley.

• **PARKING:** *Start* Lay-by, Home Park Mill Link Road, Kings Langley, WD4 8DZ. Grid ref. TL 076 019; What3Words rungs.harsh.tubes. *Finish* Rickmansworth Aquadrome car park (free), Frogmoor Lane, Batchworth, WD3 1NB. Grid ref. TQ 056 937; What3Words baked.shower.repair.

• **LAUNCHING:** Canalside.

• **PITSTOPS:** Historic pub, Kings Head, Hunton Bridge, tel. 01923 262307; sandwiches and home-made cake, Cafe @ Lock 81, Batchworth Lock, tel. 07548 747636.

• **GETTING THERE:** *Car* J20 off M25 and second exit at roundabout onto A4251 towards Kings Langley; then second exit at next roundabout towards Home Park Industrial Estate on Home Park Mill Lane. Parking lay-by on R before canal bridge; *Rail* Kings Langley rail station, 350m walk to canal; Rickmansworth tube station, 900m walk to Batchworth Lock Canal Centre.

• **SPECIAL POINTS:** 11 locks to portage.

82

GRAND UNION CANAL RICKMANSWORTH TO HAREFIELD

CANAL · HERTFORDSHIRE

Discover a stretch of canal that passes by wildlife-rich lakes and quirky landmarks, with plenty of pub and café stops along the way. Launch onto the canal, head right, and you soon reach Stocker Lock Cottage. Just beyond, the canal runs alongside Stocker's Lake Nature Reserve, home to a large variety of wintering birds like the striking goldeneye and smew, which can sometimes be seen through the trees. On the left, spot the eerie abandoned Harefield Limeworks, known for its giant toy monkey hanging from a hoist at the top, along with a bear in a kayak.

After passing the scenic Springwell Lock, the canal is bordered by Springwell Lake and Springwell Reed Bed on the right, a protected habitat full of wildlife. Shortly after, the River Colne joins the canal from the right, subtly changing the water's flow. A brief change in surroundings happens as you pass the nearby sewage works, but this is quickly replaced by pleasant views of the lovely gardens of the houses that line the canal.

After Copper Mill Lock, stop at the Coy Carp, a popular canalside pub in a converted 19th-century mill, for refreshments. Returning to Rickmansworth Aquadrome, paddle a short distance further to Batchworth Lock, where a café beside the lock offers a well-deserved treat to end the journey.

It is also possible to extend the trip 7km further south of the Coy Carp pub to Uxbridge •

- **DISTANCE:** 7km return.
- **PADDLING ENVIRONMENT:** 1.
- **ROUTE MAP:** islandeering.com/paddleboarding-rickmansworth-to-harefield/
- **ACCESS RESTRICTIONS:** Licence required, included in Paddle UK membership.
- **OS MAP:** OS Explorer 172 Chiltern Hills East.
- **STARTING POINT:** Canal adjacent to car park.
- **PARKING:** Rickmansworth Aquadrome car park (free), Frogmoor Lane, Batchworth, WD3 1NB. Grid ref. TQ 056 937; What3Words baked.shower.repair.
- **LAUNCHING:** Canalside adjacent to car park.
- **PITSTOPS:** Good food and canalside gardens, Coy Carp, tel. 01895 821471; sandwiches and home-made cake, Cafe @ Lock 81, Batchworth Lock, tel. 07548 747636.
- **GETTING THERE:** *Car* M25 J17 onto A412; first exit at roundabout, following brown signs to Aquadrome; fourth exit at Ebury Roundabout onto A404 towards London, then at the Moor Lane roundabout take the fifth exit to return along the opposite carriageway of the A404. Turn L at The White Bear along Harefield Road, then turn R into Frogmore Lane to car park on L; *Train* Rickmansworth tube station, 900m walk from Batchworth Lock Canal Centre.
- **SPECIAL POINTS:** Four locks to portage (two each way).

COY
CARP
INN

83

GRAND UNION CANAL COW ROAST TO LITTLE TRING VIA THE WENDOVER ARM

CANAL · HERTFORDSHIRE

Enjoy a peaceful paddle along a quiet stretch of the canal that takes in lush countryside, ancient mills, and historic locks, then meanders along the Wendover Arm, showcasing both industrial history and thriving natural beauty.

Head north from Cowroast Lock past a patchwork of farmland for 2km to reach Station Road Bridge in Tring, which marks an alternative starting point for those arriving by train. Continue through the peaceful woods and hedgerows that frame the canal's banks to the Bulbourne Road Bridge and the welcoming sight of The Grand Junction Arms. Once a key stop for barge workers in its 19th-century heyday, the pub now offers a peaceful spot to rest, its terrace overlooking the water and the historic buildings of Bulbourne Yard, a complex of canal lock workshops that once serviced the canal.

Just beyond, Marsworth Lock 45 marks the key point where the Grand Union Canal meets the Wendover Arm, once vital for maintaining water levels by channelling water from the Chiltern Hills. Before reaching the lock, turn left under the footbridge onto the Wendover Arm, where the canal narrows and the banks are lush with wildflowers and reeds. The clear waters attract kingfishers and herons, while perch and roach thrive beneath the surface. Built in 1797, this branch has been carefully restored and now flourishes as a peaceful sanctuary for wildlife.

Passing beneath Tringford Road bridge, the imposing Tringford Mill rises on the left. Built to harness the power of water, the mill is now known as Heygates Flour Mill and still mills wheat today. Beyond the mill, the canal traces a path through open countryside. To the right, the red-brick structure of Tringford Pumping Station is still operational, quietly regulating water levels in the canal. Built in the 19th century, this pumping station drew water from nearby reservoirs, playing a key role in maintaining the water supply to the Grand Union.

After passing beneath Little Tring Road, the canal takes a sharp bend to the right, almost folding back on itself in the final stretch of the restored Wendover Arm. The canal ends in a quiet reed-lined basin, a tranquil spot to reflect before returning the same way •

• **DISTANCE:** 14km return from Cow Roast; 9.6km return from Tring.

• **PADDLING ENVIRONMENT:** 1.

• **ROUTE MAP:** islandeering.com/paddleboarding-cow-roast-to-little-tring/

• **ACCESS RESTRICTIONS:** Licence required, included in Paddle UK membership.

• **OS MAP:** OS Explorer 181 Chiltern Hills North.

• **STARTING POINT:** Cowroast Lock, Wharf Lane, Cow Roast, HP23 5RG. Grid ref. SP 958 103; What3Words duties.truck.hears.

• **PARKING:** Wharf Lane beyond the canal bridge, free roadside parking on left.

• **LAUNCHING:** Cowroast Lock, short walk from parking.

• **PITSTOPS:** Fish and chips in the canalside garden, The Grand Junction Arms, tel. 01442 824159.

• **GETTING THERE:** *Car* From Tring take the A4251 southeast towards Berkhamsted; at the derelict Cow Roast Inn turn L into Wharf Lane just before garage; *Train* Regular services from London Euston to Tring, a short walk from the canal.

• **SPECIAL POINTS:** No locks to portage on this trip.

84

STORT NAVIGATION

RIVER · HERTFORDSHIRE

A rural journey through ancient parkland and peaceful meadows, this trip provides a quiet escape from North London's urban sprawl. With several rail stations along the route, paddlers can easily adjust the trip length, enjoying pub stops along the way. The River Stort Navigation stretches for 22.5 kilometres through the Hertfordshire countryside, connecting Bishop's Stortford to the River Lee Navigation near Harlow. In the 18th century it was an important route for transporting grain, malt, and other goods, with the river straightened and widened for barges. Today, it's a peaceful spot, ideal for a relaxing paddle.

Launch at Sawbridgeworth and head right, passing Maltings Antiques, a converted mill rich in industrial history. Soon after, portage around Sheering Mill Lock and go beneath Sheering Mill Lane, where open fields and wooded stretches now line the river. After passing through Feakes Lock, the river meanders towards Rowenbury House on the right – the former home of the Beckhams is famously nicknamed "Beckingham Palace". Continue paddling under Harlow Road (A1184) to reach Harlow Mill Lock, where the old mill has been transformed into a pub.

The river twists and turns as it skirts the northern edge of Harlow, with wooded banks offering pleasant shade. At Latton Island, the river forks; keep right to avoid the small weir and portage over Latton Lock. Walk across its gates to visit Redchurch Brewery,

• **DISTANCE:** From Sawbridgeworth to Harlow Town 7km one way; to Roydon 11.8km one way; to Rye House station 15km one way – all with rail return.

• **PADDLING ENVIRONMENT:** 2.

• **ROUTE MAP:** islandeering.com/paddleboarding-stort-navigation/

• **ACCESS RESTRICTIONS:** Licence required, included with Paddle UK membership.

• **OS MAP:** OS Explorer 194 Hertford & Bishop's Stortford and OS Explorer 174 Epping Forest & Lee Valley.

• **STARTING POINT:** West riverbank north of road bridge, off Station Road, Sawbridgeworth, CM21 9JY; Grid ref. TL 488 149; What3Words hurls.ranges.filled.

• **PARKING:** Sawbridgeworth rail station (charges); or free roadside parking on nearby Leat Close, off Station Road, CM21 9LZ. Grid ref. TL 485 151; What3Words logs.violin.reform.

• **LAUNCHING:** Leave station car park, turn left to walk 200m along RHS of Station Road over bridge, then to the end of the fence line; launch on riverbank beyond the bench.

• **PITSTOPS:** Breakfast and great sandwiches, Shed Coffee House, Sawbridgeworth, 01279 723853; well-cooked pub fare, Harlow Mill Beefeater, Harlow Mill, tel. 01279 217535; brewery bar and taproom (Sat pm) and shop (Mon–Sat), Redchurch Brewery, tel. 01279 626895; good value food and riverside garden, Moorhen pub, Moorhen Marina, tel. 01279 423066; real ales and pub grub in old-world style pub with riverside garden, Rye House just over bridge, tel, 01992 465151.

• **GETTING THERE:** *Train* Regular trains from London Liverpool Street to Sawbridgeworth and several other stations along this paddle route, greateranglia.co.uk

• **SPECIAL POINTS:** Seven locks to portage to Rye House. Check local water levels at Bishops Stortford before the trip at riverlevels.uk/flood-warning-river-stort-at-bishops-stortford

hidden gem for craft beer lovers. Back on the ver, pass Moorhen Marina on the right, where the 1oorhen pub is a good spot for a waterside meal. On ne left, Harlow Town rail station offers a convenient xit for those wanting a shorter paddle.

To continue onward, paddle through Burnt Mill ock, under the road bridge, and beneath Burnt 1ill Bridge (A414). The landscape opens up with iver Park on the left and Parndon Lock Meadows n the right. Pass Parndon Mill, a former watermill ow converted into an arts centre, before reaching arndon Lock. Beyond, fields stretch toward unsdon Lock; the river here feels more remote, vinding through beautiful countryside. The oute passes through the ancient hay meadows f Hunsdon Mead Nature Reserve, vibrant with wildflowers in spring and summer, before reconnecting with the main River Stort at Roydon Lock. The river sweeps into a wide left-hand bend beneath the railway line. Exit at the B181 road bridge if ending the trip at Roydon station.

For the onward trip to Rye House, paddle toward Roydon Marina Village, turn left under the bridge, and follow the river to Brick Lock. After passing Lower Lock, the banks become more wooded as the river curves toward the final stretch. Look out for Fieldes Weir on the left, where the River Stort joins the River Lee Navigation. Take a sharp right turn upstream into the River Lee Navigation. The final stretch passes Rye House Cartway on the right, with the historic Rye House nearby. Exit the river just before Rye Road bridge to reach Rye House station •

85

GREAT RIVER OUSE KEMPSTON TO GREAT BARFORD

RIVER · BEDFORDSHIRE

Part of one of England's longest rivers, this stretch provides a peaceful rural escape, winding through Bedford's historic waterfront and passing ancient meadows, quiet villages, and charming locks, all the way to a popular riverside pub.

Launch from Kempston and follow the river to the right as it meanders between wooded banks and fields. The peaceful start gives way to the outskirts of Bedford. Paddle beneath two adjacent railway bridges, followed by a third rail bridge, before passing under the A5141 on the approach to Bedford town.

Keep right to steer clear of the rowing clubs that frequent this part of the river. After passing under the A600 bridge, the left bank opens up to The Embankment, a popular stretch of riverside parkland known for its Victorian architecture and leafy avenues. When the river splits around an island, avoid the right fork under Abbey Bridge for now. Instead, continue straight for about 10 metres, then portage right at Bedford Lock. Walk along the lock's western side and re-enter the river, joining the right fork to continue the journey.

Continue under Longholme Bridge and the Iron Bridge, then pass beneath a concrete walkway. On the right, Fenlake Meadows, a nature reserve that's home to wildfowl, otters, and dragonflies, comes into view.

- **DISTANCE:** From Kempston Mill 16km one way; from Bedford 11km one way.
- **PADDLING ENVIRONMENT:** 2.
- **ROUTE MAP:** islandeering.com/paddleboarding-kemptston-to-great-barford/
- **ACCESS RESTRICTIONS:** Licence required, included in Paddle UK membership.
- **OS MAP:** OS Explorer 208 Bedford & St Neots.
- **STARTING POINT:** Kempston Mill adjacent to car park.
- **EGRESS:** Riverside in front of the Anchor Inn (50m walk to parking).
- **PARKING:** *Kempston* Kempston Mill car park (free), Riverview Way, Kempston, Bedford, MK42 7FB. Grid ref. TL 023 476; What3Words vanished.loafing.blemishes; *Great Barford* Roadside parking along New Road, Great Barford, Bedford, MK44 3LF. Grid ref. TL 134 517; What3Words retina.springing.feed.
- **LAUNCHING:** Riverside adjacent to car park.
- **PITSTOPS:** Café in Norwegian log cabin with riverside garden, Danish Camp, Willington (not open Mon, Tues, or Fri morning), tel. 01234 838709; real ales in historic pub, Anchor Inn, Great Barford, tel. 01234 870364.
- **LESSONS, HIRE AND TOURS:** Canoe Trail Bedford, tel. 07934 861692.
- **GETTING THERE:** Northampton/Kempston junction off A421 south of Bedford onto A6; third exit at roundabout onto Ridge Road towards Kempston; turn L onto King William Road before King William pub; L onto Riverview Way; then L onto Mill Lane and car park at end of lane.
- **SPECIAL POINTS:** Four locks to portage on this trip. Check local river conditions at Bedford, riverlevels.uk/river-ouse-bedford

On the left is the entrance to Priory Country Park and Marina. After a gentle left bend, the river flows past the gates of the Cardington Canoe Slalom Course, a popular training spot, with Cardington Lock just ahead on the left. This lock marks the start of a quieter, more rural section. Portage in front of the lock and continue below it, skirting Bedford's eastern edge. Pass under a bridge where the New Cut joins from the left, and the river starts to weave between former gravel pits now transformed into lakes that are havens for birds.

At Castle Mill Lock, portage to the right, then pass beneath the busy A421. The river takes larger sweeping bends as it approaches Danish Camp near Willington (about 13km in), a riverside café and heritage site on an old Viking settlement. It's a perfect spot for refreshments with great views of the river and countryside.

A little further along, pass through Willington Lock (portage on the right), then continue on the final stretch to Great Barford. The beautiful Great Barford Bridge signals the exit, right in front of the popular Anchor Inn. This riverside area is a favourite spot for locals and paddlers, especially on busy summer days.

For a shorter trip, the route can begin at Bedford, near the Mill Meadows car park •

86

RIVER IVEL BIGGLESWADE TO TEMPSFORD

RIVER · BEDFORDSHIRE

A true hidden gem, teeming with chub, barbel, and kingfishers. The river winds through Biggleswade's industrial edges to reach open fields and wildlife-rich nature reserves before joining the River Great Ouse at Tempsford.

Start from the grassy area near Mill Lane and take the right stream downstream. It may be overgrown, but it's passable. Pass through Biggleswade's industrial and residential areas, with open fields on the left, then under the busy A6001, followed by a sports ground and peaceful open fields.

The river widens as it meanders through Biggleswade Common, past fishing lakes and Warren Villas Nature Reserve – former gravel pits now full of life. Look out for large chub in the clear waters. The flat Bedfordshire landscape is slightly broken by a low wooded hill on the right, marking the headquarters of the RSPB at Sandy.

After passing beneath New Road, portage to the left just before reaching the weir. Walk over the stile to rejoin the river below. Paddle alongside the peaceful fields, continuing through The Riddy Nature Reserve, then beneath the A1 and the A603. The wildflower-filled riverbanks then lead to the weir at South Mills. Portage to the left before the railings and re-enter downstream at a convenient spot.

As the river narrows, it reaches Blunham's village weir. Portage on the left just before the metal railings, and re-enter the river on the gently sloping bank, overlooked by the Norman tower of St Edmund or St James Church. Moving north, the river splits; take the right-hand spur through a narrow channel over a gentle riffle, passing by old stone walls that mark a former navigation channel or bridge.

Once under the Tempsford Road bridge, the river begins to widen again, leading to Church End weir. Portage to the left before the metal railings and re-enter below the weir via the old cattle ford. The stream starts to quicken as it nears its confluence with the River Great Ouse. After crossing Church End Farm's animal bridge and the ford, the river runs straight into the Great Ouse. Paddle a short distance downstream to a footbridge and exit to the right using metal steps that lead to the footpath. From there, head towards the (now closed) Anchor Inn at Tempsford and back to the A1. Cross the footbridge and continue onto Station Road to reach your shuttle car or bus •

- **DISTANCE:** 13km one way.
- **PADDLING ENVIRONMENT:** 2.
- **ROUTE MAP:** islandeering.com/paddleboarding-biggleswade-to-tempsford/
- **ACCESS RESTRICTIONS:** No licence required.
- **OS MAP:** OS Explorer 208 Bedford & St Neots.
- **STARTING POINT:** Mill Lane, Biggleswade, SG18 8AZ. Grid ref. TL 187 444; What3Words touches.immediate.explained.
- **EGRESS:** Steps on riverbank to footpath that leads onto A1. Grid ref. TL 161 541; What3Words birds.ditching.rocker.
- **PARKING:** *Biggleswade* Mill Lane Car Park, St Andrew's Street, Biggleswade, SG18 8BB. Grid ref. TL 188 444; What3Words cheat.symphonic.name; *Tempsford* Free on-road parking, Station Road, Tempsford, SG19 2AU. Grid ref. TL 164 538; What3Words anyway.daydream.assist.
- **LAUNCHING:** Riverside in small park on RHS of Mill Lane, short walk from car park.
- **PITSTOPS:** Cooked breakfast, hot baps and more, Farmers Grill, Knotts of Tempsford, Station Road, Tempsford (check opening times), tel. 01767 669376.
- **GETTING THERE:** Regular hail-and-ride service between Tempsford and Biggleswade on bus No. 4, The Ivel Sprinter, from Station Road, Tempsford, ivelsprinter.org.uk/services.html
- **SPECIAL POINTS:** This river is popular for fishing, especially on Sundays during the coarse fishing season, so fishermen may occupy the areas you need for portaging. To avoid issues with summer weed growth, use river fins. When portaging around the three weirs, a 3m tape and karabiner can help you pull your board onto the bank or over railings. Many weirs have EA portage signs, so don't let anyone claim it's private land, but be sure to respect other water users. During low water levels, you may need to carry your board over the concrete lip at the ford near Church End Farm. For current river conditions, check Biggleswade's river levels at riverlevels.uk/river-ivel-biggleswade

87

BROGBOROUGH LAKE

LAKE · BEDFORDSHIRE

A friendly watersports hub, this lovely spot is just a short distance from Milton Keynes and Bedford. The private lake, originally clay pits used by the London Brick Company, filled naturally with water after the pits were exhausted. Though primarily focused on watersports, it has also evolved into a semi-wild habitat attracting wildlife like herons, swans, and ducks. The reed beds around the lake provide a safe haven for smaller species such as amphibians and insects. Surrounded by lush greenery, it offers a peaceful and scenic spot for a paddle •

• **DISTANCE:** Free-range.

• **PADDLING ENVIRONMENT:** 1.

• **ROUTE MAP:** islandeering.com/paddleboarding-brogborough-lake/

• **ACCESS RESTRICTIONS:** Self-launch, pre-book with Brogborough Watersports (£15/day).

• **OS MAP:** OS Explorer 193 Luton & Stevenage.

• **PARKING:** Brogborough Lake (free), Thrupp End Station Road, Lidlington, Bedford, MK43 0SL. Grid ref. SP 982 398. What3Words clinic.train.airbase.

• **LESSONS AND HIRE:** Brogborough Watersports, tel. 07999 652021, www.broglake.co.uk

• **PITSTOPS:** Great breakfasts and lunches, and treats galore, Just Baked with The Little Brownie Company (check times) facebook.com/thelittlebrowniecompany/?locale=en_GB

• **GETTING THERE:** J13 off M1; follow signs for Woburn, then Brogborough on Bedford Road. Turn R onto Thrupp End towards Lidlington; lake on R.

• **SPECIAL POINTS:** Please clean your board before you enter the water to prevent spread of non-native plants and animal species.

88

GRAND UNION CANAL WOLVERTON TO THRUPP WHARF

CANAL · BUCKINGHAMSHIRE

Blending industrial heritage with peaceful countryside views, this route passes through historic landmarks like the Iron Trunk Aqueduct and finishes at the Navigation Inn at Thrupp. Start at Wolverton, a town known for its key role in 19th-century railway development, particularly in building carriages for the British Royal Train, including for Queen Victoria and King Edward VII. Although much of the original railway works has been redeveloped, traces of this industrial past can still be seen along the canal. Launch from The Secret Garden, a community-created green space near the canal, and head left under the road and rail bridges. This section passes through an industrial area and beneath Old Wolverton Road, with The Galleon pub on the left and Ouse Valley Car Park (which also serves as an alternative starting point) on the right.

As the route transitions from urban to rural scenery, the Iron Trunk Aqueduct comes into view – a striking cast iron structure built in 1811. Standing nearly 11 metres high and 95 metres long, it carries the canal over the River Great Ouse. Continue along the straight stretch until you reach Cosgrove Lock, where the Old Stratford Cut joins from the left. There's a leisure park nearby with a café and shop – or, for a more historic stop, visit The Barley Mow pub via a horseshoe-shaped tunnel beneath the canal. Finally, pass under a road bridge to reach the Navigation Inn at Thrupp Wharf,

- **DISTANCE:** 9.6km return.
- **PADDLING ENVIRONMENT:** 1.
- **ROUTE MAP:** islandeering.com/paddleboarding-wolverton-to-thrupp-wharf/
- **ACCESS RESTRICTIONS:** Licence required, included in UK Paddle membership.
- **OS MAP:** OS Explorer 192 Buckingham & Milton Keynes.
- **STARTING POINT:** East bank of canal in The Secret Garden, Stratford Road, Wolverton. Grid ref. SP 820 413; What3Words worth.oasis.sometimes.
- **PARKING:** Wolverton Station Car Park (charges), Stratford Road, Wolverton, Milton Keynes, MK13 0DY. Grid ref. SP 820 414; What3Words toads.worked.neater.
- **LAUNCHING:** From rail station, turn R onto Stratford Road, cross railway bridge, take footpath L into Secret Garden. Launch canalside.
- **PITSTOPS:** Canalside pub with food, The Galleon, Wolverton, tel. 01908 314385; good food, The Barley Mow, Cosgrove, tel. 01908 562957; lovely canal views inside and out, The Navigation Inn, Thrupp Wharf, tel. 01908 926270.
- **GETTING THERE:** *Car* A5 to Milton Keynes, take exit towards Wolverton (A422); first exit at roundabout to Wolverton; straight over next two roundabouts, staying on V5 Great Monks St, then third exit at third roundabout onto Stratford Road to Wolverton station, follow rail signs to car park; *Train* Regular trains from London Euston to Wolverton, londonnorthwesternrailway.co.uk
- **SPECIAL POINTS:** Be mindful of other boat users, especially during peak times, and take care when crossing the Iron Trunk Aqueduct as there is no barrier on its west side.

89

RIVER THAMES MARLOW TO MAIDENHEAD

RIVER · BUCKINGHAMSHIRE

One of the most picturesque journeys along the Thames meanders past Cliveden House, charming riverside towns, steep wooded hills, open meadows, and several excellent riverside inns. Start the trip in Marlow, with its iconic William Tierney Clark suspension bridge, the cheerful sounds from the Compleat Angler Hotel, and the peaceful presence of All Saints Church. Head downstream towards Marlow Lock and Marlow Lock Island, portage around the lock cut, then continue past the bypass and Longridge Boating Centre. Soon, the steep wooded slopes of Quarry Wood come into view, featuring the castellated Quarry Wood Hall. This section of the Thames inspired Kenneth Grahame's *The Wind in the Willows*, with Quarry Wood portrayed as the "Wild Wood".

Woottens Boatyard sits opposite Gibraltar Islands at the base of Winter Hill. A quiet backwater to the right of the islands offers a peaceful paddling spot. Returning to the main river, wide flood meadows spread out on both sides. Around a large right-hand meander, the houses of Bourne End appear on the left, while the quirky and popular Bounty pub on the right makes for a perfect break.

Continue past grand riverside homes to Cookham, where the Ferry pub stands near Cookham Bridge. Beyond the bridge, the river splits into four channels – take the marked navigation channel, which is the left one of the two central channels, to the lock cut. After a portage, a peaceful detour upstream offers a chance to explore Hedsor Backwater along Sashes Island.

Further downstream, Cliveden Reach presents one of the Thames' most striking views. Towering chalk cliffs, covered in trees from around the world, rise above the river, crowned by the majestic Cliveden House and its golden tower. Land on the riverbank for a picnic or refreshments, with National Trust fees applying for further access to the grounds.

The journey ends at Boulters Lock, located a kilometre further downstream, where the right bank leads into the lock cut.

For a shorter trip, a popular option is to paddle from Boulters Lock to Cookham Lock, with a stop for refreshments at Cliveden •

- **DISTANCE:** 11km one way; car or rail return.
- **PADDLING ENVIRONMENT:** 2.
- **ROUTE MAP:** islandeering.com/marlow-to-maidenhead/
- **ACCESS RESTRICTIONS:** Licence required, included in Paddle UK membership.
- **OS MAP:** OS Explorer 172 Chiltern Hills East.
- **STARTING POINT:** Public slipway, St Peter Street, Marlow, SL7 1NQ; Grid ref. SU 852 861; What3Words peach.today.influencing.
- **EGRESS:** Boulters Lock, take right slip and land on concrete right bank.
- **PARKING:** *Marlow* Any public car park in Marlow; *Maidenhead* Boulters Lock Car Park, Lower Cookham Road, Maidenhead, SL6 8JN. Grid ref. SU 902 825; What3Words cable.take.oven.
- **LAUNCHING:** Drop kit off at slipway before parking.
- **PITSTOPS:** Lovely old pub, The Two Brewers, Marlow, tel. 01628 484140; quirky independent pub only accessible by river or foot, The Bounty, Bourne End, tel. 01628 520056; lovely riverside location and gastropub, The Ferry, Cookham, tel. 01628 525123; pop-up café and ice cream, Cliveden House riverside; good food and great views, The Boathouse at Boulters Lock, Boulters Lock, tel. 01628 621291.
- **LESSONS AND TOURS:** Paddleboard Maidenhead, tel. 07505 147957.
- **GETTING THERE:** *Car* At N end of Marlow Bridge on High Street, at two adjacent mini roundabouts take second exit at first; then second exit again onto Station Road, then R onto St Peter Street. Slipway at end of road; *Rail* Stations at Maidenhead and Marlow, with regular services from London Paddington, gwr.com
- **SPECIAL POINTS:** One lock to portage. Check local river conditions for Boulters Lock at riverlevels.uk/thames-taplow-boulters-lock

90

RIVER THAMES BUSCOT TO LECHLADE

RIVER · OXFORDSHIRE

One of the quietest stretches of the navigable Thames, this scenic route winds through lush meadows, featuring the river's first lock and island, with pub stops along the way. Start at Buscot, a charming village with its honey-coloured Cotswold stone cottages and the stately grounds of the nearby Buscot Estate. Launch from the small river beach just south of Buscot Weir into the calm waters of the weir pool. Paddle right to join the Thames below Buscot Lock, which connects two islands – Buscot Lock Island and Brandy Island, once home to a distillery run by Robert Campbell, the estate's former owner. Portage the lock, the smallest on the Thames, and continue through peaceful countryside. On the left, the spire of St. Mary the Virgin comes into view, followed by a tight right-hand bend past Cheese Wharf, a reminder of the Thames' trading past.

Continue on to St. John's Island, the first island on the Thames, with lovely picnic spots under the trees and the soothing sound of nearby weirs. Take the right channel around the island for a stop at the Trout Inn, or go left under St. John's Bridge, an elegant stone arch leading to St. John's Lock, where the statue of Old Father Thames stands, having been relocated from the river's source.

The final stretch flows through tranquil meadows before reaching Ha'penny Bridge, with its graceful bow-shaped arch. The journey ends at Lechlade's quayside, where the Riverside Inn offers the perfect spot to relax before heading back •

- **DISTANCE:** 7 km return.
- **PADDLING ENVIRONMENT:** 2.
- **ROUTE MAP:** islandeering.com/paddleboarding-buscot-to-lechlade/
- **ACCESS RESTRICTION:** Licence required, included in Paddle UK membership.
- **OS MAP:** OS Explorer 170 Abingdon, Wantage & Vale of White Horse.
- **STARTING POINT:** River beach on the weir pool south of Buscot Weir. Grid ref. SU 230 980; What3Words liners.amending.diverting.
- **PARKING:** Buscot Village Car Park (National Trust members free), Village Road, Manor Farm, Buscot, SN7 8DA. Grid ref. SU 231 976; What3Words yield.household.tabs.
- **LAUNCHING:** From car park walk R along lane and follow to riverside (250m walk).
- **PITSTOPS:** Delicious scones, Buscot Tearoom, tel. 01367 250329; good food in historic riverside inn, Trout Inn, tel. 01367 252313; lively riverside pub, The Riverside, Lechlade, tel. 01367 252534.
- **LESSONS, HIRE AND TOURS:** Hire with Cotswold Canoe Hire, adjacent to The Riverside pub, tel. 01367 252303; hire and lessons with Chilli SUP Co. The Trout, Lechlade, tel. 07359 387706.
- **GETTING THERE:** S on A417 from Lechlade towards Faringdon; turn L into no-through road marked by distinctive Buscot Village Hall and clock tower; car park on R.
- **SPECIAL POINTS:** Be cautious on tight bends when other boats are around, and always pass on the right-hand side. Check local river conditions at Buscot Lock ahead of your trip, riverlevels.uk/thames-lechlade-buscot-lock

THE RIVERSIDE

91

RIVER THAMES TADPOLE BRIDGE TO NEWBRIDGE

RIVER · OXFORDSHIRE

Pub paddle along the remotest stretch of the Thames. Start at Tadpole Bridge and head left with the gentle downstream flow. The route winds through reeds, trees, and open countryside, offering plenty of opportunities to spot wildlife. After a while, reach Tenfoot Bridge, a simple footbridge that feels far from anywhere, offering sweeping views of the surrounding countryside.

Continue to Shifford Lock Cut, where the river splits. To the right, the river flows over a weir, while the navigation channel – dug in 1897 to bypass a meandering river loop – leads through a tunnel of lush greenery. Paddle under a footbridge, enjoying the cool shade of overhanging branches on the approach to Shifford Lock. Shifford Island, formed by the cut, is one of the most remote and tranquil spots along the Thames, accessible only by foot.

This area is peaceful thanks to its proximity to Chimney Meadows National Nature Reserve, a vast floodplain teeming with wildlife like curlews, lapwings and rare wildflowers such as the snake's head fritillary.

Portage left at Shifford Lock and rejoin the main river, where the original channel merges from the right. The final stretch brings you to Newbridge, where the quiet rural setting shifts to a livelier riverside scene. Two pubs – the Rose Revived and the Maybush Inn – sit on either side of the river, offering the perfect spot to enjoy food, drink, and a well-deserved rest by the water •

- **DISTANCE:** 10km one way.
- **PADDLING ENVIRONMENT:** 2.
- **ROUTE MAP:** islandeering.com/paddleboarding-tadople-bridge-to-newbridge/
- **ACCESS RESTRICTIONS:** Licence required, included in Paddle UK membership.
- **OS MAP:** OS Explorer 180 Oxford, Witney & Woodstock.
- **STARTING POINT:** North bank of river opposite The Trout at Tadpole Bridge, grid ref. SP 334 004; What3Words wasps.continued.reserve.
- **EGRESS:** Rose Revived immediately after bridge on LHS, Newbridge, grid ref. SP 403 014; What3Words deposits.gamer.roadways; or Maybush Pub, Newbridge, grid ref. SP 403 013; What3Words flick.warns.teaching.
- **PARKING:** *Tadpole* Bridge Small lay-by, Buckland Road, Tadpole Bridge, SN7 8RF. Grid ref. SP 334 004; What3Words devoured.paradise.safari; *Newbridge* Back car park at Rose Revived (free but always polite to eat or drink in pub), Newbridge, OX29 7QD. Grid ref. SP 403 014; What3Words degree.drill.porridge. To access river, walk down track then across pub garden to bridge to access river via "steps" in bank.
- **LAUNCHING:** Short walk to drop down onto Thames Path from Tadpole Bridge to launch on north river bank.
- **PITSTOPS:** Attractive stone riverside inn, The Trout at Tadpole Bridge, tel. 01367 870382; friendly and popular Maybush Pub Newbridge, tel. 01865 300101; lovely willow-draped riverside garden, Rose Revived, Newbridge, tel. 01865 300221.
- **LESSONS AND TOURS:** Moi's SUP Tours, Rose Revived, Newbridge, tel. 07770 903860.
- **GETTING THERE:** Leave A420 onto Buckland Road following signs to Tadpole Bridge, lay-by on R immediately after pub and bridge.
- **SPECIAL POINTS**: One lock to portage. For a detour it's possible to paddle up to Duxford and back by turning immediately right downstream of Shifford Lock. Check local river conditions at Shifford Lock ahead of your trip: riverlevels.uk/thames-aston-cote-shifford-and-chimney-shifford-lock

92

RIVER THAMES CULHAM LOOP AND ABINGDON

RIVER · OXFORDSHIRE

Idyllic trip to a historic market town and a loop of Culham Island, visiting the stunningly scenic Sutton Pools with some excellent pitstops on the way. Launch at Culham Lock and head right (upstream) through Culham Cut, which runs along the northern edge of Culham Island. After a short distance, the route joins the River Thames, where a right turn continues upstream.

On a left-hand bend, pass Abingdon Marina Park, with boathouses, sailing clubs, and riverside houses on the left, and open fields on the right. Approach Abingdon, one of England's oldest towns, passing notable landmarks like the spire of St. Helen's Church and historic buildings along St. Helen's Wharf, a former trading hub reflecting the town's rich history. Continue past Margaret Brown Gardens and the slipway at the far end of the wharf. At Nag's Head Island, the right fork leads to Abingdon Riverside Café, while the left fork heads to the Nags Head pub beyond the road bridge.

On the return trip, retrace steps, bypass the exit for Culham Cut and continue along the Thames. After a long left-hand meander, the river splits around a wooded islet. The right-hand fork leads to the Endurance Boat Café. To complete the loop back to the lock, take the left fork, keeping initially to the right of the Culham hydropower scheme turbines, and portage across the narrow tip of the islet to relaunch downstream.

Continue past Sutton Pools, with its beautiful tree-lined deep inky pools and small shingle beaches along the southern banks of Culham Island. The two arms of the river rejoin, surrounded by lush vegetation. After passing under Sutton Bridge, turn left to return to Culham Lock •

- **DISTANCE:** 7.8km return.
- **PADDLING ENVIRONMENT:** 2.
- **ROUTE MAP:** islandeering.com/paddleboarding-abingdon-and-culham-loop/
- **ACCESS RESTRICTIONS:** Licence required, included in Paddle UK membership.
- **OS MAP:** OS Explorer 170 Abingdon, Wantage & Vale of White Horse.
- **STARTING POINT:** Culham Lock (see parking).
- **PARKING:** Culham Lock Car Park (free), Culham, OX14 4NE. Grid ref. SU 508 949; What3Words belt.lives.sleepy.
- **LAUNCHING:** Upstream of Culham Lock adjacent to car park.
- **PITSTOPS:** Good food in riverside gardens on an island in the Thames, Nags Head, Abingdon, tel. 01235 639023; lovely riverside spot for cake, coffee and lunch, Abingdon Riverside Café, tel. 01235 797575; delicious bakes in idyllic setting, Endurance Boat Café, nr Sutton Pools, facebook.com/Enduranceboatcafe
- **TOURS:** Adventuro, adventuro.com
- **GETTING THERE:** A4115 south of Abingdon; turn L onto Tollgate Road towards Culham; car park on R just before Culham Bridge.
- **SPECIAL POINTS:** Be mindful of other boat traffic, especially around Abingdon. Check local river conditions at Abingdon: riverlevels.uk/flood-warning-river-thames-in-abingdon

93

RIVER THAMES SONNING TO WARGRAVE VIA ST PATRICK'S STREAM AND RIVER LODDEN

RIVER · OXFORDSHIRE

Explore a peaceful tributary off the main river, passing picturesque islands and historic landmarks on a pub paddle. Launch at Sonning, heading left under the B478 bridge, and continue downstream past the lawns of The Coppa Club on the south bank, followed by open fields and meadows. After about 2 kilometres, at the end of a long right-hand bend, turn right into St Patrick's Stream. This narrow stream meanders through a quiet area, passing under a bridge near the entrance. After about 1.5 kilometres, another small bridge comes into view; pass beneath it and take the right fork just beyond, near a large farm complex. The route soon follows the River Loddon, where water lilies often bloom in summer. Passing large manicured gardens, the journey eventually rejoins the River Thames.

Once back on the Thames, turn right and continue downstream, passing marinas and leisure boats to reach the gardens of the St George & Dragon pub in Wargrave.

For the return trip to Sonning, paddle upstream along the Thames, portaging around Shiplake Lock. Along the way, pass several islands, including Shiplake Lock Island, which is divided into three sections. This peaceful island, once home to a mill and weir, has been a summer camping spot since 1889. Currently closed, its future remains uncertain.

A little further upstream is Phillimore Island, a picturesque wooded islet across from Shiplake College, named after Sir Robert Phillimore, a politician, judge, and friend of Prime Minister Gladstone. Around the next bend, two large wooded islands appear: The Lynch and Hallsmead Ait. Finally comes Buck Ait, a willow-covered islet named after the eel traps (or "bucks") once placed here. As Sonning comes into view again, the river widens, revealing the Sonning Eyots, ideal for a final bit of exploration before ending the trip •

• **DISTANCE:** 11.4km return.

• **PADDLING ENVIRONMENT:** 2.

• **ROUTE MAP:** islandeering.com/paddleboarding-sonning-to-wargrave/

• **ACCESS RESTRICTIONS:** Licence required, included in Paddle UK membership.

• **OS MAP:** OS Explorer 159 Reading, Wokingham & Pangbourne.

• **STARTING POINT:** Riverside next to car park. Grid ref. SU 753 758; What3Words groom.throw.broad.

• **PARKING:** Car park opposite French Horn pub (free, but avoid adjacent hotel car park), Playhatch Road (B478), Sonning Eye, RG4 6TN. Grid ref. SU 753 759; What3Words backup.misty.lies.

• **PITSTOPS:** Good food and river terrace at lively Coppa Club, Sonning, tel. 0118 807 8971; large riverside pub popular for food, St. George & Dragon, Wargrave, tel. 0118 940 4474.

• **GETTING THERE:** J11 M4 onto A33 to Reading, which merges with A329, take first exit at roundabout onto A4155 towards Caversham. At Playhatch, take third exit at roundabout towards Sonning; car park on R opposite The French Horn.

• **SPECIAL POINTS:** St. Patrick's Stream runs fast and narrow before opening out towards the confluence with the River Lodden, so it's best paddled downstream. A small riffle is experienced just past the bridge as you start the streamway. Check river conditions at Sonning Lock before you start, riverlevels.uk/thames-sonning-sonning-lock . Higher flows will make the return journey very challenging, so you may wish to take a one-way trip and exit further downstream at Marsh Lock (see route 94).

94

RIVER THAMES HENLEY TO WARGRAVE AND HENNERTON BACKWATER

RIVER · OXFORDSHIRE

A pub paddle that offers one of the best Thames backwaters, plus secret islands and stunning riverside homes to admire. Start at Marsh Lock, one of the most dramatic spots on the River Thames, consisting of two islands connected by an intricate weir and lock system. Wooden walkways from the Oxfordshire bank lead across the lock island, providing a scenic walking experience before launching onto the river.

Once on the water, head upstream, passing wooded hills and the manicured gardens of exclusive properties. At a right-hand bend, continue straight into Hennerton Backwater, a narrow stream that runs along the eastern edge of Wargrave Marsh Island. The Willow Marina marks the upstream tip of the island, while charming footbridges dot the way. After rejoining the main river, the St George & Dragon pub is the perfect spot for a break.

On the return, paddle downstream along the Thames, passing luxurious homes on Wargrave Marsh Island's southern bank, including the former residence of magician Paul Daniels. Continue past the beautifully landscaped Shiplake homes, encountering a series of islands: Handbuck Eyot, near the Shiplake bank, is followed by Poplar Eyot in the middle of the river, and Ferry Eyot, a group of three small wooded islets. These are named after the Bolney ferry, which once carried barge horses across the river. The journey ends back at Marsh Lock •

- **DISTANCE:** 6.5km return.
- **PADDLING ENVIRONMENT:** 2.
- **ROUTE MAP:** islandeering.com/paddleboarding-henley-to-wargrave/
- **ACCESS RESTRICTIONS:** Licence required, included in Paddle UK membership.
- **OS MAP:** OS Explorer 171 Chiltern Hills West.
- **STARTING POINT:** Marsh Lock, Grid ref. SU 774 816; What3Words giggle.wove.constrain.
- **PARKING:** Marsh Meadows car park (charges), Mill Lane, Henley-on-Thames, Oxfordshire, RG9 4HB. Grid ref. SU 770 817; What3Words tripling.curry.finalists.
- **LAUNCHING:** Pontoon on far side of lock, 400m walk from car park.
- **PITSTOPS:** Lovely café with great paninis and cakes, Mill Lane Café, Henley Town Football Club (adjacent to car park); large riverside pub popular for food, St George & Dragon, Wargrave, tel. 0118 940 4474.
- **GETTING THERE:** A4155 S of Henley-on-Thames towards Reading; turn L after Newtown Business Park into Mill Lane, car park on L towards river.
- **SPECIAL POINTS:** Leaving Marsh Lock, keep to the left bank to make it easier to find the smaller entrance to the backwater. The backwater carries very little flow so best paddled for the upstream leg (as suggested in this trip). Depending on river levels, you may have to limbo under the stone bridge just before the marina and Wargrave Island. Check water levels at Remenham Marsh Lock: riverlevels.uk/thames-remenham-marsh-lock

95

OXFORD CANAL AND RIVER THAMES WOLVERCOTE LOOP

RIVER/CANAL · OXFORDSHIRE

A circular route along the Oxford Canal connects to the Thames via Duke's Cut, with some classic pitstops and landmarks to see. Start from the Isis Lock on the Oxford Canal and head north along the canal lined with its narrowboats, back gardens, and green spaces. After 4.5km Duke's Lock House will appear; turn left under the canal bridge and into Duke's Cut. Continue beneath the rail and A40 bridges, then turn right into Wolvercote Mill Stream, heading upstream. After a tight left-hand bend, reach King's Eyot, which splits the stream. The left stream falls over Kings Weir, so follow the right stream (anti-clockwise around islet) to King's Weir Lock. Portage on the right and relaunch, passing Pixey Mead on the left and meandering gently through open countryside.

After passing beneath the A34 Thames Bridge, the stone-built Godstow Bridge comes into view. The islands ahead, Godstow Eyots, split the river – the left stream leads to a weir, while the navigation takes the right channel, passing under the bridge. To visit the famous Trout Inn, which features in Colin Dexter's *Inspector Morse*, land on the island, cross the eyot, and walk over the footbridge.

Continue downstream, keeping right to avoid the weir on the left, passing the ruins of Godstow Abbey before reaching Godstow Lock (portage right). The route then passes the ancient common land of Port Meadow, where cows are often seen swimming. Further on, land on the right bank near the pub sign for a short walk to visit The Perch at Binsey Green.

As the journey continues past Medley Sailing Club and Bossoms Boatyard, the gracefully arched and latticed Rainbow Bridge comes into view – land here to visit The Medley café, a hidden gem. Fiddler's Island splits the river at this point, so follow the right channel of the Thames, as the left stream leads into Castle Mill Stream (which is where you'll join this route if using the recommended car park).

After a kilometre or so, before a row of terraced cottages, turn left into Castle Mill Stream under pedestrian and rail bridges into Sheepwash Channel. Head towards Isis Lock, where the route ends with an exit onto the towpath, then over footbridges back to the station •

• **DISTANCE:** 11.5km return.

• **PADDLING ENVIRONMENT:** 2.

• **ROUTE MAP:** islandeering.com/paddleboarding-oxford-wolvercote-loop/

• **ACCESS RESTRICTIONS:** Licence required, included in Paddle UK membership.

• **OS MAP:** OS Explorer 180 Oxford, Witney & Woodstock.

• **STARTING POINT:** North of Isis Lock, Oxford Canal. Grid ref. SP 505 066; What3Words thus.once.herb.

• **PARKING:** Walton Well Road Car Park (charges), Walton Well Road, Osney, Oxford, OX2 6ED. Grid ref. SP 502 073; What3Words rides.afford.think.

• **LAUNCHING:** From train station 300m walk to Isis Lock, Oxford Canal side; from Walton Well Road car park, access to Castle Mill Stream is adjacent to parking. From Walton Well Road car park launch and turn R, follow for short distance (can be overgrown), pass under the footbridge to the left onto River Thames, turn left and follow route from Fiddler's Island.

• **PITSTOPS:** Rambling historic riverside pub, The Trout Inn, Lower Wolvercote, tel. 01865 510930; good beers and food, thatched Oxford institution, The Perch, Binsey, 01865 728891; wood-fired pizzas and local beers out of a refurbished caravan, The Medley, Binsey instagram.com/the_medley_oxford

• **LESSONS AND TOURS:** Moi's SUP School, tel. 07770 903860.

• **GETTING THERE:** *Car* Entrance to car park at south end of Port Meadow on Walton Well Road; *Train* Oxford rail station, with regular services from London Paddington, gwr.com, or London Marylebone, www.chilternrailways.co.uk . To walk to the launch point, turn L out of Oxford rail station, pick up pedestrian/green bike lane at entrance to short-stay car park, then turn L on Rawley Road; follow over bridge across Castle Mill Stream and turn R, following brown sign to Oxford Canal; launch on canal above Isis Lock.

• **SPECIAL POINTS:** Check local river conditions at Kings Lock, riverlevels.uk/thames-wytham-kings-lock

96

OXFORD CANAL ENSLOW TO THRUPP

CANAL · OXFORDSHIRE

Peaceful route meandering along the Oxford Canal and River Cherwell to tearooms and two excellent pubs. Launch at Enslow and head right, under the A4095 bridge, along the Oxford Canal. This historic waterway, built in the late 18th century, was originally created to transport coal from the Midlands to Oxford, playing a key role in the country's early industrial infrastructure by connecting rural areas to growing cities.

Reach Baker's Lock, where the canal joins the River Cherwell, which enters from the right.

The route then passes a quarry, which once supplied limestone and other materials for the construction of Oxfordshire's towns and villages, before going under a rail line.

When the river splits, follow the canal to the right and arrive at Shipton Stoplock, an old lock used to manage water levels where the River Cherwell intersects with the canal. Portage here and continue under Shipton Lift Bridge, a manually operated wooden bridge showcasing the canal's historical engineering.

Passing the village of Shipton-on-Cherwell, Holy Cross Church can be seen perched on the riverside. This charming 13th-century church, with its distinctive spire, has stood over the village for centuries. Shipton-on-Cherwell has a rich history, including its connections to the Victorian railway system and nearby quarries.

As the canal makes a sharp right turn, Annie's Tea Rooms comes into view – an ideal spot for a break with its home-made treats. If continuing further, the canal passes a charming row of cottages in Thrupp, a quintessential English village that has remained largely unchanged. Visitors can stop at The Morse Dining Room in The Boat Inn, famous for its appearances in the *Inspector Morse* series, or paddle 350 metres further to reach the riverside gardens of The Jolly Boatman, next to Sparrow Gap Bridge. The return journey follows the same route •

- **DISTANCE:** 8.5km return.
- **PADDLING ENVIRONMENT:** 1.
- **ROUTE MAP:** islandeering.com/paddleboarding-enslow-to-thrupp/
- **ACCESS RESTRICTIONS:** Licence required, included in Paddle UK membership.
- **OS MAP:** OS Explorer 180 Oxford, Witney & Woodstock.
- **STARTING POINT:** Canalside, Enslow. Grid ref. SP 480 183; What3Words grazes.waiter.hazy.
- **PARKING:** Lay-by parking (free) off A4095 in Enslow, OX5 3AY. Grid ref. SP 479 182; What3Words corrode.secretly.proclaims.
- **LAUNCHING:** Short walk parallel to A4095 to canalside to launch north of bridge.
- **PITSTOPS:** Home-made cakes, breakfast and lunches, Annie's Tea Rooms, Thrupp, tel. 01865 686163; friendly pub with nice garden, The Boat Inn, tel. 01865 374279; good food and canalside terrace, The Jolly Boatman, Kidlington, tel. 01865 377800.
- **HIRE:** Thrupp Canoe and Kayak Hire Centre, next to Annie's Tea Rooms, Thrupp, tel. 01865 376176.
- **GETTING THERE:** A4095 through Enslow to parking at north end of canal bridge.
- **SPECIAL POINTS:** Four locks to portage (two each way).

97

RIVER CHERWELL OXFORD COLLEGES

RIVER · OXFORDSHIRE

Explore Oxford's hidden waterways, with views of its dreaming spires, tranquil meadows, and iconic landmarks. Start from Donnington Bridge slipway and turn right upstream, passing boathouses, meadows, and wetlands. Continue past the confluence of the River Cherwell, then the college boathouses and, shortly after, the entrance to Shire Lake Ditch. Enjoy fabulous views of Christ Church Meadow, with Oxford's skyline of steeples and domes in the distance.

At Grandpont Island, take the left fork for views of Folly Bridge's stone arches, Bacon's Tower and the striking red-brick castellated house with cast-iron balconies – its recesses are filled with statues allegedly representing the fallen women from when the area hosted a brothel centuries ago. For a stop at The Head of the River pub, take the right fork around the island, passing Salter's Steamers moorings.

After a break, retrace the route to Shire Lake Ditch, turning left and joining the River Cherwell for stunning views of Christ Church and Merton Colleges. Pass under Jubilee Bridge, taking the left fork past the cricket ground and alongside the formal gardens and glasshouses of Oxford Botanic Garden. Pass by punts and under Magdalen Bridge, with its lively scene of novice punters and Magdalen Tower above.

Avoid the left stream and head slightly right to loop around Angel and Bat Willow Meadows (note that the gardens on the left are private and owned by Magdalen College). At the top of the loop, where the Cherwell splits, take the right fork under the footbridges back to Magdalen Bridge. Continue past the cricket ground and St Hilda's College, returning to Jubilee Bridge and following the Cherwell to its confluence with the Thames. Finally, turn left downstream to return to Donnington Bridge slipway

- **DISTANCE:** 6.7km return.
- **PADDLING ENVIRONMENT:** 2.
- **ROUTE MAP:** islandeering.com/paddleboarding-river-cherwell/
- **ACCESS RESTRICTIONS:** Licence required, included in Paddle UK membership.
- **OS MAP:** OS Explorer 180 Oxford, Witney & Woodstock.
- **STARTING POINT & PARKING:** Meadow Lane (free), Iffley, Oxford, OX4 4BJ. Grid ref. SP 524 044; What3Words views.longer.movies.
- **LAUNCHING:** Donnington Bridge slipway adjacent to parking.
- **PITSTOPS:** Drinks on the riverside terrace, The Head of the River, tel. 01865 721600.
- **LESSONS AND TOURS:** City tours with Oxford Kayak Tours, tel. 07816 655370; SUP lessons with Oxford SUP Club, tel. 07923 227771.
- **GETTING THERE:** A34 to Hinksey Hill Interchange, then A423/A4144 past Park and Ride. Turn R onto Weirs Lane and cross Donnington Bridge, then turn immediately L onto Meadow Lane, then immediately left into Riverside Centre. Keep left and park near river.
- **SPECIAL POINTS:** This section of the Thames is very busy with rowers so keep right wherever possible. The Cherwell is quieter but will be busy with punters, especially in summer. Check river conditions at Oxford before you leave – riverlevels.uk/oxfordshire-river-cherwell-at-oxford

98

BLENHEIM PALACE GREAT LAKE

LAKE · OXFORDSHIRE

Nestled in the rolling hills of Oxfordshire, Blenheim Palace offers the embodiment of English grandeur, and there's no better way to enjoy it than by paddling on the Great Lake. The journey to the lake is a treat in itself, with a walk through the parkland and main courtyards, passing the formal gardens before arriving at the Boat House, where LiveFree Adventures provides access to the lake for paddleboarding.

The palace, gifted to John Churchill, 1st Duke of Marlborough, after his victory at the Battle of Blenheim in 1704, is an architectural masterpiece. Its Baroque style is grand, with elegant colonnades, stately courtyards, and luxurious interiors. But it's the estate that truly sets it apart. The palace sits within a 2,000-acre park designed by Capability Brown, featuring meadows, woodlands, and water.

At the heart of this landscape is the Great Lake, fed by the River Glyme and designed by Brown. The lake stretches out beneath the palace, offering what has been called "one of the finest views in England". With ancient oaks and willows lining its shores, the lake creates a peaceful, majestic scene. The Boat House, built in the 1800s, offers the perfect spot to enjoy these views. Once used for storing rowing boats, it now serves as the base for LiveFree Adventures, where paddlers can enjoy unique views of the Palace and the Grand Bridge. The lake, part of the UNESCO World Heritage Site, is home to abundant wildlife, including swans, herons, and kingfishers, making this trip a one-of-a-kind experience •

- **DISTANCE:** Free range.
- **PADDLING ENVIRONMENT:** 1.
- **ROUTE MAP:** islandeering.com/paddleboarding-blenheim-palace/
- **ACCESS RESTRICTIONS:** Self-launch booking via LiveFree Adventures – purchase of 'Park and Gardens' pass from Blenheim Palace also required (£28). School summer holidays only.
- **OS MAP:** OS Explorer 180 Oxford, Witney & Woodstock.
- **PARKING:** Blenheim Palace (free with your booking), Woodstock, Oxfordshire, OX20 1UH. Grid ref. SP 439 159; What3Words kings.sums.disengage.
- **LAUNCHING:** 1km walk from car park along the main drive (a little further from the bus stop) to lake, through the main entrance and via the courtyards to the entrance to the formal gardens on the far side. Look out for the boathouse below.
- **PITSTOPS:** Numerous cafés in the palace courtyards.
- **HIRE:** Rowing boats, canoes and paddleboards at LiveFree Adventures Blenheim, tel. 01993 875750.
- **GETTING THERE:** *Car* A44 north of Oxford to Woodstock; then L into palace main entrance; *Train* Oxford rail station, then Stagecoach Bus S3 and S7 from station to Blenheim Palace main entrance.
- **SPECIAL POINTS:** Guidelines for Paddleboarding at Blenheim Palace include: 1) All paddleboards and associated equipment must be brought to the palace deflated and packed away. 2) Leash and buoyancy aid mandatory. 3) Only change in the boathouse and not in palace grounds or car park – water wear not allowed while walking through the palace.

99

BRAY LAKE

LAKE · BERKSHIRE

Tucked away in a scenic part of Berkshire, Bray Lake offers a mix of rich history, community spirit, and all kinds of water activities. Started in 1979 by two windsurfing enthusiasts, it has grown into one of the UK's longest-running watersports centres. Over the past 45 years, Bray Lake has transformed from a gravel pit into a lively hub for windsurfing, kayaking, canoeing, paddleboarding, and open-water swimming. The centre focuses on creating a safe, fun, and welcoming space where anyone – beginners or pros – can develop their skills or just enjoy the water.

Bray Lake is more than just about sport – it's a vibrant community that embraces nature and the wildlife around it. Over time, it's added social events, races, and a cosy café that's a popular spot on weekends. Whether it's the excitement of windsurfing or the calm of SUP and kayaking, there's something for everyone, all year round – even when they have to break the ice for winter swimmers! As the home of the British SUP Club Championships and host to many events, Bray Lake continues to bring together watersports lovers of all levels, making it a must-visit spot for anyone looking for adventure and fun •

- **DISTANCE:** Free-range.
- **PADDLING ENVIRONMENT:** 1.
- **ROUTE MAP:** islandeering.com/paddleboarding-bray-lake/
- **ACCESS RESTRICTIONS:** Private lake; for self-launch, book with Bray Lake Watersports, braylake.com
- **OS MAP:** OS Explorer 160 Windsor, Weybridge and Bracknell.
- **PARKING:** Bray Lake Watersports, Monkey Island Lane, Windsor Road, Maidenhead, SL6 2EB. Grid ref. SU 911 786; What3Words angle.detect.reap.
- **LAUNCHING:** Pontoon close to parking.
- **PITSTOPS:** Watch the action from the decking, Monkey Bar Café, Bray Lake, tel. 01628 638860.
- **LESSONS AND HIRE:** Full range of watersports equipment and lessons available with Bray Lake Watersports, tel. 01628 638860.
- **GETTING THERE:** J 8/9 off M4 onto A308(M) towards Maidenhead and Windsor, then third exit off roundabout (A308 towards Windsor). Turn L 800m after Post Office onto Monkey Island Lane, signposted for Bray Lake and Bray Marina. Follow the lane past the Marina (on R) to find entrance on L.
- **SPECIAL POINTS:** Please clean your board before you enter the water to prevent spread of non-native plants and animal species.

100

KENNET AND AVON CANAL MIDGHAM TO THEALE

CANAL · BERKSHIRE

A peaceful journey along a section of the canalised River Kennet that retains many of its chalk stream characteristics. This stretch of the canal follows the river's course through scenic pasturelands, woods, and water meadows with flowing water and abundant wildlife. Several trip options are possible, ranging from longer linear journeys with car or rail links at both ends to shorter routes starting at Aldermaston Wharf.

For the full trip, start from Woolhampton Lock, close to Midgham rail station, where the River Kennet meets the canal. Launch downstream, east of Woolhampton Bridge, next to the charming Rowbarge pub. Drift past wooded banks for 1.5 kilometres, then take the left fork (the right leads to Frouds Bridge Marina) and pass under Frouds Lane Bridge towards Aldermaston Wharf. Once a crucial hub during the Industrial Revolution, it is now a peaceful area for leisure activities, with historic buildings like the Aldermaston Wharf Tea Rooms.

Continuing along the route, pass through peaceful stretches of canal, navigating locks and swing bridges. After Sulhamstead Lock, the canal runs between two lakes, with Draper's Osier Bed Stream to the north – an area historically used for growing willows. The trip ends at Sheffield Bottom Swing Bridge, with the option to walk 400 metres to Theale station for a train ride back, or collect a shuttle car from nearby Sheffield Bottom Lock car park just a few metres away •

- **DISTANCE:** 9.4km one way with train return; shorter options available.
- **PADDLING ENVIRONMENT:** 1.
- **ROUTE MAP:** islandeering.com/paddleboarding-midgeham-to-theale/
- **ACCESS RESTRICTIONS:** Licence required, included in PaddleUK Membership.
- **OS MAP:** OS Explorer 159 Reading, Wokingham & Pangbourne.
- **STARTING POINT:** The Rowbarge, Woolhampton Bridge, Woolhampton, RG7 5SH. Grid ref. SU 572 665; What3Words september.abandons.swaps.
- **PARKING:** *Woolhampton* Midgham Station Car Park (charges), Station Road, Woolhampton, RG7 5SE. Grid ref. SU 573 666; What3Words roofer.masking.backhand; *Theale* Sheffield Bottom Lock Car Park (free), Hangar Road, Theale, RG7 4AJ. Grid ref. SU 647 704; What3Words asks.bonds.visits.
- **LAUNCHING:** Canalside near The Rowbarge, 200m walk from car park.
- **PITSTOPS:** The Rowbarge, tel. 0118 971 2213; hearty breakfasts and great cakes, Tea Rooms Aldermaston Wharf, tel. 07917 631730.
- **GETTING THERE:** *Car* A4 between Thatcham and Newbury to Woolhampton. Opposite The Angel pub, follow signs to rail station; *Train* Stations at Midgham, Theale and Aldermaston, regular services to London Paddington, gwr.com
- **SPECIAL POINTS:** Six locks to portage.

101

KENNET AND AVON CANAL NEWBURY TO HUNGERFORD

CANAL · BERKSHIRE

A gentle trip with chalk stream characteristics through the beautiful Berkshire countryside, crisscrossing the River Kennet and railway. The Kennet and Avon Canal, a historic waterway stretching for 140 kilometres, connects the River Thames at Reading with the River Avon at Bristol. Built between 1794 and 1810, it played a vital role in the Industrial Revolution, helping transport goods between London and the Bristol Channel.

Begin at Newbury Wharf, head left under Wharf Road Bridge and pass through the town centre beneath the charming Bridge Street bridge. Pass The Lock, Stock & Barrel pub near Newbury Lock, portaging on the right. After passing under West Mills Swing Bridge, the town fades into the countryside as the route winds past moored boats. Several locks require portage on the towpath side before reaching the picturesque village of Kintbury, where the Dundas Arms, a popular riverside pub, offers a great place to pause and watch the horse-drawn barge trips.

The trip can end in Kintbury, with a train ride back to Newbury, or continue onward to Hungerford. Nea Hungerford, Dun Mill Lock is the final lock before reaching the rail station, marking the journey's end and a convenient spot for a return train trip •

- **DISTANCE:** 9km to Kintbury one way; 14.4 km to Hungerford one way.
- **PADDLING ENVIRONMENT:** 1.
- **ROUTE MAP:** islandeering.com/paddleboarding-newbury-to-hungerford/
- **ACCESS RESTRICTIONS:** Licence required, included in Paddle UK Membership; or Canal and River Trust permit.
- **OS MAP:** OS Explorer 158 Newbury & Hungerford.
- **STARTING POINT:** Newbury Wharf (see parking).
- **PARKING:** Newbury Wharf Car Park (free), Wharf Road, Newbury, RG14 5AP. Grid ref. SU 473 672; What3Words charmingly.froth.bounty.
- **LAUNCHING:** Wharf adjacent to car park.
- **PITSTOPS:** Great cakes by the canal, The Teashop by the Canal, Newbury Wharf tel. 01635 522609; popular canalside inn, Dundas Arms, Kintbury, tel. 01488 658263.
- **GETTING THERE:** *Car* Off A339 in Newbury, follow signs to Wharf; *Train* Rail stations at Newbury, Kintbury and Hungerford enable a linear trip of varying lengths; regular services to London Paddington, gwr.com
- **SPECIAL POINTS:** If you encounter a horse-drawn barge, move to the non-towpath side of the canal. Nine locks to portage for full trip to Hungerford. Trip can be done in reverse – especially good when the River Kennet has higher flows.

GO FURTHER 14
McConks

102

HORSESHOE LAKE

LAKE · BERKSHIRE

A popular family destination on the doorstep of Sandhurst. Once part of an extensive network of working gravel pits that have now been flooded, Horseshoe Lake covers about nine hectares and sits within the attractive Blackwater Valley.

A great place to spot wildlife including a wide variety of birds, grasshoppers, crickets, dragonflies, and butterflies. With a much-visited café loved by walkers and paddlers alike, it is also a great place to watch the sun set •

- **DISTANCE:** Free-range.
- **PADDLING ENVIRONMENT:** 1.
- **ROUTE MAP:** islandeering.com/paddleboarding-horshoe-lake/
- **ACCESS RESTRICTIONS:** Self-launch via booking with Horseshoe Lake Activity Centre.
- **OS MAP:** OS Explorer 159 Reading, Wokingham & Pangbourne.
- **PARKING:** Horseshoe Lake Activity Centre (free), Mill Lane, Sandhurst, GU47 8JW. Grid ref. SU 820 621; What3Words vibe.images.decks.
- **LAUNCHING:** Pontoon.
- **PITSTOPS:** Rustic Italian sandwiches, pizza, pastries etc., Lakeview Café, Horseshoe Lake.
- **LESSONS AND HIRE:** Horseshoe Lake Activity Centre, tel. 01252 871808, horseshoelakeactivitycentre.co.uk . Pre-booking essential; bouyancy aid mandatory, waiver must be signed.
- **GETTING THERE:** Head northwest on A321 from Sandhurst towards Wokingham. Turn L in front of St Michael's CE School, then follow brown signs to Horseshoe Lake along Lower Church Road. Turn L at T-junction onto Mill Lane, then R to lake.
- **SPECIAL POINTS:** Please clean your board before you enter the water to prevent spread of non-native plants and animal species.

103

JUBILEE RIVER

RIVER · BERKSHIRE

Options for peaceful routes from meadows and wetlands to the iconic skylines of Eton and Windsor. The Jubilee River is a man-made flood relief channel, designed to divert water from the River Thames to reduce flood risk in Maidenhead, Windsor, and Eton. Stretching for 11.6 kilometres and designed to look like a natural river, it offers a quiet boat-free alternative to the Thames, especially when the Thames is in flood. The river is lined with meadows, woodlands, and wetlands, providing a rich habitat for birds and aquatic life and perfect for wildlife spotting.

Paddling routes start at Lake End, with options both upriver and downriver. For an 8km round trip to Taplow Weir, paddle left under Lake End Road bridge, passing meadows and the M4 bridge, and portaging at Marsh Lane Weir. Continue through meanders, under Amerden Lane road bridge (with Engage Watersports, Taplow Lake, and a café a short walk along the lane), and beneath the railway and footbridge to reach Taplow Weir.

For an 8.5km round trip through Dorney Wetlands to Slough Weir, turn right from Lake End and, after 1.6km, portage Manor Farm Weir (on the right). The wetlands, designed as a wildlife refuge with reedbeds, scrapes and islands, host birds such as great crested grebes, grey herons, red kites, and kingfishers, along with many migratory birds. A longer 15km round trip to Eton and Windsor includes portaging Slough Weir at the Jubilee River Riverside Centre and Black Potts Weir. After a short walk, join the Thames and head upstream past Eton College Masters Boathouse. Keep left at an island and portage Romney Lock for views of the spires and Gothic towers of Eton College, and the imposing towers and battlements of Windsor Castle. Return the same way •

• **DISTANCE:** 8km to Taplow Weir return; 8.5km to Dorney Wetlands and Slough Weir return; 15km to Windsor Castle and the Thames return.

• **PADDLING ENVIRONMENT:** 2–3.

• **ROUTE MAP:** islandeering.com/paddleboarding-jubilee-river/

• **ACCESS RESTRICTIONS:** No licence required on the Jubilee River; licence required on the Thames, included in Paddle UK membership.

• **OS MAP:** OS Explorer 172 Chiltern Hills East, and OS Explorer 160 Windsor, Weybridge & Bracknell.

• **STARTING POINT & PARKING:** Dorney Wetlands car park (free), Lake End Road, Dorney, SL4 6QS. Grid ref. SU 928 795; What3Words sticks.move.foster.

• **LAUNCHING:** Riverbank adjacent to parking.

• **PITSTOPS:** "Famous" sandwich menu, The Pineapple, Dorney, tel. 01628 662353; Lake House Café, Taplow Lake (exit river at Amerden Lane Bridge), tel. 01628 782113.

• **LESSONS, HIRE AND TOURS:** Lessons and hire either on the lake or river, Engage Watersports, Taplow Lake, tel. 01628 671131; lessons and pub and picnic trips, Jubilee River Riverside Centre, Slough, tel. 07776 997255.

• **GETTING THERE:** Leave M4 at J7 onto A4 towards Slough; first exit at roundabout to stay on A4, then first exit at roundabout onto B3026 towards Eton. After Dorney Bridge, car park on L.

• **SPECIAL POINTS:** One weir to portage each way on route to Taplow Weir; also on trip to Dorney Wetlands and Slough Weir. There are two weirs and one lock to portage each way on route joining the Thames to Windsor Castle. Jubilee River is still navigable when the Thames has been red-boarded, however always check local levels and flow at riverlevels.uk/jubilee-river-taplow ; for the trip to Windsor, check conditions at Romney Lock riverlevels.uk/thames-eton-romney-lock

104

RIVER THAMES WINDSOR TO STAINES

RIVER · BERKSHIRE

Journey through history past Windsor Castle and Runnymede, the birthplace of the Magna Carta, with islands and tranquil backwaters along the way. Start in Windsor, launching and heading downstream under the wrought-iron Windsor Rail Bridge, which sits on Baths Island. To the left, Brocas Park, owned by Eton College, stretches out, while Snap and Firework Aits lie on the right. Ahead, Windsor Castle dominates the skyline. Pass under Windsor Bridge for views of Eton's spires, then keep to the right of Romney Eyot and follow the marked channel through Romney Lock.

After the rail bridge, the Jubilee River joins the Thames near Black Potts Ait. The right bank offers views into the royal ground of Home Park. Continue past Victoria and Albert Bridges, and soon Lion Island marks the approach to a weir. The New Cut branches right, carving out Ham Island, now occupied by a bird sanctuary and sewage works. Follow the cut to Old Windsor Lock, rejoining the main river at Friday Island, a small isle with a footprint-like shape reminiscent of Robinson Crusoe's Man Friday. The charming cottage here was once the home of Dr. Julius Grant, a forensic scientist famous for exposing forgeries, including the "Hitler Diaries".

Paddle past the homes of Friary Island to reach the wooded Pat's Croft Eyot. The Runnymede Boathouse makes a good spot nearby to stop for a café break and a chance to explore Runnymede, the historic site where the Magna Carta was sealed in 1215. Notable memorials include the Air Forces Memorial, honouring Allied airmen and women of World War II.

Back on the river, Magna Carta Island appears, with its secret back channel and overgrown ruin. Inland, the grounds of Ankerwycke Priory add to the sense of mystery. Continuing downstream, the wide fields of Runnymede Pleasure Grounds come into view; along with the quieter backwater of The Island, they make an interesting detour. The Runnymede Hotel signals the approach to Bell Weir Lock, where murals commemorate the signing of the Magna Carta. Portage on the right, then paddle under the M25.

Next, pass Holm Island and its calm backwater, followed by Hollyhock Island. Exit here if parked at the Lammas Recreation Ground car park, or continue for another 500 metres past Church Island and under Staines Bridge, its three white granite arches designed by George Rennie. Just beyond the bridge is a replica of the London Stone, which once marked the tidal limit of the Thames. Exit just after for Staines rail station to return •

• **DISTANCE:** 12.5 km one way.

• **PADDLING ENVIRONMENT:** 2.

• **ROUTE MAP:** islandeering.com/paddleboarding-windsor-to-staines/

• **ACCESS RESTRICTIONS:** Licence required, included in Paddle UK Membership.

• **OS MAP:** OS Explorer 175 Reading & Windsor.

• **STARTING POINT:** Windsor Leisure Centre, Clewer Avenue, Stovell Road, Windsor, SL4 5JB. Grid ref. SU 957 772; What3Words shades.hops.ritual.

• **PARKING:** Windsor Leisure Centre (charges); Lammas Recreation Ground car park (charges), Wraysbury Road, Staines, TW18 4YZ. Grid ref. TQ 027 719; What3Words shin.dips.soap.

• **LAUNCHING:** Slipway, Windsor Leisure Centre.

• **PITSTOPS:** National Trust's Magna Carta Tea Room at Runnymede.

• **GETTING THERE:** *Car* A332 exit for Windsor Racecourse and Thames Valley Athletics Centre; first exit at roundabout towards town centre then L, following sign to leisure centre along Stovell Road; *Train* Windsor & Eton Riverside station is 150m walk from Thameside where there are steps down to the river; Staines rail station, 600m walk from river. Regular services to both from London Waterloo, southwesternrailway.com

• **SPECIAL POINTS:** Three locks to portage. Check local river conditions at Romney Lock riverlevels.uk/thames-eton-romney-lock

KEEPING SAFE ON THE WATER

For safe paddling, always use the equipment described below and follow the procedures recommended, especially in an emergency.

SAFETY EQUIPMENT

Buoyancy aids: These are mandatory for access to some locations in this book and we recommend wearing one at all times, except if you are SUP surfing or racing where support is close to hand. Buoyancy aids come in two forms. **Chest/vest** buoyancy aids are designed not to obstruct paddling; they can be worn like a jacket that's zipped up at the front or pulled over the head with buckles to tighten, and they usually have a useful front pocket. Ensure you wear a brightly coloured, well-fitting, and well-maintained buoyancy aid that is appropriate for your weight and size. Consider attaching a whistle and a small strobe light for darkness. A **waist belt** features an inflatable sack that is inflated by a single-use gas cylinder; it is activated by pulling a cord in an emergency, transforming it into a device resembling a life jacket. The paddler must pull it over their head and secure it; this is easier in open water than in fast-flowing, turbulent environments.

Leash: This key piece of safety equipment keeps the board close to you in the event of a fall. We recommend wearing one without exception. A useful guide to leash options is provided by Paddle UK paddleuk.org.uk/stand-up-paddleboard-sup-safety-choosing-the-right-leash/. Our recommendation is a leash attached to a quick-release waist belt, as this is easy to detach if the leash catches on an obstruction in the water. In stronger flows it is not always easy to reach down to an ankle and release the leash. There are other quick-release devices on the market – but whatever you use, practise detaching it so that it becomes second nature.

Phones and VHF radios: Always take a fully charged mobile phone in a waterproof case on a lanyard tied to a buoyancy aid or float. Preload it with emergency numbers – including 999 or 112 – so you can call for assistance or contact the Coastguard in an emergency on the ocean/estuary. VHF radio is recommended for coastal/estuary paddling. Always keep phones and radios on your person as you may not be able to reach them in an emergency if they are stowed away in bags.

SAFETY PROCEDURES

Let someone know: Leave details of where you're going, time on and off the water, and where you're parked. Alternatively, use an app such as Paddlelogger (iPhone only). The RNLI suggests downloading the free Royal Yacht Association SafeTrx app, which monitors your journeys and alerts emergency contacts if you fail to return home on time.

In an emergency: On the ocean/estuary, call the Coastguard – using 999 or 112 – giving your location, how many people are with you, how you can be recognised, and what the problem is. Alternatively, attract attention using continual blasts on a whistle or kneel on the board with paddle in one hand, stretch out arms and move arms up and down to attract help when close to others. If help is further away, such as on the cliffs or headland, raise both arms above your head in a Y shape, which signifies "I want help". Stay with your craft and, if possible, raise as much of your body out of the water as you can to keep warmer.

If you have a **VHF radio**, for emergencies use Channel 16, activate DSC if fitted, then press and hold the transmit button. Say "Mayday" three times, use your call sign, give your position, give details of number in group, assistance required, and explain what the emergency issue is. Then say "Over" and wait for response.

Visibility: It's always important, but during a rescue good visibility can be a lifesaver. Stick SOLASpproved reflective tape to your craft and paddle, and isplay appropriate lights if out at dusk or night-time. lso, if you lose any gear while you're out paddling, lease contact the Coastguard so they know that ou're safe and won't launch a search. It's a good idea use a permanent marker and label your craft with our name and emergency contact details.

EALTH ISSUES

old Water Shock (CWS): This can happen when your ody is suddenly or unexpectedly immersed into water f less than 15°C. In the UK, average sea temperatures e just 12°C, with rivers and lakes often colder – even the summer. Warning signs of CWS include:

- Breathing rapidly, gasping for breath
- Heart racing or beating irregularly
- Movement becoming more difficult or laboured

et out of the water and try to warm up with a hot ink, high-energy foods, and a hot water bottle. If ossible, change into dry clothes and move around get the blood flowing through the body again. If omeone else has fallen in, notice if their breathing ecomes sporadic, they struggle to move or talk, or ey become confused. These are signs to seek help. the person is shivering, pale, and cold to touch, this ight indicate that they're struggling to warm up. asping for breath or rapid breathing from sudden mersion can even be triggered by water as warm 25°C, especially on a hot day.

eventing CWS:

- Check conditions first, including sea water mperature, at surfline.com or take a floating ermometer and record the lake or river mperature before you set out.
- Dress for the water temperature, not the air mperature, and include a buoyancy aid.
- ake spare dry clothes and keep them in your drybag.
- Pack a blanket and a hot water bottle in the car.
- ake warm drinks in a flask.

aterborne illness: Weill's Disease (leptospirosis) can be ntracted when the urine of some animals penetrates ough cuts or abrasions on the skin, or through the ng of the nose, mouth, throat, or eyes. If flu-like mptoms develop 1–3 weeks after contact with water, consult your GP. This is most prevalent after heavy rain when the water from burrows washes out into the river.

Blue-green algae (cyanobacteria) are commonly found in fresh and brackish water during mid- to late summer, particularly during long periods of warm, settled weather. The blooms produce allergens and/or toxins that can cause eye irritation, dermatitis, and joint/muscle pain. More seriously, they can lead to gastroenteritis, pneumonia, liver damage, and certain neurological conditions.

Gastrointestinal illness risks from inland and coastal waters depends on the number and proximity of sewage effluent discharges. The Surfers Against Sewage (SAS) Safer Seas and River Service app (sas.org.uk/safer-seas-service/) provides information on the latest pollution incidents, as does The River Trust's app.

Hepatitis, a virus in faeces, may also be contracted from water contaminated with sewage. Onset can be abrupt and symptoms include fever, jaundice, and abdominal discomfort. Beware of other agricultural and industrial pollutants, too. Generally, if the water looks or smells bad there is a likelihood of pollution and the potential to cause ill health. More information and how to avoid illness can be found at gopaddling.info/weils-disease-and-other-waterborne-diseases-to-be-aware-of/ As a general rule, clean hands with antibacterial hand gel before eating and after all river and coastal trips.

Weaverfish and jellyfish stings can be issues in certain areas. **Weaverfish** can grow up to 50 cm in length and are usually buried in sand or mud. If you step on them, even when dead, the neurotoxin venom in their spines can cause a serious reaction. Symptoms may include severe pain, itching, swelling, heat, redness, numbness, tingling, nausea, vomiting, joint aches, headaches, abdominal cramps, light-headedness and tremors. More severe reactions involve abnormal heart rhythms, weakness, paralysis, shortness of breath, and seizures. With warming seas, more onshore winds and overfishing of predators, **jellyfish** are increasingly encountered in UK waters or found stranded on beaches. Some species have stings that are barely noticeable, while others can leave you with painful welts and scarring. Common types include:

- Moon jellyfish: Identifiable by four pink rings within their transparent bodies; mild sting may cause a small rash or reddening of the skin.
- Barrel jellyfish: Can weigh up to 30kg; mild sting that usually goes unnoticed.

Cuckmere Haven and Seven Sisters (25)

- Compass jellyfish: Yellow/white and brown jellyfish with lines extending from the centre and v-shaped markings around the circular rim; very painful sting.
- Lion's Mane jellyfish: Up to 2m in diameter with a reddish/brown body and a mane of hair-like tentacles; very painful sting.
- Portuguese Man-O'War: Looks like a purple plastic bag with blue ribbon tentacles; very painful sting.

Most stings from sea creatures in the UK are not serious and can be treated with first aid; very occasionally hospital treatment may be necessary. The NHS advises the following if you are stung:

- Get help if possible.
- Ask a lifeguard or someone with first-aid training for help.
- If help is not available:

DO
- Rinse the affected area with seawater (not fresh water).
- Remove any spines from the skin using tweezers or the edge of a bank card.
- Soak the area in very warm water (as hot as can be tolerated) for at least 30 minutes – use hot flannels or towels if you cannot soak it.
- Take painkillers like paracetamol or ibuprofen.

DON'T
- Use vinegar
- Pee on the sting
- Apply ice or a cold pack
- Touch any spines with your bare hands
- Cover or close the wound

Other hazards: Always pass to the right of **boats** as long as conditions allow, and respect **anglers**, giving them space and avoiding their lines. **Rowers** often have their back to you, so let them know you are there and give their oars a wide berth. **Swans** can be aggressive, especially when defending nests (May–June), so move away from them or exit the water so that they can pass. **Barbed wire** lining riverbanks can get washed in after floods and lie unseen •

PADDLING RESPONSIBLY

HE PADDLER'S CODE

ritish Canoeing and Natural England launched this ɔde in 2022. Aiming to mirror what the Countryside ɔde does for dry land, it provides guidance on how addlers can stay safe, respect the environment nd others, and enjoy their time on the water. Most the code is covered in this book, but additional commendations include: keeping group sizes small nd discreet; avoiding damage to fences and walls hen lifting craft over them; being respectful to those ɔu meet along the water and passing them on the ght where possible. To protect nature, paddlers are ked to avoid dragging boats on riverbanks and to oid gravel beds, which can be important spawning ounds for fish. Also, consider sharing cars to avoid ɔllution and congestion, park respectfully, and be screet when getting changed. And, of course, leave ɔ trace. See paddlerscode.info for the full guide.

ILDLIFE

ɔast, rivers, lakes, and canals in the South East are essed with plentiful wildlife, so please minimise sturbance and protect precious habitats.

als: These creatures are very sensitive to humans; even racting their attention so they look at us indicates that e have disturbed them. The Seal Research Trust and ddle UK recommend that you restrict your time with als at sea to less than 15 minutes – any more and you ay distract them from feeding and resting. When on the ater, keep at least 100m away from seals on the shore d on rocks. If they stampede or "tombstone" into the ater they can suffer from grazed flippers, ripped-out ws, gashes, or broken jaws and ribs. Let curiosity be e only reason for the seals to visit you; they must always in control of their encounter with you.

ds: On some routes, especially around islands, ding is prohibited to protect breeding bird colonies and other sensitive wildlife. British Stand Up Paddleboarding Association (BSUPA) and the Royal Society for the Protection of Birds (RSPB) have teamed up to promote a code of conduct to help paddlers enjoy bird life without adversely impacting breeding areas or negatively affecting the bird life in other ways. It's available to read online at www.bsupa.org.uk/2021/06/15/bird-life-paddle-boarding-guide-the-rspb-and-bsupa-code/ Always be aware of wild birds on the water and paddle at a safe distance. If birds change their behaviour by calling out or bobbing up and down, you are too close. Don't linger, and make sure you check out local or seasonal restrictions and by-laws around sensitive wildlife sites. These are mentioned in the book, but do look out for additional signage asking you to give wildlife space and keep to designated launching points and paths.

Other mammals: Lucky paddlers may see dolphins and porpoises when paddling in the Solent, along with otters in estuaries and rivers. Some of the best advice for avoiding disturbance is given by Whale and Dolphin Conservation at uk.whales.org/our-goals/create-healthy-seas/watch-out-for-dolphins-when-you-are-on-the-water/.

Invasive non-native species (INNS): Many of the 50 INNS in UK waters can wreak havoc across our rivers, lakes, canals, and other waterways, with detrimental impacts on indigenous British species and ecosystems. Four of the most prolific INNS you may encounter are killer shrimps, floating pennywort, signal crayfish, and giant hogweed. These species can survive in damp clothing, get caught around rudders, stick to the surface of craft, or get stranded in puddles at the bottom of poorly drained canoes. Paddle UK recommends adopting a clean-check-dry biosecurity procedure for your craft and clothing to halt the movement of such undesirable species. More information on the species and how to minimise transmission is at gopaddling.info/how-to-clean-your-kayak-or-sup-and-stop-the-spread/.

MAKE YOUR VOICE HEARD

Demanding better-quality water, protecting wildlife, and promoting better access to UK waterways are causes we can all get behind. The organisations below run campaigns and citizen science projects, and undertake beach cleans and fundraising activities.

- **Whale and Dolphin Conservation:** The largest charity dedicated to the protection o whales and dolphins and their ocean home, uk.whales.org.
- **National Trust:** A charity and major landowner in the South East that looks after beaches, cliffs, estuaries, and rivers and aims to keep them open for all. It also has significant appeals to raise money for waterways (the Riverlands Appeal) and looking after the coast (Neptune Appeal), nationaltrust.org.uk.
- **Wildlife Trusts:** A UK-wide conservation organisation that protects nature including on our waterways, islands, and seas, wildlifetrusts.org.
- **Canal and River Trust:** A charity that cares for 2,000 miles of canals and rivers, reservoirs, and a wide range of heritage buildings and structures in England and Wales, canalrivertrust.org.uk.
- **Paddle UK:** A national governing body for canoeing with a current "Clear Access, Clear Waters" campaign for "fair, shared and sustainable open access to water for all", clearaccessclearwaters.org.uk/about-clear-access-clear-water-campaign/.
- **Surfers Against Sewage (SAS):** An environmental charity dedicated to cleaner, safer oceans. It offers the Safer Seas and Rivers Service app and organises the Million Mile Beach Clean, sas.org.uk.
- **River Action UK:** A campaigning organisation committed to addressing the severe problem of river pollution caused by agricultural and food industry practices, riveractionuk.com.
- **Captain Paul Watson Foundation UK (formerly Sea Shepherd UK):** A campaigning organisation that organises river and canal cleans and removal of ghost netting from UK waters, paulwatsonfoundation.org
- **Planet Patrol:** A global movement of paddleboarders who remove litter from waterways and where you can join the ever-growing community of water quality testers planetpatrol.co.
- **The 2 Minute Foundation:** A charity that promotes the 2-minute beach clean, litter pick, and street clean. It has funded over 1,000 clean-up stations on the coast and green spaces, 2minute.org.
- **Seaful:** A charity dedicated to helping more people reconnect to the ocean and waterways, for their mental health benefits, and to nurture stewardship of our blue spaces, seaful.org.uk.

LICENCE AND PERMITS

A Waterways Licence is required for kayaks, paddleboards, and canoes on canals and rivers managed by the Canal and River Trust, the Environment Agency and Broads National Park. You can be fined £1000 if you fail to purchase or display one. There are numerous options for day and annual licences from a number of issuing bodies, which can be confusing. The following tips may be useful to help you choose:

- Look at all the waterways you intend to paddle in a year. Those requiring a licence are listed on paddleuk.org.uk/waterways-licences/ and the GoPaddling app gopaddling.info/paddlepoints/.
- If you are only going to paddle for one day on a waterway that requires a licence, the cheapest option is to buy a day pass/short-term pass from that licensing body.
- If you are likely to paddle multiple routes over multiple days, the best option is to become a member of Paddle UK, paddleuk.org.uk/membership/ Annual membership includes an annual Water Licence for over 4,500 km of waterways, liability insurance, and numerous other benefits.
- Some private lakes and Harbour Authorities require a permit that is not covered by the above; these can be purchased locally or online. They will require liability insurance, so if you are not a member of Paddle UK you will have to arrange this separately.
- A UK Waterways Licence is not required to paddle on the UK coastline, including tidal rivers and estuaries. The sea surrounding the UK is free to paddle, except for a few off-limits areas as stipulate by the Ministry of Defence (MoD).
- The Waterways Licence fee contributes towards the maintenance and protection of the waterways, ensuring they are kept clean and safe •

River Stour (76)

Paddle Boarding London & South East England
100 Places by SUP, Canoe & Kayak

Words:
Lisa Drewe

Photos:
Lisa Drewe
and those credited

Design and layout:
Gary Nickolls

Editorial:
Alex Davidson

Proofreading:
Tania Pascoe

Distributed by:
Central Books Ltd
Freshwater Road,
Dagenham, RM8 1RX, UK
Tel +44 (0)20 8525 8800
orders@centralbooks.com

Published by:
Wild Things Publishing Ltd
Freshford, Bath, BA2 7WG, UK
www.wildthingspublishing.com

hello@wildthingspublishing.com

PHOTOGRAPHS

All photographs © Lisa Drewe except pages: 46 (Shutterstock), 48 right (Botley Brewery), 74 (Marathon), 76 (Shutterstock), 102 (Shutterstock), 104 (The Coastguard Inn), 122 left (Oast House Archive), 122 right (hedera.baltica), 129 top (Mote Park Watersports Centre), 135 top (Chatham Maritime Watersports Centre), 167 top and bottom right (Lee Valley White Water Centre), 187 bottom right (Curve Watersports), 231 top left (@Bods), 232 bottom right (Steve Daniels).

ACKNOWLEDGEMENTS

First and foremost, a huge thank you to Charlie, my paddling partner-in-crime. Whether we were ducking under the leafy chaos of Surrey's "jungle," coaxing a large motorhome through central London's traffic, or tackling the million and one curveballs last year threw at us, you were there with unflinching enthusiasm and rock-solid support.

A heartfelt thanks to Mum and Dad, too—for those waterside picnics, chats, and shared moments that always ended in laughter. They were, as always, highlights of this book-writing journey.

A massive shoutout to Andy McConks, who gifted us the unsinkable hero of this story: our paddleboard. It endured every absurdity we threw at it—hauling ridiculous amounts of camera gear, moonlighting as a drone launchpad and snack station, and serving under the unpredictable command of Goose, our loveably maddening spaniel. Her nose led us on detours that defied both maps and logic, but the board took it all in stride, proving its worth in waters of every kind.

To everyone we met on the water—the cheerful wave-sharers, accidental philosophers, and the "isn't this just the best way to spend a day" tribe—you were the heartbeat of this journey. Time and again, you reminded me that paddleboarding is more than a hobby; it's an invitation to connect—with the water, with a paddling community, and with the wild blue spaces that need our care more than ever. Thank you for the chats, the encouragement, and the occasional pint.

Finally, an enormous thanks to Daniel and the team at Wild Things Publishing. Your books don't just spark ideas—they inspire adventure. Thank you for believing in another watery journey and bringing it to life.

OTHER BOOKS FROM WILD THINGS

Snorkelling Britain
Wild Guide West Ireland
Wild Guide North East
Wild Guide Wales
Wild Guide Scotland
Wild Guide Central England
Wild Guide Lakes & Dales
Wild Guide South-West
Wild Guide London South-East
Wild Guide Isle of Man
Wild Guide Morocco
Wild Guide Scandinavia
Wild Guide Portugal
Wild Guide French Alps
Wild Guide Greece
Wild Guide Andalucia
Wild Guide Balearic Islands
Wild Fishing Britain
Wild Sauna Britain
Lost Lanes South
Lost Lanes Wales
Lost Lanes West
Lost Lanes North
Lost Lanes Central
Wild Swimming Walks Yorkshire
Wild Swimming Walks Bristol Bath
Wild Swimming Walks Cornwall
Wild Swimming Walks Dorset
Wild Swimming Walks Dartmoor
Wild Swimming Walks Exmoor
Wild Swimming Walks London
Wild Swimming Walks W Wales
Wild Swimming Walks S Wales
Wild Swimming Walks Eryri
Wild Swimming Walks London
Wild Swimming Walks Lake Dist
Wild Swimming Walks Peak Dist
Wild Swimming Britain / France
Wild Swimming Italy / Spain / Alp
Wild Swimming Croatia Slovenia
Paddle Boarding South East
Paddle Boarding South West
Paddle Boarding Wales
Hidden Beaches Britain / Spain
Bikepacking / France en Velo
Magical Britain / France
Wild Running Britain
Wild Ruins / Ruins B.C.
Wild Garden Weekends
Scottish Bothy Bible / Walks
Outdoor Swimming London